McClure's Magazine
and the
Muckrakers

McClure's Magazine
and the
Muckrakers

By Harold S. Wilson

Princeton, New Jersey
Princeton University Press
1970

Preface

McClure's Magazine, which appeared as an inexpensive monthly in 1893, became by common assent the leading muckraking journal. The pejorative term "muckraking" was a popular misnomer. Its usage by Theodore Roosevelt in 1906 was deceptive, for whether the term was borrowed from Henry George's *Progress and Poverty* or from John Bunyan himself, it was mainly applicable to Roosevelt's malefactors of great wealth: the main principals raking treasure without lifting their gaze to the Celestial City. Although the expression remained as a description of exposures of economic and political privilege, Roosevelt was careful to inform the leading muckrakers at *McClure's* that they were excluded from the odium of the phrase.

Indeed, the muckrakers were more than exposers; they were the vanguard of a revolution in thinking. Their writings accurately reflected the growing public interest in literary realism, pragmatic philosophy, institutional economics, the cult of efficiency, sociological jurisprudence, and experimental psychology. It is not surprising, then, that the magazine press, and especially *McClure's*, should have become a forum for new questions about the nature and direction of American society and government.

The growth of industry and population created an unprecedented national problem. In a half century the United States had grown from an economic power comparable to the Kingdom of the Two Sicilies to the most powerful in the world. The specialization of labor and its growth into national organizational groupings, the increased concentration of financial wealth in Wall Street, and the professionalization of traditional middle-class pursuits of law, medicine, and education created dissensions which strained the fabric of American pluralistic culture. In the newly grown urban areas these problems were compounded when an immense European immigration placed considerable stress upon traditional political institutions. These and other questions were the subjects of numerous exposés.

Rather self-consciously these propagandists for the progressive movement worked their way towards substantive answers. At the heart of reform journalism lay a quest for order and higher law in a society fragmenting into special interest groups. Before either Croly or Weyl, the muckrakers generated nationalist sentiments for a new and more powerful structure of government. They felt that a new, perhaps unitary, state should undertake such reforms as the direct primary, postal savings banks, workers' compensation, minimum wages, child labor laws, woman suffrage, and graduated income tax. The proposed state would prevail over each and all of its parts. The *McClure's* group employed the techniques and championed the causes of traditional reform; they dallied with socialism, but in the end they found their own motivations and radical conclusions in calling to heel the financial and political oligarchy threatening the country.

ANY STUDY owes deep obligations to those who gave aid and comfort. James Harvey Young of Emory University first fanned my old interest in Lincoln Steffens' *Autobiography* and suggested the possibilities of a group study of *McClure's* muckrakers. Richard Griffin (Northern Virginia), James W. W. Daniel (Wesleyan College), and William Wade (King College), fellow historians, have given both friendship and scholarly encouragement. Special appreciation is also due Louis Harlan (University of Maryland) and John Braeman (University of Nebraska), who enriched a long summer of research at the Library of Congress. Additional obligations I owe to the seminars of C. Vann Woodward (Yale), Charles Barker (Johns Hopkins), and Walter Posey (Emory).

The interdisciplinary seminars of the Graduate Institute of the Liberal Arts at Emory University, directed by James Smith, have afforded a truly unique contact with many original and stimulating scholars such as Richard Hocking,

Charles Hartshorne, Thomas J. J. Altizer, and Gregor Sebba. But in this profession, which is much like a priesthood with the transmission of its own occult arts, my greatest debt of gratitude is to James Harvey Young and Gregor Sebba, who have always mixed forbearance and kindness with the sternest academic criticism.

Of many helpful librarians, special appreciation is due the staff of the Lilly Library, University of Indiana.

This research in part has been generously financed by the National Foundation on the Humanities, the Old Dominion University Foundation, and the Shell Foundation.

Contents

McClure's Magazine
and the
Muckrakers

Chapter I. The Imprint
of Abolitionism

WHEN *McClure's* Magazine was founded in 1893, it was staffed to a great extent by graduates of Knox College located in Galesburg, Illinois. The two dozen Knox alumni who edited, sold, and financed *McClure's* carried to the New York publishing world many of the reform traditions of the Great Revival. All of this was consistent with the aims of Rev. George Washington Gale, who founded Knox on the Illinois prairie in 1837. Thus evangelical Christianity—although greatly modified—with its injunctions to transform an evil world, helped to provide the purpose, technique, and content of many of the progressive reforms championed by the muckraking movement in a later era.

George Washington Gale was a mild-mannered, unobtrusive Presbyterian preacher in western New York's "burned-over district" in 1821, when his quiet, doctrinal preaching surprisingly led to the conversion of Charles G. Finney, a rather notorious young lawyer.[1] Finney himself, turned evangelist, shortly afterwards converted the youthful Theodore Dwight Weld, a student at Hamilton College. The Great Revival commenced with these three men guiding it towards a wide area of humanitarian reform. Peripheral to the movement's central principles of "abolition and temperance" were such diverse sentiments as sabbath observance, feminism, and anti-Masonism.[2] The need for ministers with the proper zeal and values to spread the faith became so acute that Gale resigned his pastorate and founded the Oneida Institute in New York, a manual labor school, to instruct the "called."[3] The immediate success of the Oneida Institute led to the founding of Oberlin and

1 Whitney R. Cross, *The Burned-over District* (New York, 1950), 152.
2 *Ibid.*, 226.
3 See Alice Felt Tyler, *Freedom's Ferment* (New York, 1944), 491-93.

3

Knox Colleges, the former by Finney and Weld, the latter by Gale, where the principle of manual labor was applied.[4]

The dedicated men and women who came to the unsettled plains of Illinois at the insistence of Gale to found a college and a community were grounded in religious enthusiasm and believed in an educated elect. They also shared a common distaste for human bondage. Benjamin Lundy edited his *Genius of Universal Emancipation* in the neighboring county, and Owen Lovejoy, brother of the murdered Elijah P. Lovejoy, lived a few miles away at Princeton, called in Congress the "greatest Negro stealing town in the west."[5]

Galesburg, founded around Knox College, became in time "probably the principal Underground Railroad station in Illinois," and a hotbed of abolitionist activity.[6] The Galesburg home of Edward Beecher, one of the famous children of Lyman Beecher of Lane Seminary, was one of the locality's more notorious refuges for runaway slaves.[7] Eventually Edward Beecher became a trustee of Knox, and his brother, Charles, became a professor of rhetoric. The college served as a meeting ground for New England and Midwestern emancipators. Such abolitionists as William Lloyd Garrison, Henry Ward Beecher, John P. Hale, Cassius M. Clay, Theodore Parker, and Wendell Phillips received an enthusiastic welcome when they visited and lectured at Knox.[8]

The early settlers were humble families who lived peaceably with the Illinois Indians and dreamed of Calvin's experiment at Geneva. A feminist reformer characterized them as walking under the "sun of reform."[9] Successively

[4] See Hermann R. Muelder, *Fighters for Freedom* (New York, 1959), 1-62.

[5] *Bureau County Republican*, Jan. 2, 1868.

[6] Muelder, *Fighters for Freedom*, 191.

[7] Earnest Elmo Calkins, *They Broke the Prairie* (New York, 1937), 180ff. Calkins later supervised the advertising of both *McClure's* and the *American Magazine*.

[8] Muelder, *Fighters for Freedom*, 341.

[9] *Ibid.*, 335.

4

the Liberty Party, the Free Soil Party, and the Republican Party found militant leaders and supporters in the community. In 1843 the first president of Knox, Hiram H. Kellogg, served as one of the nine delegates from the United States to the World Anti-Slavery Convention in London, and in 1845 he was succeeded in office by Jonathan Blanchard, a nationally known abolitionist who later founded Wheaton College.[10] Galesburg was committed to militant reform long before the Baptists and Methodists split in 1845.

When Abraham Lincoln and Stephen Douglas debated on the Knox campus in 1858, in the fifth of their famous addresses that year, a large sign confronting the podium read, "Knox College for Lincoln." The community's partisanship was shown more clearly two years later when the college awarded Lincoln, before his election, its first honorary doctorate. Present on these occasions were many men who were to guide the college through the next half century and leave their impression on a score of the muckrakers who graduated in the decade after Reconstruction.

Most important was the so-called Knox "Triumvirate." It consisted of George Churchill, a trustee's son who was principal of the Academy; his brother-in-law, Albert Hurd, professor of natural philosophy; and Milton L. Comstock, professor of mathematics. Churchill taught at Knox from 1855 until 1899, Hurd from 1851 until 1906, and Comstock from 1851 until 1899.[11] Both Churchill and Hurd married daughters of George Washington Gale. Perhaps the most capable of these men was Albert Hurd. Hurd was a descendent of Barbara Heck, the New York feminist who had introduced Methodism into the United States. His own family, because of loyalist sympathies during the Revolution, had migrated to Canada, where he was born. Graduating from Middlebury College in 1850 and from Harvard

[10] Marshall Max Goodsill and Arthur Galvin Walton, eds., *Knox Directory*, 1837-1963 (Galesburg, Ill., 1963).
[11] *Ibid.*, 371-86.

shortly afterwards, Hurd commenced his long teaching career in Galesburg.[12] Several other faculty members from the pre-Civil War era remained at Knox during the 1875-1900 period and long perpetuated the school's unique traditions. Teaching in the Academy at the time of the great debate was Ellen Browning Scripps, later a co-founder with her brother of the Scripps newspaper syndicate.[13] She undoubtedly influenced many of the school's neophyte journalists.

Newton Bateman, more than any other resident, knew and loved Lincoln, saw him proudly feted on the Knox campus, and, as president and teacher from 1874 to 1896, personified the Free Soil tradition. Bateman's life was shaped by adversity. Born in New Jersey in 1822, the son of a crippled weaver, he migrated to Illinois in 1833 in a covered wagon. His mother died on the trip and was buried in an unmarked grave. The family settled in Jacksonville, Illinois, where Edward Beecher was currently serving as president of the newly founded Illinois College. Bateman, who was a classmate of Thomas Beecher, struggled through Illinois College by "almost unbelievable industry and economy, living at one period in a hollow tree, and subsisting on mush and milk, at an expense of eleven cents a week."[14]

After graduating from Illinois College in 1843, Bateman took an M.A. at Lane Theological Seminary, Lyman Beecher's school in Cincinnati, where Henry Ward Beecher taught. In time Bateman became intimately acquainted with nearly all of the Beecher family. Working his way through seminary with a "peddler's pack on his back," Bateman eventually turned to education and was elected the first Republican State Superintendent of Schools in Illinois, a position which he held for fourteen years.[15] For

[12] *Middlebury Catalogue, 1850*, n.p., n.d.
[13] *Knox Directory*, 371-86.
[14] Calkins, *They Broke the Prairie*, 384; see *Galesburg Evening Mail*, Oct. 22, 1897 for obituary.
[15] Calkins, *They Broke the Prairie*, 384-85.

many years Bateman and Lincoln shared adjoining offices in the old state building at Springfield, and "Lincoln, with the uneducated man's exaggerated respect for learning, found relief in chats with the little schoolmaster."[16] The friendship lapsed after Lincoln became president.[17]

The students and teachers attracted to Knox during the Reconstruction years were on the whole devoted to the same religious and moral principles as had been the founders of the college. Such professors came as Miss Malvina M. Bennett, whose father knew Charles Sumner, William Lloyd Garrison, and Henry Wilson, and was counted "one of the founders of the abolitionist movement" in New England.[18] Miss Bennett, young and pretty, arrived in 1880 from Boston, and immediately attracted a large following to her elocution classes, from which many of her students went forth to achieve honors in inter-collegiate oratory contests, often speaking on Civil War topics.[19] Later she returned to Boston, where she lived with her brother and taught at Wellesley.

Another addition was Melville Best Anderson, who assumed the chair of English in 1881. Anderson not only inaugurated a popular Anglo-Saxon course, in which a number of boys did secret courting, but contributed regular articles to the *Dial*, a Chicago journal considered the leading literary magazine of the West.[20] "The *Dial* was a journal with standards," writes Mott, ". . . Melville B. Anderson . . . kept it so" with the aid of several New England contributors.[21] The *Dial*, though rather conservative, maintained that many subjects demanded the attention of maga-

16 *Ibid.*

17 *Ibid.*, 389; *Galesburg Evening Mail*, Oct. 22, 1897.

18 *Knox Student*, IV (Jan., 1882), 56. The Knox magazines and memorabilia were examined at the Knox College Library.

19 See *Galesburg Evening Mail*, May 7, 1898.

20 Calkins, *They Broke the Prairie*, 387ff; see Melville B. Anderson, *The Happy Teacher* (New York, 1910) and Nicholas Joost, *Years of Transition: the Dial, 1912-1920* (Barre, Mass., 1967), 11.

21 Frank Luther Mott, *History of American Magazines* (4 vols., Cambridge, 1930-57), III, 541.

zines, such as "those of political administration, of good government, of municipal socialism, of economics as they relate to social and individual prosperity and comfort."[22] Anderson later moved to Stanford University, where he published a well-considered translation of the *Divine Comedy*. Knox replaced him with Jeremiah Whipple Jenks, a Halle Ph.D., who was to become one of the country's leading experts on trusts and municipal corruption.[23]

On the whole the postwar years saw the faculty and students maintaining a solid phalanx in defense of the ideals of Gale and Finney, if not those of the martyred John Brown and Abraham Lincoln. In no area was life more circumspect than that of religion. "No instructor," asserted President Bateman, "could teach at Knox College if there was the slightest doubt about his orthodoxy," and in each annual report to the trustees he listed the number of Christians in the college.[24] Bateman kept a patrician's eye on students temporarily out of school and working. "I miss your sympathetic face when I try to talk to the boys in chapel," he wrote to one student, urging him to maintain a high moral life.[25] Nearly all of the members of the faculty occasionally addressed the students in chapel or Sunday school. Absence from chapel could be excused only by a vote of the faculty, and on Sunday there were six different church services.

Yet Bateman seems to have tolerated a good deal of theological divergency among his faculty. Albert Hurd alone was trained to address himself authoritatively to the conflict between science and religion, an old battle renewed after the war in evolutionary terms. Hurd had further prepared himself for such discussion by taking a leave of

22 *Ibid.*, IV, 9.

23 Calkins, *They Broke the Prairie*, 387ff; *Galesburg Daily Mail*, Sept. 28, 1894.

24 Calkins, *They Broke the Prairie*, 390; Albert Britt, *An American That Was* (Barre, Mass., 1964), 59, 67, 78, 170-71.

25 Newton Bateman to S. S. McClure, Oct. 19, 1878, McClure Papers, Lilly Library, University of Indiana.

absence in 1854 to study under the Lamarkian Louis Agassiz at Harvard, where Alexander Agassiz, the son, had been his classmate.[26] Back at Knox, with the help of his oldest daughter, Harriet, Hurd gathered up geological samples from lime quarries for a small museum he supervised, and prepared charts for his lectures. When he was scheduled to speak in morning chapel, according to his daughter, many of the townspeople would come to listen. "Father used to present all there was to be said on his chosen subject from both points of view," Harriet later wrote, "always coming to the final conclusion that the glorious poetry of the first two chapters of Genesis could not possibly be regarded as the expression of literal, scientific fact, but was to be considered as an allegorical picture. . . ."[27] If this recollection be correct, then Knox possessed one of the earlier advocates of the religious implications of evolution. Yet Hurd definitely believed in the revelatory nature of the Bible, since it furnished "all the factors which produce the noblest human character, it authoritatively tells us what to believe and what to do. . . ."[28]

On the other hand, following Aquinas' natural reason, Hurd felt that God had left another record in the rocks for man's understanding. This reconciliation of reason and faith, Harriet wrote, probably speaking for numbers of the student body, "greatly impressed me."[29] Doubtless the collective moral injunctions of Hurd, Bateman, Willard, and Anderson left their impression upon the fallow minds of the Knox students.[30] For example, after an emotional sermon in February, 1879, the college *en masse* pledged itself to temperance.[31] Enthusiasm was far from finished. And

[26] *Harvard Catalogue, 1854-55*, n.d., n.p.

[27] *Knox Alumnus*, May, 1929.

[28] Enclosure in Albert Hurd to Harriet Hurd, Oct. 29, 1882, McClure Papers.

[29] *Knox Alumnus*, May, 1929.

[30] Albert Hurd to Harriet Hurd, Oct. 29, 1882, McClure Papers.

[31] *Knox Directory*, 370; *Knox Student*, I (Feb., 1879), 13.

9

somehow Lamarkianism and the Gospel seem to have coexisted quite pleasantly in the post-Reconstruction years.

Nonetheless, extreme religious unorthodoxy was still dangerous. In 1871 a student led some trustees to question whether he should be awarded his degree when he gave a negative answer in his senior oration to the question, "Is Orthodoxy in Theology Necessary for the Christian?" He finally got his degree and later helped found the Ethical Cultural Society.[32] But Hurd lamented, "How sad a sight it is to see a man in the prime of life walking the streets of Galesburg with one of Ingersoll's lectures before his eyes."[33] Hurd's fear of widely propagated heresy was unfounded. Knox still prepared a tenth of its graduates for the ministry, and his own daughter's valedictory address in 1877 was a far more common type: "What Woman Owes Christianity."[34]

Reminiscences of the war competed with religion as a chapel topic. Newton Bateman's favorite subject was Abraham Lincoln. He gave a regular series of lectures at Knox, as well as across the country, on the abolitionist movement in Illinois.[35] Other faculty members frequently reminisced in chapel about the Beecher family, John Brown, the Lincoln-Douglas debates, or the founding of the college.[36]

A Methodist advocate of the Social Gospel, C. W. Blodgett, gave a typical address as late as 1896. His father-in-law had attended the Republican convention in Chicago in 1860 and supported the nomination of Lincoln. Blodgett thought Lincoln's opposition to the Compromise of 1850 as inspired as the Decalogue. Divinity further revealed

[32] "John Edward Sumner Salter," *Dictionary of American Biography*, ed. by Dumas Malone (20 vols., New York, 1935), XVI, 315-16. Henceforth cited as *DAB*.

[33] Enclosure in Albert Hurd to Harriet Hurd, Oct. 29, 1882, McClure Papers.

[34] "Knox College Graduation Program," 1877.

[35] See *Knox Student*, IV (March, 1882); *Galesburg Daily Mail*, May 22, 1896; Calkins, *They Broke the Prairie*, 387.

[36] *Galesburg Evening Mail*, Oct. 24, May 26, 25, 1898, Oct. 10, 1894.

itself through Lincoln's plans as president, and for this reason his administration was flawless. The service closed with the students singing "Guard That Banner While We Sleep."[37] Blodgett was also an expert on the subject of the "Saloon and its Relation to Society," on which he frequently lectured. Intemperance, he thought, was responsible for the fact that there was not a well-governed city in America and for the increase in poverty, crime, and taxes.[38]

Another speaker, a short time later, insisted: "we cannot doubt that the success of the Union cause was due to the moral sentiment that supported and inspired it" because "out of the calm wisdom and the pure purpose of Lincoln's mind and heart, came like a divine revelation the one sentiment and the one thought that could overmaster all others. It was the sentiment of patriotism. . . ."[39] With the intertwining of patriotism, orthodoxy, and social reform, it was not surprising that most of the Knox students in the postwar generation wrote themes and orations on Civil War heroes, made *Uncle Tom's Cabin* the most popular play ever presented in Galesburg, and went into the world with a deep commitment to the ideals of the Great Revival.[40]

Probably a large percentage of the four hundred colleges in the country in 1880 had a similar environment. Certainly those schools in the West and Northwest had their YMCA and Prohibition clubs in large numbers. Most colleges were small and informal—Wabash, Illinois, and Allegheny as well as Harvard, California, and Kansas—and the student bodies were personally exposed to the raconteurs who explained to the new generation the meaning of the Civil War, often from experience, and the ways of God, apes, and Victorians. This was the breeding ground of the next generation's political progressives. At any rate, at

[37] *Ibid.*, Feb. 17, 1896.
[38] *Galesburg Daily News*, Dec. 12, 1884.
[39] *Galesburg Evening Mail*, April 1, 1896.
[40] See *Galesburg Daily Mail*, June 5, Nov. 5, 1894; *Galesburg Evening Mail*, 9 May, 1896; *Knox Student*, IV (Dec., 1881), 35.

Knox, if not on numerous campuses, students and faculty condemned drinking, gambling, prostitution, slums, sabbath breaking, racism, and political corruption; and upheld feminism and public charities.[41]

On the occasion of the college's semi-centennial, the *Galesburg Evening Mail* evaluated the impact of Knox upon its times. Out of a thousand graduates had come six college presidents, twenty college professors, forty physicians, eighty lawyers, one hundred ministers, and twenty-five journalists. Most of the journalists were those who made *McClure's Magazine.*[42]

Mary Hatton made the earliest contribution. She attended the Knox Academy between 1856 and 1861. Her son, William Allen White, helped create *McClure's* reform journalism. Converted from Catholicism to Congregationalism, Mary Hatton sat with the Hurd family in Edward Beecher's church, and, on occasion, heard Henry Ward Beecher, of Beecher's Bibles fame, lecture on abolitionism.[43]

After the Civil War, she left Galesburg, possibly because a son in her employer's family fell in love with her and asked Edward Beecher to intercede.[44] Although she had formed close relationships with many of the Knox community, including Albert Hurd, Mary Hatton went west to teach in Kansas without the benefit of her degree. In Kansas her radical abolitionist ideas about integrating her school only precipitated an imbroglio with the public school officials. A Democratic physician, whose admiration was earned by her radical politics, came to the rescue and married her.[45] In time Mary Hatton's deep ties with Knox and the abolitionist traditions were bequeathed to her only son who became one of the most popular writers for *Mc-*

[41] *Galesburg Daily Mail*, Sept. 28, 1894; *Galesburg Evening Mail*, June 8, 1898, Jan. 30, 1897.

[42] *Galesburg Evening Mail*, June 11, 1896.

[43] William Allen White, *The Autobiography of William Allen White* (New York, 1946), 7, 8. Henceforth cited as *Autobiography*.

[44] Mamie Hurd to Harriet Hurd, March 28, 1900, McClure Papers.

[45] White, *Autobiography*, 10, 17.

Clure's.[46] William Allen White pioneered the fields of political and juvenile writing for the magazine when barely out of his adolescence.

Charles Edward Churchill, a son of George Churchill, Hurd's brother-in-law in the department of mathematics, graduated in 1882. Eventually he became an advertising manager for *McClure's* and a close friend of William Allen White.[47]

Edgar A. Bancroft and Frederick Bancroft, who left Knox in 1878 and 1882 respectively, became aides-de-camp and friends of the *McClure's* group. Edgar took a law degree at Columbia and subsequently became general counsel to International Harvester.[48] Frederick Bancroft collaborated with McClure writers and became a reputable historian of abolitionism. After receiving his Ph.D. from Columbia, he published *The Negro in Politics* (1885), *The Public Life of Carl Schurz* (1908), and his classic *Slave Trading in the Old South* (1931). In the muckraking era Bancroft always remained in the *McClure's* wings, frequently contributing articles on Civil War themes and snatching such plums for the magazine as Carl Schurz's memoirs.[49]

But the leading man in Knox's dramatis personae for *McClure's* was Samuel S. McClure. In his exciting and readable *Autobiography* Sam McClure has portrayed his student years at Knox College as being dominated by a romantic crisis precipitated when he fell in love with Albert Hurd's daughter, Harriet. In fact, during those years he was assimilating ideas, mastering techniques, and making friendships that were to usher him into national prominence later.

Sam McClure and his three brothers, John, Thomas, and

[46] *Ibid.,* 20.

[47] Later he worked for *McCall's* and founded the Churchill-Hall Advertising Agency in New York.

[48] *DAB,* I, 562-63; see Edgar Bancroft, *The Sherman Law and Recent Decisions* (n.p., 1911) for his position on government and regulation.

[49] Frederick Bancroft to McClure, Nov. 25, 1906, McClure Papers.

Robert, were immigrants from County Antrim, Ulster, Ireland. Their mother had brought the family to Valparaiso, Indiana, in 1866, after the accidental death of their father, a ship's carpenter. Though only nine years old, Sam McClure must have been forming the hostility which he later articulated against "Irish Landlordism," the Anglican Church, and the English.[50] Upon their arrival in Indiana the McClures lived with relatives, among whom was Joseph Gaston, Sam McClure's young uncle who was shortly to become a ministerial student in the Academy at Knox.

Within a year Elizabeth McClure had made a permanent home for her four sons by marrying Thomas Simpson, another Ulster immigrant who owned a farm of one hundred acres near Valparaiso.[51] The farm work was arduous, and Simpson needed the young laborers. In spite of this, in 1871, at fourteen, Sam McClure, urged by his mother, moved into Valparaiso to work his way through school.[52] On his own, McClure attended school, while living with and working for, first, a local physician, and then a more congenial family because it was a "place with only one cow and one stove."[53]

The depression of 1873 forced McClure to leave school. With work hard to find and harder to keep for a sixteen-year-old boy, he worked in quick succession as a printer's devil for the *Valparaiso Vidette*, a grocery clerk, a butcher, a section gang laborer, and an iron foundry hand. When his step-father died within the year, McClure returned to the family farm to help his brothers with the harvest.

In the fall Joseph Gaston happened by and persuaded McClure to enroll at Knox. Escaping the farm with relief, McClure arrived in Galesburg with but fifteen cents in hand and very few material possessions. That same fall Newton

[50] *Knox Student*, III (March, 1881), 5.
[51] Samuel McClure, *My Autobiography* (New York, 1914), 39, Henceforth cited as *Autobiography*.
[52] *Ibid.*, 46.
[53] *Ibid.*, 50; see *Tacoma Tribune*, Oct. 20, 1917.

Bateman began his long presidency. In 1882, eight years later, McClure was to receive his B.A. degree.[54]

Unable to pay two dollars per week to live in the college dormitory, McClure secured lodging in the home of the town's Congregational minister, M. L. Williston, a successor to Edward Beecher, who had left town four years previously.[55] Within a short while McClure had impressed the Williston family as having a "very mature mind for nineteen, and very pioneering," and Mrs. Williston thought he could hardly "pass my door but that I felt the influence" of his vitality.[56]

In a rather unusual move the faculty gave McClure free tuition during his years in the Knox Academy, and when his brothers, Thomas and John, followed during the next three years, this benefit was extended to them.[57] Later in his collegiate years, when he began to take Bateman's advice and earn money by peddling, McClure moved into the one-story "West Bricks," an ancient dormitory which Frederick Bancroft insisted "might cause some of our eastern friends to wonder as to which part of Northern Siberia we were brought up in."[58]

At first the impoverished but ambitious McClure had thought of raising money by publishing a book, but he ceased because he "ought to be something of an original investigator before he compiles the results of others."[59] One endeavor, a dictionary of etymological copyings from Lidell and Scott, never grew beyond sixty pages.[60] Still later, in 1881, McClure had finished what "I don't think is a very good novel. . . ."[61] It was at this juncture that he

[54] McClure, *Autobiography*, 60-61.
[55] See Muelder, *Fighters for Freedom*, 249.
[56] Louise Williston to Harriet Hurd, Nov. ?, 1876, McClure Papers.
[57] "Knox College Faculty Minutes," n.d., 246, 266, 281, Mss in Knox College Library.
[58] Frederick Bancroft to John Phillips, Dec. 6, 1913, Bancroft Papers, Columbia University.
[59] Louise Williston to Harriet Hurd, July 31, 1878, McClure Papers.
[60] Mss in *ibid.*
[61] McClure to Harriet Hurd, Dec. 3, 1881, *ibid.*

took to the road as a peddler. Selling pins, hosiery, handkerchiefs, and lampwicks, McClure, often accompanied by his roommate, Albert Bird Brady, like scores of students working their way through college, toured the back country. One summer they sold microscopes all the way to Minnesota.[62] Another year McClure obtained the western franchise for a new coffee condenser and unsuccessfully tried to organize high school boys to sell it.[63] By the end of his senior year, McClure was subsisting principally on loans from Edgar A. Bancroft and Professor Thomas Willard, although he was teaching a class in shorthand and assisting in mathematics.[64] McClure's financial difficulties left him with a life-long feeling of insecurity, a desire to succeed, and an inability to manage money. In his own mind his romantic problems were tumultuous.

McClure fell in love with Harriet Hurd at a dinner given by the Willistons, and suddenly encountered paternal objections to the courtship. Albert Hurd, said Harriet, was "deeply prejudiced and very jealous in regard to me," since he expected her to "teach for the next thirty years," and planned that "nobody will ever have anything to say about me but himself."[65] Unlike her only sister, Mary, she had no desire to make a career teaching French at Knox. "How can a sane person look at life in such a way?" she asked.[66]

Before the adamant Hurd could be reconciled to the marriage, McClure was involved in several campus squabbles, significant only because they established a pattern of conduct that plagued him in his professional life later. These disputes involved the eruption of a long-standing rivalry between the school's literary societies. Beginning in 1873

[62] McClure, *Autobiography*, 128, 130.
[63] Louise Williston to Harriet Hurd, July 31, 1878, McClure Papers.
[64] *Knox Student*, III (Oct., 1880), 10-13; *Knox Directory*, 377; notes dated April, 1882 and August 5, 1882 in McClure Papers.
[65] Harriet Hurd to McClure, Dec. ?, 1881, *ibid.* Harriet's nickname was Hattie.
[66] *Ibid.*

the Adelphi Society, one of the two, had sponsored a popular Inter-State Oratorical Contest. In 1877, with representatives from a number of colleges participating, Edgar A. Bancroft, in the same class as Harriet Hurd, became the first Knox student to win first place. Subsequently competition for places on the speaker's list became so keen that the faculty considered abolishing the event.

Henry T. Rainey was dropped by the faculty from the oratory list during McClure's junior year because after several weeks of preparation he had gotten sick.[67] The faculty's decision might be questioned in the light of Rainey's later career. He became a successful lawyer, member of Congress for twenty-five years, and the first Speaker of the House of Representatives under Franklin D. Roosevelt. At any rate, McClure and several of his friends, John S. Phillips, Albert Brady, and Frederick Bancroft, took up Rainey's cause when he claimed an injustice was done.

John S. Phillips at twenty was four years younger than McClure. He was a son of the organizer of Knox County and a relative of Wendell Phillips. His father, Dr. E. L. Phillips, of Council Bluffs, Iowa, had moved to Galesburg, where John Phillips and his two sisters, Elizabeth and Julia, attended Knox.[68] Later a brother, Ed Phillips, also briefly attended the school.[69]

Albert Brady, already mentioned as McClure's roommate, was also from Iowa, the son of Edwin W. Brady and the younger brother of Curtis Brady, the co-editors of the *Davenport Daily Times*, a temperance journal.[70] A Democrat and a prohibitionist, he, like John Phillips, planned

[67] See "Knox College Faculty Minutes," Knox College.

[68] *The Independent Republican*, Jan. 2, 1940; clipping, n.p., n.d. in Phillips Papers, Lilly Library, University of Indiana; John S. Phillips, "A Legacy to Youth," 138, 260, a manuscript in possession of Dorothy P. Huntington, New York City.

[69] *New York Times*, March 2, 1949; Frances Sisson to McClure, April 25, 1923, McClure Papers.

[70] *New York Times*, Dec. 25, 1900; Curtis P. Brady, "The High Cost of Impatience," 5, manuscript memoir in possession of Mr. Peter Lyon, New York City.

to make journalism a career.[71] Frederick Bancroft was another member of this coterie.

For somewhat specious reasons this student clique accused the incoming president of Adelphi Society, Robert Mather, of precipitating the faculty's adverse decision which excluded Rainey from the oratory competition. Mather, the son of a mechanic on the Chicago, Burlington, and Quincy Railroad, in time was to become president of the Rock Island Railroad and director of thirty others, chairman of Westinghouse, and trustee and vice-president of the S. S. McClure Company.[72]

The affair ended abruptly in favor of Mather and the faculty, and several students left school in disgust, Frederick Bancroft and Rainey going to Amherst College.

Student hostilities grew over the summer. In the fall of 1881, McClure and his friends almost disrupted campus life in a struggle to capture control of the company that published the school magazine, the *Knox Student*. Successful, McClure hastily had the company chartered by the state in Springfield.[73]

By agreement Albert Brady was responsible for financing the new magazine. He set the subscription rate at $1.00 a year, and started soliciting local merchants and national concerns for advertising. Over a rival magazine founded by Mather, McClure garnered in the patronage of several national firms, including that of the Pope Manufacturing Company of Boston, which produced the Columbia Bicycle.

Under the editorship of McClure and Phillips, the *Knox Student* inaugurated several reforms. It expanded to sixteen pages, started an exchange section with eastern colleges, and began printing book reviews. One of the first

[71] See *Knox Student*, IV (May, 1882).

[72] McClure, *Autobiography*, 132.

[73] The struggle can be reconstructed from McClure to Mrs. Everett, April 9, 1934, McClure Papers; Bonty to McClure, Oct. 15, 1881, *ibid.*; *The Coup d'Etat*, I (Oct., 1881), 5-8; *Knox Student*, IV (Oct., 1881), 15.

books reviewed was Albert Hurd's *The Elements of Chemistry*. Further irritating the father of his beloved, McClure found many weaknesses, including "inferior typography" in the book.[74]

The only quality literary magazines to which the *Student* staff had access were those in John Phillips' home. It was there that McClure read the last copy of the old thirty-five-cent *Scribner's* before it was transmuted into the *Century* later in the year. In the new *Century* he followed "to the end with intense interest" William Dean Howells' "A Modern Instance."[75] Save for occasional newspaper fiction, it was the first serial McClure had ever read. Soon he was reviewing the magazines for the *Student*.[76]

McClure's editorial policy was to characterize him all his life. "He works," wrote a student who knew him well, "by fits and starts; weeks, almost months go by, and he does no work to amount to anything and then crowds all into a few days and nights."[77] At times he disagreed with the staff over the contents of the magazine. When some items were submitted by Nannie Bateman, the President's daughter, or others "that did not seem worth printing I rejected them," he wrote, and yet translations of short prose by Harriet Hurd were most printable.[78] But McClure ignored the dissent, let Phillips do the detailed busy work, and dashed off after other projects.

McClure organized an intercollegiate news service. Taking notices from various colleges, the *Student* published them in a weekly bulletin to which all the campuses subscribed.[79] Later, he fondly recalled that this was his first syndicate. He helped found a Western College Associated Press and under its auspices published a *History of Col-*

[74] *Ibid.*, 16.   [75] McClure, *Autobiography*, 149.
[76] *Knox Student*, IV (Oct., 1881), 16.
[77] Fanny Hague to Harriet Hurd, June 21, 1881, McClure Papers.
[78] McClure to Mrs. Everett, April 9, 1934, *ibid.*
[79] *Knox Student*, IV (Dec., 1881), 35.

lege Journalism.[80] A year later Phillips and John McClure
published a similar volume for eastern schools.[81] McClure
was delighted with the impression made by his business
acumen. "Several of the boys want to 'go in' with me in
some business next year, and tonight Prof. Anderson said
the same thing," he wrote Harriet, by then his fiancée.[82]

During his senior year McClure also served as president
of the oratory contest association, and in that capacity, he,
Phillips, Harriet Hurd, and Emma West, who was to marry
Phillips within the year, welcomed speakers to the state
intercollegiate contest. One speaker whom McClure entertained was William Jennings Bryan from Illinois College,
who took only second prize.[83]

McClure's own oration on the nature of enthusiasm
hardly impressed the judges. Nevertheless, he gave this
same address, so revealing of his character, when called
upon to speak at graduation. He pointed out that, "it was
when they believed in what seemed impossible that the
Abolitionists did the most good, that they created the sentiment which finally did accomplish the impossible."[84]
John Phillips gave a graduation address on the "Inner
Self," and Robert Mather, the valedictorian, with deep
irony, spoke on "The Cynic and his Kinsman."[85]

Upon graduation McClure had determined to become a
"Publisher, Importer & Dealer in Books."[86] Several of his
classmates accompanied him as he approximated this intent. Of invaluable aid throughout the next decade in the
making of his syndicate and magazine were Harriet Hurd,
who married McClure in 1883; the meticulous John Phil-

80 See *ibid.*, IV (March, 1882); Samuel McClure, ed., *History of College Journalism* (Chicago, 1882).

81 John Phillips and John McClure, eds., *History of American College
Journalism* (Cambridge, 1883).

82 McClure to Harriet Hurd, May 20, 1882, McClure Papers.

83 Julian J. Wadsworth to McClure, June 2, 1929, *ibid.*

84 McClure, *Autobiography*, 139.

85 "Knox College Graduation Program," 1882.

86 McClure to Harriet Hurd, Nov. ?, 1881, April 10, 1882, McClure
Papers.

lips and his wife, Emma West; and John's brother, Ed Phillips.

Albert Brady grew from his experiences at Knox to be something of a financial genius. After he became treasurer of *McClure's*, he brought his brothers, Oscar W., Curtis, and Ed from the family paper to be advertising and financial executives of the magazine.[87] A brother of Mable Sisson, who graduated with McClure, was also destined to work on the advertising staff. Francis H. Sisson and his friend Charles May at McClure's behest joined the magazine staff and inaugurated distinguished careers.[88]

Subsequently other Knox alumni were to join McClure in New York. Probably the most important was Albert Augustus Boyden, who came after taking Knox and Harvard degrees. Boyden was the youngest of four sons in a family that had migrated from New England before the Civil War, becoming deeply involved in Congregational Church affairs and Republican politics.[89] The elder Boyden was part owner in a department store and a banker. One of the sons, George W. Boyden, became Vice President of the Illinois State Bankers' Association. Another became a businessman and a Knox trustee. Still another son, William C. Boyden, became Vice President of the Chicago Bar Association. His law partner, the prime mover behind much of Chicago's progressive reform, was Walter Fisher, who became Secretary of the Interior when Ballinger resigned from Taft's cabinet.[90]

In his own boyish, country way Albert Boyden served as an effective link between his family and their connections and McClure's publishing empire. This proved an invaluable way of getting personal accounts of political ineptitude

87 *New York Times*, Nov. 25, 1900.

88 Frances Sisson to McClure, April 5, 1933, McClure Papers; Lincoln Steffens, *The Autobiography of Lincoln Steffens* (New York, 1931), 363, henceforth cited as *Autobiography*.

89 *New York Times*, May 3, 1925; *Bureau County Republican*, Jan. 20, 1876.

90 *Ibid.*, Jan. 6, 1875; *New York Times*, March 8, 1940.

21

in Illinois and the Midwest. Boyden's only sister, Martha, married John Houston Finley, later president of Knox, editorial assistant at *McClure's*, and editor of the *New York Times*. Finley's circle of friends included the leading liberal intellectuals of the country.

John Finley and his brother, Robert, were, like the Boydens, children of early Illinois immigrants of staunch Presbyterian persuasion. Both boys were born during the Civil War at Grand Ridge, Illinois, near Galesburg. Each worked his way through Knox and both graduated in the same year, 1887, when John Finley, like E. A. Bancroft before him, won the Inter-State Oratory Contest. His oration was a eulogy of John Brown. Together the boys went to The Johns Hopkins University, then only a dozen years old, and studied under Professors Frederick Jackson Turner and Richard T. Ely. Eventually John Finley was associated with Ely in the authorship of his *Taxation in American States and Cities*, and both of the brothers absorbed the economist's interest in municipal charities.[91]

Robert helped pay for his study in Baltimore by editing a monthly, *The Record and Guide*, and by assisting with the *Chautauquan*, on whose staff he met Ida M. Tarbell. One summer he edited the daily *Chautauquan* newspaper. Leaving Hopkins to write his dissertation, Robert Finley worked with several New York newspapers; finally in 1890 he became associate editor of Albert Shaw's remarkable reform journal, *The Review of Reviews*, which was published in the same building as *McClure's*. McClure admired Finley's "wonderful capacity for work" which was demonstrated when he practically assumed the editorship of the *Review* during a prolonged illness of Shaw.[92] In 1896 Finley was appointed manager of McClure's syndicate business, a position he held until his death.[93]

---

[91] *Knox Directory*, 166; *New York Times*, March 8, 1940, June 10, 1897; *Galesburg Evening Mail*, June 10, 1897.

[92] *Ibid.*, Dec. 16, 1897.

[93] *New York Times*, June 10, 1897; *Galesburg Evening Mail*, June 10, 1897.

John Finley, like his brother, had a talented interest in humanities and a penchant for reform. He left Hopkins after two years and went to New York, where he became secretary of the extremely influential Charities Aid Association.[94] While there he edited the *Charities Review*, a journal befriended by Jane Addams and Jacob Riis and "the first review on that subject in America."[95] After three years, at the age of twenty-eight, he returned to Knox as the youngest college president in the country, a position which he held until 1899 when he joined *McClure's*. Although Finley edited the *Charities Review* until 1896, the public platform served him equally well as a means of spreading reform sentiments. He often presided at public meetings in Illinois dealing with such topics as charities, civil service, and municipal reform.[96] His audiences included the State Board of Supervisors, the Christian Endeavor fellowship, which he helped found, a Christian Citizenship League, and the Knox student body.[97]

In his inaugural address in 1893 Finley called upon the Knox students to reform not only public institutions, but social institutions, and bring about the needed changes in immigration, taxation, sanitation, charities, and alcoholism.[98] In 1894 Finley sponsored a Christian Endeavor convention at Knox that heard a theologian from the Palmer Settlement House in Chicago declare that the politics of the country were "so bad the conscience of the church and the conscience of the nation" were becoming jaded, concluding that "when the country reaches this point there comes a John Brown, who arouses public sentiment against

[94] See Irwin Yellowitz, *Labor and the Progressive Movement in New York State, 1897-1916* (Ithaca, 1965), 40, 82.
[95] *New York Times*, March 8, 1940; Mott, *History of American Magazines*, IV, 741ff.
[96] *Galesburg Daily Mail*, Jan. 16, 1895.
[97] *Galesburg Evening Mail*, Jan. 20, Jan. 30, 1898, Nov. 12, 1897; *Galesburg Mail*, June 9, 1893.
[98] *Ibid.*

these evils."⁹⁹ In the same year Finley led an excursion to the Hull House of Jane Addams, who had "many friends at Knox. . . ."¹⁰⁰ One commencement the daring young president even broached the benefits of bi-metalism: It would, he said, help pay off the national debt.¹⁰¹ McClure was hardly ready for such strong medicine, but he appreciated Finley and hired him. "He is," he wrote Harriet, "just like Phillips or Brady."¹⁰²

During Finley's administration the usual flow of students from Knox to *McClure's* continued unabated. Florence M. Bates, Earnest Elmo Calkins, and John W. Clark, intimates of the *McClure's* group, arrived during these years.¹⁰³ Albert Britt was another such addition. As a Knox debater in 1898 Britt asked a visiting Beloit team, "Are we to allow Rockefeller to translate Providence for himself?" and answered, "we maintain that unjust accumulation of wealth is an inherent evil."¹⁰⁴ Knox lost the debate. In the following summer the young Britt, a future president of Knox, came to New York, "very ill at ease and very homesick."¹⁰⁵ Ray Stannard Baker, a new journalist at *McClure's* himself, befriended the boy, and soon Britt was working for *Public Opinion*, a transitory McClure holding supervised by Robert McClure.¹⁰⁶ For five years Britt worked for the magazine, which made "some ventures in muckraking," and eventually he became its editor.¹⁰⁷ Later, with Thomas Harper Blodgett, a former classmate, he bought the *Out-*

---

⁹⁹ *Galesburg Daily Mail*, Oct. 20, 1894.

¹⁰⁰ *Knox Student*, new series, I (May 1, 1895), 5.

¹⁰¹ *Galesburg Mail*, June 8, 1893.

¹⁰² McClure to Harriet McClure, May 14, 1895, McClure Papers.

¹⁰³ *Knox Directory*, 169, 175; Robert McClure to J. C. Clark, March 1, 1898, McClure Papers.

¹⁰⁴ *Galesburg Evening Mail*, April 16, 1898.

¹⁰⁵ Albert Britt to Ray Stannard Baker, May 22, May 25, 1928, Baker Papers, Manuscript Division, Library of Congress. Unless otherwise cited these are the Baker papers referred to.

¹⁰⁶ *New York Herald*, May 11, 1906.

¹⁰⁷ Mott, *A History of American Magazines*, IV, 651.

ing magazine, and ran it for a decade before going to *Munsey's*.[108]

By the turn of the century it was a practice for "every man who had graduated from Knox in the last few years to write McClure's asking for some position."[109] Numerous young men with Finley's recommendation helped fill the editorial department, reading and correcting manuscripts.[110]

In his appointments, McClure did not eschew nepotism. Each of the McClure brothers was given an executive position in one of the family enterprises. Sam McClure's youngest brother, Robert, remained in charge of the London office.[111] Thomas Carlyle McClure managed the newspaper syndicate for several years, and John F. McClure worked on *McClure's*. A cousin, Henry Herbert McClure, joined the syndicate immediately after graduating from Wabash College in 1894.[112] Henry, along with another cousin, W. H. P. Walker, started the McClure Lecture Bureau in 1899. Later he was advertising manager of the book company and, in 1906, helped found the *American Magazine*.[113] This recitation hardly exhausts the list of McClures, Phillipses, and Bradys who found their way into the New York publishing world.[114]

The Knox alumni often made significant contributions at *McClure's*, and on the whole they developed a climate of opinion that attracted other young Midwestern Republi-

[108] Albert Britt to Baker, May 22, 1928, Baker Papers; McClure to Janet Grieg Post, Feb. 4, 1936, McClure Papers.

[109] Harry H. Boggs to McClure, March 17, 1900, John H. Finley Papers, New York Public Library; *Knox Directory*, 178.

[110] P.J.M. Gladden to John Finley, Aug. 21, 1901, Finley Papers.

[111] *New York Times*, May 31, 1914.

[112] McClure, *Autobiography*, 105.

[113] Henry McClure to Ida Tarbell, May 17, 1899, Phillips Papers; *New York Herald Tribune*, Nov. 25, 1938.

[114] John Siddall to Baker, n.d., Baker Papers; W. A. Brady to Baker, Feb. 13, 1908, *ibid.*; Finley Peter Dunne to H. N. Phillips, Nov. 5, 1904, quoted in Elmo Ellis, *Mr. Dooley's America: A Life of Finley Peter Dunne* (New York, 1941), 190-91.

cans to the magazine. To say that this collective background —a religious atmosphere, flavored with reform sentiments associated with the Civil War—explains muckraking is an extreme simplification. John Phillips, always conscious of family heritage, was probably exaggerating when he wrote William Allen White that the fact his family had taken their turn "being abolitionists and running a station on the under-ground railway" explained "why a man feels as he does, and why he works as he does, and why things interest him as they do in public matters." Such a background, he said, provided some "suggestion as to why the sense of justice is active and quickly aroused."[115] Yet these people, those from Knox and those who joined McClure from similar environments later, had a deep sense of the pattern of history and saw the brave new century in the categories of their fathers. Some problems, stated violently in the Civil War, were eternally current, it seemed.

McClure, in his political maturity, thought, "What a curious thing it is that in entering upon this new era of intelligent and moral government, the same parties that wanted to perpetuate slavery under the guise of state rights, are now trying to perpetuate corrupt government under the same guise."[116] William Allen White, to whom this remark was made, responded in the *Emporia Gazette* that "The slaveholding oligarchy was never more solidly arrayed against the free people of the nation than is this bondholding aristocracy today. It places property above men."[117] And yet muckraking, by its very nature, had to grow out of the stuff of life, out of a confrontation with current evils, trusts and bosses. In 1882, when McClure graduated, Standard Oil was a trust. It was to be twenty years exactly before these two forces met head on.

[115] John Phillips to White, Sept. 24, 1912, White Papers, Manuscript Division, Library of Congress.

[116] McClure to White, Sept. 9, 1910, *ibid.*

[117] William Allen White, *The Editor and His People*, ed. by Helen Orden Mahin (New York, 1924), 280-81.

Sam McClure left college driven by only two immediate desires: to earn a living and to win the hand of Harriet Hurd. Having gotten ahead of our story, let us revert to seeing how he solved these problems, launched his publishing empire, and helped revolutionize American journalism.[118]

[118] A number of the progressive reformers were eventually given honorary degrees by Knox, including Sam and Harriet McClure, John Phillips, Edgar and Frederick Bancroft, Robert Mather, Albert Boyden, John and Martha Finley, Ida Tarbell, Jane Addams, Albert Britt, and Will Irwin. See *Knox Directory*, 387ff.

Chapter II. An Apprenticeship in the Publishing World

THERE WAS little anticipation of the career that awaited him when Sam McClure journeyed from Galesburg, via Boston, to New York, where he founded his famous and successful newspaper syndicate in 1884. Unknown to him, the publishing world was in a springtime of change that would open new opportunities.

Between 1860 and 1900, while the American population was doubling, the number of daily newspapers grew from 387 with an average circulation of about 4,000 to 2,190 with an average circulation near 12,000, and the number of weeklies grew fivefold to 15,813.[1] The number of dailies almost doubled again between 1890 and 1915.[2] Periodicals, often little more than newspapers themselves, grew from 700 in 1865 to 5,500 in 1900, with the peak growth coming in the decade after McClure left college, during which more than a thousand new magazines were founded.[3]

The reasons for this phenomenal growth lie partly in governmental action. In both 1870 and 1874 copyright laws were tightened, and by 1891 American participation in an international copyright law became effective, though cumbersome to comply with and still more difficult to enforce.[4] Coupled with this protection for authors was the development of additional services by the Post Office Department. In 1879 second-class mailing privileges were extended to magazines. Shortly thereafter, free rural delivery was

[1] Bernard A. Weisberger, *The American Newspaper* (Chicago, 1961), 111, 146; *Printer's Ink*, ixx (May 10, 1893), 595.

[2] Frank Luther Mott, *American Journalism, A History: 1690-1960* (New York, 1962), 549.

[3] Frank Luther Mott, *A History of American Magazines*, iii, 5; *ibid.*, iv, 11.

[4] *Ibid.*, iv, 42.

added. These developments enabled the subscriber to get his magazines quickly and inexpensively.[5]

If the government made concessions to the press which amounted to a subsidy, it was because of the demands of an increasingly literate public tutored by the new public schools and colleges. Between 1870 and 1890 illiteracy fell from 20 to 13.3 percent.[6] The new public wanted reading matter, not just in the traditional fields of general literature, but in specialized areas of religion, education, finance, agriculture, home-making, and recreation. Luther Mott, who has counted the journals, writes that by 1892 almost every organized fraternity or society, certainly every national one, had its official organ.[7] And in America's new industrial society the number of organizations was multiplying rapidly. There were 200 college papers, for example, such as the *Knox Student*, giving an average of almost one paper per 1,000 college students. Faddish recreational journals, such as the *Wheelman*, a Boston magazine for bicycle enthusiasts, were also added to the flood of literature directed towards the new market. By count of *Printer's Ink* in 1894 there were 168 prohibition and temperance journals, over 100 unofficial Methodist papers, and 20 publications of the G. A. R. alone!

Another ingredient in the easy availability of literature was the series of technical advancements in the art of printing. By 1886 a workable linotype machine was finally developed. Almost simultaneously a rapid multiple cylinder press that allowed even the largest city papers to print an entire edition in a few hours was marketed. The hand-tooled woodcuts for illustrations of the 1870's were superseded by the halftone photo-engraving process, which permitted swift duplication of tonal grays in photographs. By 1893 even Gilder's stylish *Century* was employing this

[5] James P. Wood, *Magazines in the United States* (New York, 1957), 74.

[6] Mott, *American Journalism*, 507.

[7] Mott, *A History of American Magazines*, IV, 10.

method to reproduce illustrations. At the same time the first regular four-color printing was inaugurated by the Chicago *Inter-Ocean*.[8] The next major innovation, which came swiftly, was the direct reproduction of live photographs, and by the Spanish-American War even provincial newspapers were availing themselves of this advancement.[9] These and still other technological advances ushered in a media revolution and paved the way for careers such as McClure's.

Significant developments occurred in the manufacture of paper. Cloth was replaced by wood as the basic ingredient in paper immediately after the Civil War. By 1900 the price of paper had declined from 8 cents to 2 cents per pound.[10] Thus, although the recurrent depressions of 1873, 1886, and 1893 may have hurt the older, established magazines and papers, the reduced price of paper and the lower cost of depression labor actually made these decades timely for new journalistic ventures.[11] In 1890, for example, the young John Moody, who later started *Moody's Monthly* and worked with the *McClure's* staff, edited a small magazine with a circulation of two hundred that cost him only four to eight dollars per issue.[12] In the early years of the syndicate, McClure got his printing done free by a special arrangement with the *Boston Globe*. Even advertising cost only 35 cents a column line in a good paper.

Perhaps more important to publishing growth than either governmental action or the price of raw materials was the rise of an industrial society of abundance, for a time aggressively competitive, that demanded advertising media to sell its wares. By 1900 two-thirds of all publish-

[8] Mott, *American Journalism*, 585.
[9] Mott, *A History of American Magazines*, IV, 5ff.
[10] Weisberger, *The American Newspaper*, 122.
[11] Mott, *A History of American Magazines*, IV, 5.
[12] John Moody, *The Long Road Home, An Autobiography* (New York, 1937), 57.

ing revenue came from this source alone.[13] Thereafter magazines and papers were economically dependent. Their alliance with and reliance upon the industrial sector of the nation for advertisements, free passes, and financing grew as circulation revenue became correspondingly less important. In millions, advertising grew from 39 in 1880 to 71 in 1890 and 95 in 1900, a tenfold increase since the Civil War.[14] As David Potter has explained, the country's industry was moving from a market of scarcity to one of abundance—and the advertising media were necessary to distribute its wares.

Publishers were increasingly to find themselves in a dilemma. Their journals had to increase capitalization to afford advanced mechanical means of production, and simultaneously the price of the magazine had to be cut to increase circulation, because the more important advertising revenue depended upon this factor. The problem was made more acute when the centralization of business into monopolistic trusts caused a similar centralization of advertising available for the press. In some instances a decline resulted. For example, in the March, 1896, issue of *Cosmopolitan*, thirty-eight bicycle manufacturers advertised their products. A year later bicycle supplies still accounted for about ten percent of all national advertising revenues.[15] But by the fall of 1899, a gigantic bicycle trust of the same companies had been formed with a concomitant loss of advertising. In addition the *Wheelman* and other cycling journals were founded solely to promote bicycle sales, thus absorbing revenues formerly destined for the general periodicals.

Scripps, Munsey, Hearst, and Pulitzer adopted the methods of the financier and survived. It was not, wrote Ed-

13 Weisberger, *The American Newspaper*, 149; David Potter, *People of Plenty: Economic Abundance and American Character* (Chicago, 1954), 180; Mott, *American Journalism*, 597.
14 *Ibid.*, 503.   15 *Ibid.*, 545.

ward Bok of the *Saturday Evening Post,* "so much the survival of the fittest as the survival of the largest capital."[16] It was a law true of the financial community as a whole. While the great newspaper chains survived, the individual publisher faced grave problems.

There were few like Frank Munsey or Edward Bok or William Randolph Hearst who possessed the alchemical powers to turn the printed word into gold. Often manufactured news was employed to survive, such as Stanley's fabled trip in search of Livingston or much of the Cuban news prior to the war. But severe competition, overproduction, and declining prices tied survival more closely to the new advertising firms with their bag of gimmicks.

Sam McClure initially gave slight thought to these problems of American publishing after his graduation in 1882. He only hoped to intercept and win Harriet Hurd in Utica, New York, where she was visiting. "I presume that the most daring, hairbrained, venturous, absurd, bold, risky, presumptuous, wonderful plan I ever conceived was laying siege to your heart," the future editor wrote.[17] "My ambition in that case was certainly vaunting," and it was.[18] Temporarily foiled in love McClure decided to go from Utica to Boston, where his pretty teacher of elocution, Malvina M. Bennett, was living. After a few days' visit, McClure searched for employment and came upon the Pope Manufacturing Company, which had advertised in both the *Knox Student* and the *History of College Journalism.* "Every boy in the West," he later wrote, "knew the Pope Manufacturing Company and the Columbia Bicycle," an old-fashioned high-wheeler.[19]

Founder and owner, Col. Albert A. Pope, was the first American bicycle manufacturer, and, by controlling forty principal patents, he made ten dollars off every high-

[16] Quoted in Mott, *A History of American Magazines,* iv, 15.
[17] McClure to Harriet Hurd, Oct. 15, 1881, McClure Papers.
[18] McClure, *Autobiography,* 144.
[19] *Ibid.,* 145; *The Wheelman,* ii (April, 1883), 73.

wheeler manufactured in the country.[20] But already his wheel was facing overwhelming competition from the "safety" bicycle which, with two pneumatic tires of equal size, soon replaced it. By good fortune McClure talked himself into a job teaching beginners how to ride the 60-inch-high, unbalanced bicycle at Pope's arena—no mean feat since he himself had never learned.[21] Pope later jested that McClure got the job by conjuring up pitiful visions of the large prospective family he would be called upon to support. For a dollar a day, McClure worked until he heard the Colonel remark that he had thought of founding a magazine as an advertising medium for his bicycles. Sensing greater opportunities, McClure encouraged the plan by going to Galesburg for a complete file of the *Knox Student* to serve as credentials for his own role in such a venture.[22]

Pope was impressed and agreeable. Paying McClure only ten dollars a week as editor, equal to an apprentice newspaper salary, Pope felt the whole project, with receipts from advertising, might be placed on a profitable basis. There were hundreds of bicycle clubs in the country which made a ready and enthusiastic market for such a publication. A Manhattan club flaunted its wealth by announcing a million-dollar project to build an indoor arena. As early as 1878 Colonel Pope had sold only 92 bicycles. In 1882, the *Wheelman* estimated the total number of bicycles in the country at 20,000; by 1895, the yearly sales were close to half a million, and *Scribner's* estimated there were 10,000,000 bicycles on the road.[23] Almost one out of every seven people had purchased a vehicle worth $100.[24] The census reported over one million bicycles sold in 1899 alone. Galesburg was in the midst of the craze, and John

20 McClure, *Autobiography*, 146.

21 *Ibid.*, 147.   22 *Ibid.*, 148.

23 *The Wheelman*, I (Oct., 1882), 71; Mott, *A History of American Magazines*, III, 212; *ibid.*, IV, 378; *Printer's Ink*, XIII (July 3, 1895), 3.

24 Mott, *American Journalism*, 545.

Finley proudly owned one of the several hundred cycles used in that town.

Professor Melville B. Anderson of Knox gave McClure detailed advice on the magazine, and in October, 1882, McClure's first issue of the *Wheelman*, a "high-class organ of bicycling and tricycling operation and sentiment," was ready.[25] The *Wheelman* cost two dollars a year or twenty cents per issue, as did the *Outing*, another bicycling magazine brought out five months earlier by William B. Howland in Albany, New York.

The first issue contained a well-illustrated article called "A Wheel Around the Hub." McClure had seen this piece in Roswell Smith's *Century* two years earlier, and, with Pope's permission, he had gone to New York and paid the extravagant price of three hundred dollars for the plates. To keep the style uniform, he imitated the format of the *Century*, "somewhat to the astonishment of the publishers of the latter magazine, who had never intended to sell me their idea of make-up along with the plates of the article on bicycling."[26] The *Wheelman*, one of eventually over thirty periodicals devoted to cycling, retained its style even after Pope bought the *Outing* and merged the two.[27] In some respects the *Wheelman's* contents of short fiction, factual articles, and book reviews resembled the *Knox Student*. But, in addition, the new magazine was profusely illustrated with woodcuts. Reviews of the *Wheelman* were flattering. The *Nation* called it "among the most attractive of the monthly magazines," and the *London World* thought "both the letter press and illustrations of this magazine are equal to the costliest and most elaborate got-up art magazines in England," while *Puck* insisted "no conscientious bicycler should neglect subscribing for it."[28]

[25] McClure to Anderson, Aug. 18, 1882, McClure Papers; McClure to Anderson, Sept. 15, 1882, *Ibid.*; *Wheelman*, I (Oct., 1882), 2.

[26] McClure, *Autobiography*, 150.

[27] Mott, *A History of American Magazines*, IV, 379.

[28] Quoted in Peter Lyon, *Success Story* (New York, 1963), 38; Mc-

Soon John Phillips and John and Robert McClure arrived from Galesburg to commence work in the *Wheelman's* office, and as on the *Student,* the twenty-five-year-old McClure, probably on a bicycle, fled the office routine to push circulation and acquire material. Professor Anderson's considerable work with the *Dial* had acquainted him with New England writers from whom McClure solicited material to fill the *Wheelman's* modest eight, then sixteen, pages.[29] Although Howland of *Outing* was often buying from the same group, McClure's successful entries and the intimacy he gained upon acquaintance with these writers, more than any other single ingredient, made a success of his magazine.

Down to tiny Deer Island, just outside of Newburyport, a suggested bicycle tour, McClure went to visit Harriet Prescott Spofford, a minor but popular writer of New England lore, who often wrote for the *Chautauquan* and *Scribner's.* To his profit the young red-headed editor began a friendship that was to last thirty years.[30] On the same trip to Newburyport McClure met the aging James Parton, biographer of Horace Greeley and Andrew Jackson. Parton was an Englishman, and McClure thought him impressed by his idea to found an *Eclectic Magazine* to publish French, German, and Italian articles along with an index of important foreign articles.[31] McClure's impressions of his excursion to Newburyport were so lasting that ten years later in the first issue of *McClure's Magazine* he published a sketch of the writers who lived there.[32]

Charles Eliot Norton, who was president of the Dante Society, and who, like Anderson, worked on a translation

---

Clure to Anderson, April 30, 1883, McClure Papers; *Wheelman,* III (Oct., 1883), vii.

[29] McClure to Anderson, March 4, April 30, Feb. 4, 1883, McClure Papers.

[30] McClure, *Autobiography,* 153.

[31] McClure to Anderson, April 30, 1882, McClure Papers.

[32] See J. J. Currier, "Ould Newbury," *McClure's Magazine,* I (June, 1893).

of the *Divine Comedy*, was another upon whom McClure called for *Wheelman* material. Norton had edited the *North American* and helped found the *Nation*, but neither he nor Oliver Wendell Holmes, from whom McClure got a cycling poem, was much interested.[33] Of more benefit was Charles E. Pratt, a Bostonian who had edited the defunct *Bicycling World*, the first magazine of importance on the subject.[34] Pratt became the *Wheelman's* contributing editor, and, after McClure, editor.[35] As the circulation of the *Wheelman* slowly rose, McClure continued to gain acquaintances within the New England literary circle, meeting Charles Dudley Warner, Mark Twain's collaborator, and Thomas Bailey Aldrich, William Dean Howells' successor as editor of the *Atlantic Monthly*.[36]

McClure hoped to publish serials, later to be collected and issued as books, but by the summer of 1883 he was frustrated by the seeming impossibility of building "quite a publishing business."[37] "The *Wheelman* is really an anomaly," he wrote in depression. "It seems that the *Wheelman* can never pay."[38] William B. Howland, editor of *Outing*, and later publisher of *Outlook*, felt the pinch of bankruptcy too. He first offered to consolidate the *Outing* with the *Wheelman*, then, when rebuffed, privately offered McClure $2,000 a year salary if he would accept editorship of the *Outing*.[39] Pope responded by raising McClure's salary to fifteen dollars a week, permitting him to accomplish his long-delayed marriage with Harriet Hurd in September, 1883. Still McClure was not satisfied. He wanted either a third of the *Wheelman's* stock or a larger salary

---

[33] McClure to Anderson, April 30, 1883, McClure Papers.

[34] Mott, *A History of American Magazines*, III, 213.

[35] McClure to Harriet Hurd, April 22, 1883, McClure Papers; William B. Howland to McClure, Dec. 18, 1883, *ibid.*

[36] McClure to Mrs. Albert Hurd, Jan. 13, 1884, *ibid.*; McClure to Anderson, April 30, 1883, *ibid.*

[37] McClure to Harriet Hurd, April 9, 1883, *ibid.*

[38] McClure to Harriet Hurd, July ?, July 12, 1883, *ibid.*

[39] McClure to Harriet Hurd, July ?, Aug. 10, 1883, *ibid.*

because the profits, he felt, were going to remain hypothetical.[40] The owner was no less discontented as circulation lagged.

Colonel Pope, whose losses on the magazine were reported at $20,000 a year, bought the *Outing* in the fall of 1883, consolidated it with the *Wheelman*, and promptly installed Howland as business manager of the new magazine.[41] Circulation soon reached 20,000. But McClure was jealous and hurt by this pruning of his authority, and decided that the time had come for a move to a position of greater opportunity.[42] Having just read Emerson's "Uses of Great Men," he was convinced that, "almost every sentence is applicable to myself."[43] So, in the spring of 1884, while John Phillips and John McClure attended Harvard, he moved to New York with his new bride and prepared to plow his acres of diamonds. Roswell Smith, editor of the *Century*, had been favorably impressed with McClure's activities on the *Wheelman*. In 1883, he offered McClure a job working on a new dictionary *Century* was preparing but got no response.[44] After McClure finally moved to New York, Smith hired Harriet to work on the dictionary and obtained employment for McClure with Theodore De Vinne, his printer. McClure chafed under the "slavery of being employed by others," and when the De Vinnes discovered an inordinately large number of proofing errors in his work, quietly and quickly moved over to the Century Company.[45] McClure was promised a sub-editorship under the tutelage of Maurice Thompson, who was to move from the reformist *New York Independent* to edit a new magazine projected by *Century*, *Boys' Book*.[46] But, when the project fell through, Thompson went to the *Saturday*

40 McClure to Harriet Hurd, Jan. 26, 1883, *ibid.*
41 McClure to Anderson, Nov. 6, 1883, *ibid.*
42 McClure, *Autobiography*, 159.
43 McClure to Harriet Hurd, Jan. 5, 1883, McClure Papers.
44 McClure to Anderson, March 4, 1883, *ibid.*
45 McClure to Mrs. Albert Hurd, June 6, 1885, *ibid.*
46 Maurice Thompson to McClure, April 25, 1884, *ibid.*

Evening Post and McClure went to work for *St. Nicholas,* a reputable children's magazine published by Smith.[47] The work was congenial, and numerous possibilities for improving the operation presented themselves to his restless mind.

While at home one Sunday, possibly reading a Sunday supplement, McClure strangely experienced what seemed to be "huge transparent globes like soap bubbles" floating in the atmosphere, and immediately he drew up a sixteen-page prospectus which suggested that the Century Company create a syndicate, selling the old stories of *St. Nicholas* to newspapers.[48] With the Western College Associated Press experience behind him, McClure certainly knew that the "thing was in the air at that time. . . ."[49]

The increased competitiveness among the publishing media helps to explain the development of the syndicate, a business designed to sell quality material to several newspapers at reduced rates for simultaneous publication. Ansel Nash Kellogg pioneered this field in the days following the Civil War by circulating a four-page sheet to county weekly editors which had "patent insides," or material of general interest already printed on pages two and three. Thus, by subscribing, the local editor halved his labor and retained two pages for local news. By 1880 there were 3,000 weeklies alone—two-thirds of those in the country—using matter syndicated by twenty-one companies.[50]

"Boilerplate," or cheap stereotype that could be shipped to editors, eventually replaced the "patent insides." Soon special departments were added such as fiction, children, women, and farmers, and in 1882 the enterprising Ameri-

---

[47] McClure, *Autobiography,* 42-43.

[48] McClure, Manuscript autobiographical material in McClure Papers.

[49] McClure, *Autobiography,* 164.

[50] Mott, *American Journalism,* 479; Elmo Scott Watson, *History of Auxiliary Newspaper Services in the United States* (Champaign, Ill., 1923), 22ff.

can Press Association entered the field attempting to attract daily papers with such literary fare as the comical verse of Eugene Field, also a Knox alumnus.[51] But McClure was probably ignorant of these developments.

McClure's interest in syndicates was aroused early in the summer of 1884. William Frederic Tillotson, the English publicist, who owned five weekly papers in South Lancashire, came to New York to procure material for a syndicate he operated among his journals. The arrival of the Tillotsons, who among other novelties used carrier pigeons between their papers and published one of the earliest magazines on cycling in England, was duly noted by McClure.[52] Almost simultaneously Charles Dana, of the *New York Sun*, announced that a half-dozen papers had formed a syndicate to buy the works of leading American writers. "And these two things coming together," wrote McClure, "led me to realize that there might be a big business in syndication."[53]

Other possibilities of syndication presented themselves. One suggestion was made by Frederick Bancroft, who was finishing up his Ph.D. at Columbia University. In the fall of 1884, Bancroft was hard at work fighting James B. Blaine in the New York headquarters of the Independent Republicans. "Let us get together," he urged McClure, "and get up some scheme whereby we can do good service vs. Blaine. . . . Couldn't we work up a literary bureau and furnish short articles to friendly papers? Yours for reform."[54] While McClure turned a deaf ear to this proposal, it is interesting that Frank Munsey, likewise a newcomer to New York, joined the donnybrook as a Blaine ally and made his fortune by turning the short-lived *Munsey's Illustrated*

---

[51] Weisberger, *The American Newspaper*, 147ff.

[52] Frank Singleton, *Tillotsons, 1850-1950* (Boston and London, 1950), 16, 17, 27, 33, 61.

[53] McClure, Manuscript autobiographical material in McClure Papers.

[54] Quoted in Lyons, *Success Story*, 56.

Weekly into a mouthpiece for the Republican National Committee.[55]

Not surprisingly, Roswell Smith and the Century Company had no intention of creating a syndicate. *Century* prestige could hardly stand the tarnish of handling boilerplates. Instead, McClure was given a leave of absence to attempt the scheme himself. Even John Phillips was hesitant to endorse the project, thinking that though a syndicate might give writers "larger remuneration for stories," still they would prefer to publish in a "choice journal like the Century to a broader circulation through the medium of second and third rate papers."[56] In addition, he thought the scheme was "monopolistic," "too extensive," and on the whole, "impracticable."[57] But professional journalists thought otherwise. J. A. Elwell of the *Portland Transcript* in Maine wrote encouragingly that the scheme was "decidedly original" and "would save trouble to editors, who often have so much to attend to that they accept a poor story without reading it. . . ."[58] A month and a half behind in rent, with a forced leave of absence and a baby on the way, McClure had little choice but to try the syndicate.[59]

McClure and his wife wrote almost a thousand copies of the first circular announcing the Literary Associated Press, and mailed them on October 4, 1884, to the major newspapers in the country.[60] McClure claimed to be able to "secure the best work by the best authors," by which he meant Harriet Spofford, William Dean Howells, and Helen Hunt Jackson, whose friendship he had already cultivated.[61]

A circular sent to authors explains some of McClure's

[55] George Britt, *Forty Years–Forty Millions: The Career of Frank A. Munsey* (New York, 1935), 70-71.
[56] Phillips to McClure, Aug. 10, 1884, McClure Papers.
[57] *Ibid.*
[58] J. A. Elwell to McClure, August 22, 1884, *ibid.*
[59] L. M. Long to McClure, June 23, 1884, *ibid.*
[60] Harriet McClure to Albert Hurd family, Oct. 9, 1884, *ibid.*
[61] Syndicate circular, Oct. 4, 1884, *ibid.*

non-financial motives behind founding the syndicate: "Millions of people will be led to appreciate good literature, and the book-buying public will be largely increased," and this would be a "powerful agency in destroying the market for vile literature."[62]

With no capital McClure had to live on the money due the writers for their stories. Six anxious weeks after leaving *Century*, he made his first sale. The editor of the *San Francisco Argonaut* bought a half dozen stories.[63] To sell the syndicate idea to newspapers, McClure took to the road. W. B. Merrill of the *Philadelphia Press* was already receiving material from one syndicate but took several stories, though he did not think Miss Spofford's story "worth printing."[64] In Washington, Baltimore, Albany, Boston, and Rochester, where the syndicate principle was rather new, McClure found papers interested in subscribing to his service, if he could produce the New England authors he announced.[65] Still many problems plagued the enterprise.

All stories had to be copied by hand and sent to newspapers who might reject them or, worse, reject the entire service. Many newspapers served overlapping areas and could not carry the same stories, and some weekly newspapers were published on different days of the week and found simultaneous publication, necessary for copyright, impossible.

In addition there was the threat from competing syndicates, many founded prior to McClure's.[66] In the fall of 1884, Allen Thorndike Rice, editor of the *North American Review*, announced the sale of four or five non-fiction articles a week, and Sara Orne Jewett, the spinster New

62 Syndicate circular, Feb. 10, 1886, *ibid.*
63 Jerome A. Hart to McClure, Nov. 8, 1884, *ibid.*
64 W. B. Merrill to McClure, March 2, 1885, *ibid.*
65 McClure to Harriet McClure, Nov. 19, 1884, *ibid.*; McClure, *Autobiography*, 168-69.
66 Page Baker to McClure, Oct. 12, 1884, McClure Papers.

England writer, advised McClure to merge.[67] St. Jacob's Oil, a patent medicine, also organized a syndicate and offered to take out in advertising an amount equal to the cost of the paper's subscription. Even Edward Bok attempted to launch a syndicate in 1886. The strongest competitor was Irving Bacheller, a New York reporter who authored the best seller, *Eben Holden*. Bacheller strengthened his position in 1886 by merging his syndicate with Ansel N. Kellogg of "patent insides" fame.[68] McClure responded by inaugurating illustrated stories, offering daily short stories, and varying his non-fiction with a diet of adventure, travel, folklore, and biography, topics of appeal to the isolated households over the land.[69]

Fortunately for McClure the newspapers were also facing crushing competition. Newspaper editors such as Charles Dana of the *New York Sun*, himself a bicycle enthusiast, incidentally, and Charles Taylor of the *Boston Globe* saw dozens of daily papers die in their provinces during the eighties.[70] Both became strong allies of McClure's service, and the *Globe* eventually did all of the syndicate's printing. Another ally was Richard L. Howland, publisher of the *Providence Journal* for twenty years, who quickly saw the "advantage we derived from the use of your syndicate in the early days when we were publishing the Sunday edition at a loss of $200 to $300 every week."[71] Most of the syndicate's material went into the newly organized Sunday supplement.[72]

Kate Field's sensational article on Mormonism, one of McClure's earliest offerings, was a welcome success. Miss Field was a "well-known lecturer, daughter of a St. Louis journalist, and a chatty, witty, prejudiced, and sometimes peevish commentator on public affairs and Washington

---

[67] McClure, *Autobiography*, 182-83.
[68] *Ibid.*, 183.
[69] Syndicate circular, Jan. 16, 1885, McClure Papers.
[70] Mott, *A History of American Magazines*, III, 211.
[71] Richard L. Howland to McClure, March 5, 1914, McClure Papers.
[72] Mott, *American Journalism*, 480-82.

doings."[73] She strongly favored low tariffs, woman's rights, justice to the Indians, and prize fights. While perhaps not a reformer, she certainly was a disturber of the Victorian peace, and her magazine, *Kate Field's Washington*, had a long run.

Articles with this kind of punch made editors friendly towards the Associated Literary Press and brought Mc-Clure's business out of the red. In March, 1885, McClure had lost $125.00 per week out of funds due his writers, but by the first of June, eight months after inaugurating his venture, he was out of debt and clearing $75.00 a week above expenses. "I never expected to make much money," he wrote his incredulous in-laws, the Hurds, "and I hadn't built any great hopes on the scheme at all, but everyone thinks that I have established a business that will give me an independent income and make me rich besides."[74] But he hardly got rich his first year: The total volume of business was $8,378.[75]

While the syndicate was to be presided over by men of widely different personalities, Thomas A. McClure, Harry H. McClure, or Robert Finley—usually working also on various other projects that Sam McClure dreamed up—its output always remained rather typed. Its content was directed towards the rural folk that McClure had met on his tours around Galesburg. McClure's early fiction was dominated by such New England Victorian writers as Harriet Prescott Spofford, Sarah Orne Jewett, Elizabeth Stuart Phelps Ward, author of the popular *The Gates Ajar*, Julian Hawthorne, Edward E. Hale, and Margaret Deland, whose *John Ward, Preacher* signaled a more realistic, religiously unorthodox, approach to literature when it was published in 1888.[76]

---

73 Mott, *A History of American Magazines*, IV, 61.

74 McClure to Mrs. Albert Hurd, June 6, 1885, McClure Papers.

75 Syndicate circular, fall, 1892, *ibid.*

76 Syndicate Scrapbook, "1885-1888," Dec. 25, 1886, *ibid.*; Syndicate Scrapbook, "1888-1892," Jan. 6, 1889, *ibid.*; Syndicate Scrapbrook,

The bent of the syndicate towards religious offerings was pronounced. Quite early Rev. E. P. Roe contributed ten articles on his impressions of the West; Dr. Donald Mac-Leon, a chaplain of the Queen, talked about matrimony; Elizabeth Phelps Ward prepared a series of the "Time of Christ." H. Rider Haggard's "Esther" was announced in September, 1889, and George Ebers' "Joshua" came shortly later, followed by William T. Stead's "Letters from the Vatican." Even the popular Rev. Thomas DeWitt Talmage took time off from his Brooklyn Tabernacle to write a "Life of Christ." McClure, Hamlin Garland later insisted, was always after a "snappy" life of Christ.[77] The reader's fare of religion included discussions on the Mormon Temple, the state of religion in the colleges, the fine arts' view of Christ, and the biblical defense of celibacy, the latter written by the happily married Tolstoi.

In the spring of 1887, the syndicate also did its share to create a revival of Lincoln literature. First, there was offered a 100,000-word novel on the Civil War by Jules Verne, called "North and South."[78] Then, as *Century* commenced publishing its $50,000 *Life of Lincoln* by Nicolay and Hay, McClure offered "The Real Lincoln" by Colonel Ward H. Lamont, advertised as a former law partner of Lincoln, at twenty-five dollars per article.[79] This was followed by Colonel Alexander K. McClure's reminiscences

---

"1885-1888," Jan. 2, Jan. 9, Jan. 16, 1887, *ibid.*; Syndicate circular, Feb. 21, 1886, *ibid.*; Jerome A. Hart to McClure, Nov. 8, 1884, *ibid.*

[77] For examples of this religious material see: Syndicate Scrapbook "1885-1888," Jan. 16, Feb. 6, June 5, May 29, 1887, *ibid.*; Syndicate Scrapbook, "1888-1892," Jan. 25, 1891, Dec. 22, 1889, June 22, 1890, *ibid.*; Syndicate Scrapbook, "1892-1896," April 6, 1893, *ibid.* Even P. T. Barnum, the showman, joined the ecclesiastics in giving "A Temperance Talk to Young Men," Syndicate Scrapbook, "1885-1888," May 29, 1887, *ibid.*; Hamlin Garland, *Roadside Meetings* (New York, 1930), 341.

[78] Syndicate Scrapbook, "1885-1888," Feb., 1887, *ibid.*

[79] Syndicate Scrapbook, "1885-1888," June, 1887, *ibid.*

of Lincoln which were later developed into a series for the *Saturday Evening Post.*[80]

The syndicate carried a surprisingly large amount of material dealing with the trusts, prohibition, and civil service reform. Theodore Roosevelt, then a Civil Service Commissioner, wrote an article on "The Civil Service of the United States."[81] Senator John J. Ingalls of Kansas, like Henry Cabot Lodge and others, contributed articles on government and civil service reform, a question of great current interest.[82] In addition to Roosevelt, reformers such as Henry George, Edward Bellamy, Gustavus Myers, and William T. Stead, editor of the London *Review of Reviews,* appeared in the syndicate along with liberals from the Civil War era like Moncure D. Conway, Mrs. Henry Ward Beecher, and Susan B. Anthony.[83] Syndicate articles on the rise of crime and prostitution in the United States were also frequent copy.[84]

As McClure's organization grew, it employed a large number of strong-minded women on its staff, like other New York publishing houses of the period. In 1889 McClure secured the services of Frances Hodgson Burnett, whose *Little Lord Fauntleroy* had been one of the most famous *St. Nicholas* serials of the eighties. Mrs. Burnett not only supplied fiction to the syndicate, but edited a Youth's Department that supplied up to three-quarters of a newspaper page of material each week.[85] Mrs. Charles S. Pratt, editor

[80] Syndicate Scrapbook, "1888-1892," July, 1889, *ibid.*; Mott, *A History of American Magazines,* iv, 689. See Syndicate Scrapbook, "1892-1896," April 11, 1893, McClure Papers.

[81] Syndicate Scrapbook, "1888-1892," Feb. 2, 9, 1890, *ibid.*

[82] See Syndicate Scrapbook, "1888-1892," Dec. 9, 1888, March 2, April 6, 1890, *ibid.*

[83] Syndicate Scrapbook, "1888-1892," Oct. 28, 1888, March 2, 1890, Jan. 25, 1891, *ibid.*; Syndicate circular, May 19, 1901, *ibid.*; Mrs. Henry Ward Beecher to McClure, Oct. 22, 1891, *ibid.*; "Prospectus," Oct. 8, 1900, *ibid.*

[84] Syndicate Scrapbook, "1888-1892," Feb. 1, Dec. 8, 1889, *ibid.*

[85] Syndicate Scrapbook, "1888-1892," July 1889, *ibid.*

of *Wide Awake,* one of the Boston periodicals for children, worked with Mrs. Burnett in the Youth's Department.[86] In time, Mrs. Frances A. Humphrey, who also edited *Wide Awake,* joined the syndicate.[87]

A former editor and writer for the *Chautauquan,* Ida Tarbell, was studying at the Sorbonne when called upon for feminine subjects. Her titles included "French Women and the Legion of Honor," "The French Academy and its Relation to Women," "French Politeness," and the "Paris Exhibition of the Arts of Women."[88] In addition to Miss Tarbell, McClure secured the part-time services of Miss Mary Bisland in 1892. She supervised the women's page, "one of the most successful departments I ever organized."[89] Miss Bisland, an instructor of nurses at Johns Hopkins, supplied such fascinating pieces as "The Truth about Green and Black Tea" and "Is Coffee a Food?"[90] These pressing problems received Miss Bisland's full-time efforts in 1894, after her journal, *The American Woman,* failed in the depression.[91] Attuned to average folk, she eventually found a more prestigious place in the McClure organization when Robert Finley assumed direction of the syndicate in 1896.

After seven years of operation, the Associated Literary Press was an unqualified success, furnishing fifty thousand words and forty to fifty pictures a week to customers located in the United States, Canada, and other English-speaking parts of the world. A great deal of the literature may have been poorly written, but in 1891 McClure estimated that he was paying from $800 to $2,000 a week for

[86] Harriet Hurd to Albert Hurd family, Dec. 2, 1886, *ibid.*; Mott, *A History of American Magazines,* III, 177.

[87] Syndicate Scrapbook, "1892-1896," Aug. 12, 1892, McClure Papers.

[88] Syndicate Scrapbook, "1892-1896," Aug. 8, Oct. 22, 1892, *ibid.*; James Morgan to McClure, 24 Dec., 1891, Tarbell Papers, Allegheny College.

[89] Syndicate Scrapbook, "1892-1896," Aug. 8, Sept. 3, 1892, McClure Papers.

[90] *Ibid.*

[91] Syndicate Scrapbook, "1892-1896," May 26, 1894, *ibid.*

matter and from $200 to $300 a week for illustrations. His annual volume of business had risen to $103,874.[92] A compliment to the quality of some of the syndicate's offerings was paid when *Godey's Lady Book* and other established periodicals requested its services.[93]

McClure's own daring astuteness, aided by the ever-increasing size of the reading public and the growing competitiveness of newspaper publishing, had brought him remarkable success. But he had no time to count laurels, for Bacheller's syndicate was also successful and closing hard behind. McClure's vistas naturally turned back to Europe, scene of many pleasant memories. Could his familiarity with England be made into an asset for the syndicate?

[92] Syndicate Scrapbook, "1892-1896," June 13, 27, 1892, *ibid.*; Syndicate circular, fall, 1892, *ibid.*

[93] *Godey's Lady Book* to McClure, June 17, 1895, *ibid.*

Chapter III. "My Blood Is
Like Champagne"

McClure HEARD rumors that Irving Bacheller was going abroad for literary material in the spring of 1887, and immediately he left for London, intending to be the first American to tap the resources of the English writer's market.[1] The move was to make his reputation as an American agent for the best British writers.

Being unfamiliar with the current works of European authors, McClure was forced to rely on recommendations and intuition. Every English literary figure and American expatriate he heard mentioned was bombarded with notes requesting manuscripts. A brother-in-law of *Century's* esteemed Richard Watson Gilder told McClure about a "very remarkable story of adventure, *Kidnapped*," which had been published by Robert Louis Stevenson the year before.[2] When written, Stevenson ignored McClure's letters. Henry Drummond, the Scottish divine, was also coldly disinterested.[3] McClure even ferreted out the obscure Margaret O. Oliphant, the once celebrated English novelist and biographer. She wrote acquaintances asking for the identification of McClure, "who quotes various names of writers here as having dealings with him."[4] It was soon obvious to McClure that writers hesitated to deal with an editor who accosted them with such great exuberance and poor credentials.

Frustrated with authors, McClure quickly turned to British literary agents, such as A. P. Watt and William Tillotson, the Lancashire publisher. McClure found Watt, upon whom he first paid a lengthy call, a "most agreeable

[1] McClure, *Autobiography*, 183.   [2] *Ibid.*
[3] Henry Drummond to McClure, July 2, 1888, McClure Papers.
[4] Margaret Oliphant to C.S.S. Windsor, May 10, 1888, Margaret Oliphant Papers, Princeton University. She had a story "Seen and Unseen" in *McClure's*, II (Dec., 1893).

man."[5] Despite being in the agent's "good graces," McClure was unable to buy any manuscripts. Instead, Watt suggested that McClure approach Tillotson and Son, who had a number of unsold stories by both Bret Harte and Henry Rider Haggard.[6] McClure, sensing success, immediately proposed "to see them and make as favorable terms as possible for the American rights."[7] His enthusiasm mounted as his fortunes changed, and he came away from Watt feeling "able to found a great publishing house."[8]

It was two days before McClure called on William Tillotson, and then only to learn of "treachery."[9] One of Bacheller's employees had already written the English publisher asking for his services. McClure worked furiously. For nine hours he kept the great publisher in conversation. No doubt, if this interview followed the course of others, most of the time was spent talking about Knox College, the courtship of Harriet Hurd, and the founding of the syndicate. At any rate Tillotson was eventually reduced to concluding a "treaty offensive, and defensive to monopolize the syndicate serial service of the world."[10] Since Tillotson was not realizing any substantial revenue from the foreign sale of his material, anything that could be peddled to McClure represented a profit. By the terms of the agreement, which served to enhance McClure's reputation, each firm was to pay sixty percent of the total realized from the sale of the other's material.

Tillotson was world-famous, being the agent for such writers as Robert Louis Stevenson, Bret Harte, Gerald du Maurier, Anthony Hope Hawkins, John Ruskin, J. M. Barrie, H. G. Wells, Israel Zangwill, Thomas Hardy, and R. D. Blackmore, of *Lorna Doone* fame.[11] On the other hand the only McClure writer in whom Tillotson was interested was Frances Hodgson Burnett, whose English rep-

[5] McClure to Hattie McClure, March 7, 1887, McClure Papers.
[6] *Ibid.*   [7] *Ibid.*   [8] *Ibid.*
[9] McClure to Phillips, March 9, 1887, *ibid.*   [10] *Ibid.*
[11] Frank Singleton, *Tillotsons, 1850-1950*, 43-44.

utation was based on *Little Lord Fauntleroy*. McClure
sold her material in his possession for $4,000. With scant
reason McClure persisted in thinking his "most dreadful
and most successful" negotiations with Tillotson had "succeeded, absolutely, perfectly."[12]

Predictably the alliance did not last. In the first place
McClure was not content to buy from English agents while
the writers themselves were accessible. The "natural Mc-
Clure," Henry James wrote Stevenson shortly thereafter,
was embarrassingly attendant upon them both rather than
their agents.[13] More significant than buying directly from
English authors, in 1888 McClure began to syndicate
British material in England. This brought him into direct
competition with English literary agents and violated
the letter of his agreement with Tillotson.

In reprisal Tillotson made McClure pay a "large share
of whatever I had ahead," and the next fall came to America himself to push his fiction and establish a branch
office.[14] This only increased McClure's bent towards buying and selling in England. In 1889 he finally opened a
permanent office in London under the supervision of Robert McClure.[15] In spite of these vagaries of business, Mc-
Clure's connections with the English literary agents remained friendly, useful, and life-long. Their sufferance
towards an Ulsterman gave him an added advantage in
the rooster-pit jungle of New York publishing.

With some literary exaggeration McClure wrote Stevenson that within a year the London office was "almost as

12 McClure to Phillips, March 9, 1887, McClure Papers. McClure
correctly felt that the published news of his contracts in London
would deter Bacheller. (McClure to John F. McClure, March 4, 1887,
ibid.).
13 Henry James to Robert Louis Stevenson, July 31, 1888, copy in
ibid.
14 McClure, *Autobiography*, 202; Singleton, *Tillotsons, 1850-1950*, 33,
42.
15 Samuel Storey of London *Echo* to McClure, Nov. 14, 1884, McClure
Papers; Syndicate Scrapbook, "1888-1892," Aug., 1189, *ibid.*

large as my business in New York."[16] For eighteen years this branch office was semi-independent of the other McClure holdings. During that period a disproportionately large share of the fiction used first by the syndicate, then by the magazine and publishing house, was supplied from London. Robert McClure often sent back as many as fifty-three short stories on one packet for the New York office to peruse, and as a result *McClure's* always had a leaning towards European writers.[17]

The most important English writer whose work was acquired by McClure was Robert Louis Stevenson. Ending his initial aloofness, Stevenson had his stepson, Lloyd Osbourne, make an unexpected call on McClure in New York. This led to frequent meetings between Stevenson and McClure and their families, and, finally, to an agreement that went far towards making the American reputation of both men.[18] During Stevenson's brief stay in America in 1888, McClure succeeded in buying *The Black Arrow,* published a year later, which was illustrated by Will H. Low, a noted artist and an old friend of Stevenson since their Barbizon days. The novel was serialized as *The Outlaws of Tunstall Forest,* with Charles Scribner's Sons handling the American book rights. Before Stevenson left America for the South Seas in June, 1888, McClure offered him $10,000 to write a short essay each week about his travels, a venture that paid dividends only in anxiety. Thus within a period of six months Stevenson was paid $18,000 for *Black Arrow* and the *South Sea Letters,* certainly a contemporary record.

Later McClure paid Stevenson $8,000 for a sequel to *Kidnapped,* an act which McClure insisted caused the author to blush.[19] Stevenson accepted, knowing he was under contract to Scribner's Sons for all his American publica-

16 McClure to Stevenson, Sept. 12, 1890, *ibid.*
17 Shumer Sibthrop to T. C. McClure, March 13, 1901, *ibid.*
18 Hattie McClure, "Notebook," July ?, 1888, *ibid.* For a discussion of McClure's relationship with Stevenson see McClure's *Autobiography,* 184-189.
19 McClure, *Autobiography,* 184-89.

tions, and feeling "a little sore as to one trick I played" on McClure.[20] *St. Ives* finally fulfilled this obligation. For all of this expense McClure capitalized upon Stevenson's name in America and upon his coterie of literary friends in England.[21]

Close to Stevenson stood such scholars and writers as Andrew Lang, the Scottish man of letters, from whom Mc-Clure occasionally got syndicate pieces but, more important, upon a visit to Lang's favorite haunt, St. Andrews, in the spring of 1889, he had his attention directed to a new writer, a Scottish physician named A. Conan Doyle.[22]

Doyle had published two mysteries, *A Study in Scarlet* and *The Mystery of Cloomber*. Looking for a wider public which would allow him to escape the physician's waiting room, he wrote Tillotson that same spring asking if a market existed for his short stories. Though Longman's had just bought *Micah Clarke*, Doyle was still in need of money.[23]

Leaving St. Andrews, McClure dashed back to London, reading one of Doyle's stories on the way. Impressed, he went to A. P. Watt, with whom he was currently on friendly terms, and negotiated the sale of twelve Sherlock Holmes stories at sixty dollars each, one of the best purchases he ever made.[24] Shortly he wrote Hattie that, "I find all England wild over Sherlock Holmes," and rushed off to Paris to corner the author himself.[25] Later he purchased numerous works of Doyle, including *The White Company*.

Within the year McClure was back in London visiting Sidney Colvin, who a dozen years earlier had introduced Stevenson to literary society. Colvin, a Trinity fellow, was Curator of Prints and Engravings at the British Museum.

20 Robert Louis Stevenson, *The Letters of Robert Louis Stevenson* (2 vols., New York, 1901), 276.
21 Hattie McClure, "Notebook," July ?, 1888, McClure Papers.
22 McClure, *Autobiography*, 205.
23 Singleton, *Tillotsons, 1850-1950*, 46.
24 McClure, *Autobiography*, 205.
25 McClure to Hattie McClure, April 9, 1889?, McClure Papers.

When Colvin mentioned a new writer from India with whom he was much taken, like a hound after a hare Mc-Clure pursued the suggestion. It was a name, Rudyard Kipling, that had to be written down to be remembered.[26] Stalking the new writer, McClure wore him down with talk, and bought some of his work. Within six months the syndicate was touting the twenty-five-year-old Kipling as the English "literary sensation of the hour," and offering his short story, "At the End of the Passage," at bargain rates.[27] And within the year *The Light That Failed* was also being serialized. McClure was even more generous to Kipling than to Stevenson. He paid Kipling $12,000 for serial rights to *Captains Courageous* and $25,000 for the longer *Kim*.[28] McClure, Kipling wrote, remembering the long negotiations, was "as clean and straight as spring water."[29]

Another Stevenson friend was George Meredith, the dean of all English writers. At a dinner party given by Meredith, McClure first heard the name of James Matthew Barrie. He took the bait, and before Kipling's serials were finished, was writing, "I have discovered a new author, J. M. Barrie. *He is great*, almost equal to Stevenson."[30] Soon Barrie, too, had an American publisher. A lead from A. P. Watt brought Anthony Hope Hawkins into the fold shortly afterwards.

McClure knew little of literature, but by good judgment he picked the brains of men who knew more than he. His introduction of Barrie and Kipling, as well as Stevenson

[26] McClure to Stevenson, Sept. 12, 1890, *ibid.*
[27] Syndicate Scrapbook, "1888-1892," Nov. 2, 1890, *ibid.*
[28] Mott, *A History of American Magazines*, IV, 41. McClure gained a reputation for paying writers well. Stephen Crane later wrote, when a story earned above his expectation, "that sounds very much like a McClure price." (Stephen Crane to Mr. Reynolds, Oct. 24, 1898, Crane Papers, Syracuse University.) An account of McClure's largess is in Curtis P. Brady, "The High Cost of Impatience," 122-23.
[29] Rudyard Kipling, *Something of Myself* (New York, 1937), 134.
[30] Meredith to McClure, March 21, 1891, McClure Papers; McClure to Hattie McClure, April 2, 1891, *ibid.*

and Doyle, to the American public bespeaks an intuition amounting to genius.

Perhaps because he was an Ulsterman, McClure had a penchant for Scottish writers. Such were Ian MacLaren, the Presbyterian minister who wrote the popular *Bonnie Briar Bush,* and Henry Drummond, Free Church Professor of Natural Science at Glasgow. Both found themselves being drawn into the McClure orbit and their works being broadcast across America. By the fall of 1889 McClure had appointed a general European editor to work with the London office in acquiring the works of such men as these. Edmund Gosse, Leslie Stephen's successor at Oxford and a good friend of Stevenson, accepted the post and attempted to coordinate purchases on the European market. Later Gosse contributed a series of weekly literary letters to the syndicate himself. His first was on Ibsen, whom he is credited with having introduced to English-speaking audiences.[31]

Back in Galesburg, John Finley, presiding over Knox, penned a brief ode to the prowess of "Mac, my brawny friend," who was bringing the best of Victorian literature to America:

> You've lured both sage and stripling
> "Ian" by Tochly's rippling
> Doyle, Drummond, Hope and Kipling
> Oe'r treacherous seas the best. . . .[32]

Indeed the quality of syndicate material reflected its owner's conquests. In 1890, for example, Meredith's *One of Our Conquerors* and Doyle's *The White Company* appeared along with a Tolstoi novel. These were followed the next year by William Dean Howells' *The Quality of Mercy,* which he wrote between *A Hazard of New Fortunes* and *A Traveler from Altruria,* and Mark Twain's *Letters from*

[31] Syndicate Scrapbook, "1888-1892," August, 1889, Oct. 27, 1889, *ibid.*
[32] Item, n.d., *ibid.*

Europe. Subsequently both Twain's *An American Claimant* and Stevenson's *David Balfour* and *Ebb-Tide* were syndicated in years when stories appeared by Henry James, Richard Harding Davis, Joel Chandler Harris, Robert Barr, Joseph Conrad, Anthony Hope, H. G. Wells, and William Allen White.[33] McClure even persuaded the young Randolph Winston Churchill to file correspondence from South Africa during the Boer War.

Such success only whetted McClure's appetite to fill larger spaces. In 1890 he negotiated a contract with a "large publishing firm in the country," apparently John W. Lovell's United States Book Company which specialized in reprints, by which McClure would purchase outright for them manuscripts from English novelists.[34] "During '91 I shall handle nine, during '92, eighteen, and in '93 thirty or forty. There will be no more A. P. Watt nor Tillotson & Son. There is room for one person in this business of mine, and I am that person," he boasted to Stevenson ensconced in distant Samoa.[35] Few were left in doubt about his optimistic aims. McClure confided to Harriet that, "I propose to down *all* competition, and in a short time I can dominate the *world* in my line. . . . My blood is like champagne."[36]

Through his New York office McClure was soon approaching the new journals, *Cosmopolitan* and *Munsey's Magazine,* seeking their contracts for serials.[37] This was like bearding the lion, but the efforts were not without success. William Allen White soon complained because the syndicate was selling his material to *Collier's* at rates far below what he himself could get.[38] A more lucrative field

[33] See Syndicate Scrapbook, "1892-1896," Jan. 13, 1893, Oct. 21, 1892, *ibid.*; Syndicate circular, Feb. 2, 1901, *ibid.*; Robert McClure to McClure, Feb. 6, 1900, *ibid.*

[34] McClure to Stevenson, Sept. 12, 1890, *ibid.*

[35] *Ibid.*

[36] McClure to Hattie McClure, Oct. 28, 1891, *ibid.*

[37] Robert McClure to T. C. McClure, Jan. 2, 1900.

[38] White to Phillips, May 27, 1902, White Papers.

was the Sunday supplement. Many American newspapers such as the Philadelphia *Enquirer,* the Louisville *Courier-Journal,* and the Atlanta *Constitution* made up their own weekly magazines from the offerings of the agency.[39]

Some of the best customers for American stories were often British magazines such as *Pearson's* and *Black and White.* Much of the syndicate's material also went to *The Illustrated London News* and its sister magazine, *The Graphic,* and for a while at the turn of the century these magazines submitted all of their advance proofs to the syndicate for its utilization.[40]

Only a few years of operation had brought McClure to an eminent position in American journalism, and yet he restlessly dreamed of new empires. In the summer of 1890 he decided upon a venture that may well have cost him his fortune. The new scheme was twofold. First, McClure hoped to expand to the continent and win the syndicate business available there. Robert McClure was moved from London to Germany, and Theodore Stanton, of the European Correspondents' Bureau in Paris, became head of the French office. John Phillips in turn assumed control of the London bureau, and W. B. Merrill, one of McClure's old friends on the *Philadelphia Press,* agreed to replace Phillips in the New York office.[41]

Next McClure hoped to forge an alliance with the United States Book Company to exploit the cheap reprint business across Europe. John W. Lovell, who owned the company, had two partners in London who negotiated with McClure. One was Wolcott Balestier, an unsuccessful American novelist. Balestier had migrated to England, where he made the acquaintance of Kipling, who married his sister. The two men collaborated on *The Naulahka,*

39 Syndicate Scrapbook, "1892-1896," Feb. 20, 1893, McClure Papers.
40 Robert McClure to T. C. McClure, Nov. 11, 1899, *ibid.*
41 McClure to Hattie McClure, July 30, 1890, *ibid.*; McClure to Stevenson, Sept. 12, 1890, *ibid.*; Mary C. Hurd to Hattie McClure, Sept. 4, 1890, *ibid.*; McClure to Hattie McClure, Oct. 1, 1890, *ibid.*; Syndicate Scrapbook, "1888-1892," Oct., 1890, *ibid.*

and as Kipling's agent Balestier had sold McClure the American rights to *The Light That Failed*.[42] A partner of Balestier in the projected reprint business was William Heinemann, an enterprising young London publisher.

The plan was simple. McClure hoped to launch a book reprint business in partnership with Balestier which would "supplant Tauchnitz's library," a huge German concern.[43] The expanded syndicate would be used to acquire literary materials. Edmund Gosse, a close friend of both Stevenson and Balestier, was to become general editor of the project. As ever, McClure was confident of success: "Balestier and I are true and faithful allies and we have the world at our feet."[44]

McClure hoped to use the fifty South Sea letters, contracted for two years previously, as bait to get this international organization launched. "By publishing these letters in England simultaneously with their publication in the United States, I secure English copyright," he wrote to Samoa.[45] "I believe that you understand the nature of my contract in regard to these letters. *The New York Sun* pays $10,000 for the American rights. The European rights will be worth about $5,000 more."[46] The success of the entire project depended absolutely upon the acquisition of this capital.

The *Sun*, though well disposed towards McClure, was hesitant to pay the $10,000 (which McClure had advanced Stevenson) until the letters actually began to arrive. And Stevenson, sequestered away from publishers, had numerous other works in hand, including a novel, *The Wrecker*, with McClure cast as the character Pinkerton.[47] Stevenson had originally planned to send McClure about fifty "patches" from a travelogue volume he was writing,

---

[42] See Charles E. Carrington, *The Life of Rudyard Kipling* (New York, 1956), 134-52, especially 137, 141, 147.
[43] McClure to Hattie McClure, July 30, 1890, McClure Papers.
[44] *Ibid.* [45] McClure to Stevenson, Sept. 12, 1890, *ibid.*
[46] *Ibid.* See John S. Phillips, "A Legacy to Youth," 269.
[47] See Phillips to McClure, Nov. 3, 1892, McClure Papers.

but finally he submitted *The South Seas,* a published book.[48] This was not acceptable to the *Sun*; the syndicate was short $15,000 capital.

Without the income from the Stevenson letters, Phillips and McClure thought it feasible to "capitalize for $50,000, one half to go to us and $25,000 in money to be secured."[49] This was to be done by getting "Col. Taylor of the 'Boston Globe,' Laffan of 'the Sun,' or Bennett of the 'Herald,' and possibly the owner of the 'Philadelphia Press,' and Nixon of the 'Inter-Ocean'—to each take a few thousand of the shares, and thereby secure for their own papers a chance of the services furnished by the company."[50] But more serious problems than finances plagued the enterprise.

Walcott Balestier, the chief promoter, hesitated to do business "with the McClures, as he did not regard them as straightforward."[51] Balestier, it seems, suspected the syndicate of "working behind his back to hurt his position with English authors," particularly Kipling, and in turn he was suspected of prejudicing Kipling against McClure. Both William Heinemann and Edmund Gosse attempted to mediate the dispute, and by the end of 1890 McClure was placated enough to regard himself "as pledged" to the project.[52] Yet one-quarter of the company's shares had to be sold before it could be registered in England, and neither did Stevenson's Samoan letters arrive nor did American newspaper editors show any appreciable inclination to finance the venture.

Fundless and dissident, McClure had no choice but to withdraw from the business scheme which, at any rate, was permanently dissolved when Walcott Balestier died shortly thereafter.[53] The whole project was assumed by the Methuen Company, to whom McClure was to pay court a decade later.

[48] Stevenson, *The Letters of Robert Louis Stevenson,* II, 276.
[49] McClure to probably Phillips, 1891, McClure Papers.
[50] *Ibid.*   [51] *Ibid.*   [52] *Ibid.*
[53] The letters finally came. See Stevenson to McClure, Jan. 1, 1893?, *ibid.*

McClure, whose heights of ecstasy were often baseless, took the defeat in stride, "I have abandoned German scheme, cabled Phillips to return at once & shall confine my operations to English speaking countries for a year or two."[54] His was a mind filled with innumerable schemes, and the failure of one only moved him to new creations.

One new ambition was the founding of his own periodical. Since the days of the *Student,* the *Wheelman,* and the proposed *Eclectic Magazine,* editing a periodical had never been far from his mind. After a half dozen years, when the syndicate business seemed relatively secure, John Phillips and McClure spent long hours in informal talk about the possibilities of founding a magazine.[55] Clients and writers, such as Kipling, were not spared from giving their opinions on the topic.[56] It was in this mood that McClure opened a conversation with William Dean Howells in the spring of 1890. Howells' imagination was even more vivid than McClure's. Why could they not together establish a journal modelled on the one described in *A Hazard of New Fortunes?*[57] McClure needed only a spark to burn. For weeks he kept the scheme alive, proposing that he and Howells each advance $16,000. Money from advertising and distributing agents could be called upon to raise the total capital to $97,000.[58] Howells retreated. He wanted no part of the financing, suggesting that McClure publish the magazine and call upon him to be its editor.[59] The pipe dream finally collapsed when Howells went to *Cosmopolitan* in the summer of 1890.[60] The pioneering of inexpensive magazines was left to others.

[54] McClure to Hattie McClure, Dec. 30, 1890, *ibid.* Heinemann published an "International Library" with Gosse's aid commencing the next year. See Frederick Whyte, *William Heinemann: A Memoir* (New York, 1929), 61.
[55] Hattie McClure, "Notebook," Sept. 8, 1892, McClure Papers.
[56] Kipling, *Something of Myself,* 134.
[57] Hattie McClure to Albert Hurd family, April 11, 1890, *ibid.*
[58] McClure, Notebook, "December, 1889," *ibid.*
[59] Hattie McClure to Albert Hurd family, April 11, 1890, *ibid.*
[60] McClure to Hattie McClure, June 14, 1890, *ibid.*

By 1892 both *Cosmopolitan* and *Munsey's Magazine,* priced a dime beneath the thirty-five-cent *Century,* were proving that low-priced journals could succeed financially. McClure watched closely, noting the success of *Strand* and *Country Life* in England as well as Bok's *Ladies' Home Journal* and William T. Stead's *Review of Reviews.*[61] The time seemed propitious, and in the fall of 1892 Phillips and McClure decided to establish an even cheaper magazine, one priced at fifteen cents per issue, the same price as the *Knox Student.* McClure wanted a yearly rate of a dollar, but agreed to a dollar and a half, still the cheapest price for any quality magazine.[62]

It was only the resources of the syndicate that made this plan practicable. The magazine could be filled with stories and articles from the nine-year-old file of the syndicate. Likewise, syndicate publicity could be used to build magazine circulation. Newspapers could be allowed to pay up to one-half of the cost of the syndicate service by advertising the magazine.[63] Although in later years both Albert Brady and John Phillips frowned on such activities, this proved an effective method of getting cheap advertising.

Control of the syndicate gave McClure one additional advantage when competing for literary material. He could offer writers premium prices and wider dissemination of their works, because after being used in the magazine, and possibly published in a book, their writings could be sold to newspapers. For this reason the Associated Literary Press, though presided over by Mary Bisland, Robert Finley, or a McClure, was always to work closely with the book department and the magazine. But the syndicate had reached the maximum extent of its growth. Although it added a news service to its various departments, and although it was finally consolidated with the International Syndicate Serv-

---

61 McClure, *Autobiography,* 207.
62 McClure to Hattie McClure, Nov. 25, 1892, McClure Papers.
63 Syndicate Scrapbook, "1892-1896," Dec. 31, 1895, *ibid.*

ice of Baltimore, its business grew very little.[64] It was for this reason that the impatient McClure, hot after a publishing empire, decided to take his and Phillips' practically nonexistent capital and risk it on a new magazine in the depression year of 1893. His years on the syndicate and his many trips to Europe had given McClure his principal asset—the trust and friendship of the greatest living writers.

[64] Phillips to McClure, Nov. 9, 1892, *ibid.*; Syndicate circular, June 18, 1901, *ibid.*

Chapter IV. The Making of
a Magazine

McClure's Magazine was begun with $7,300 worth of capital, most of which came from John Phillips. McClure's assets, after eight successful years in the syndicate, amounted to $2,800 in cash and two thousand syndicate manuscripts in the safe.[1] But the magazine, it was planned, would pay only for its own printing and paper, while all other expenses—those for administration, literature, and circulation—would be assumed by the syndicate or come from the minuscule capital. Most of the capital was immediately expended when Albert Brady was hired as treasurer in January, 1893, at $5,000 per annum.[2]

More money was urgently needed when the sudden stock market crash of May, 1893, sent the country into the worst depression since 1837. "Money," wrote McClure with one meager issue published, "cannot be borrowed on any terms."[3] But by luck it was obtained. A stepsister died, leaving Robert McClure several thousand dollars which he invested in the magazine.[4] Shortly thereafter, Professor Henry Drummond of Glasgow, who had an article on "Where Man got His Ears" in the first issue of the magazine, provided $3,000.[5] In addition Colonel Pope, when called upon, agreed to supply $6,000, part of which was payment for future advertising. Dr. Phillips, John Phillips' father, mortgaged and rented the family home in Galesburg for further capital, and Arthur Conan Doyle, sensing a good investment, turned over a $5,000 lecturing fee for stock.[6] Tileston

1 McClure, *Autobiography*, 208-209.

2 *Ibid.*, 210; McClure to Hattie McClure, Jan. 2, 1893, McClure Papers. Brady reinvested much of his money in the magazine.

3 McClure to Hattie McClure, June 9, 1893, *ibid.*

4 McClure to Hattie McClure, Dec. 26, 1889, *ibid.*; McClure, *Autobiography*, 210.

5 *Ibid.*, 212-213.

6 *Galesburg Daily Mail*, Jan. 14, 1894; McClure, *Autobiography*, 214, 217.

and Hollingsworth, the Boston paper merchants, extended considerable credit. Still there was a scarcity of money.

The magazine barely survived. Despite a page advertisement run free by Dana in the *New York Sun* on May 28, 1893, the day the first issue of *McClure's* appeared, 12,000 copies of the initial 20,000 magazines printed were returned by distributing agents. The $600 realized did not even cover the first printing bill.[7] A profit had been originally anticipated with a circulation of only 12,000, but when that figure was reached the magazine continued to lose $1,000 a month.[8] Such was the inexact nature of McClure's calculations. But perseverance was to win.

Within a year of *McClure's* appearance, the gradual return to prosperity stimulated publishing. The magazine went to press in November, 1894, a year later, with 60,000 subscribers and carried sixty pages of advertising.[9] It was a good showing for a depression and compared favorably with *Century's* circulation, which had fallen from 200,000 to 75,000. At this point *McClure's* was making money, though "not a great deal to be sure."[10] Undoubtedly, the most important ingredient in this success was the popular price of the fifteen-cent magazine. But other factors certainly contributed to the company's improved fortunes: well-written articles, engaging prospectuses designed by the well-known Will H. Low, prolific newspaper advertising, an abundant use of pictures and color illustrations, and favorable reviews by other established journals.[11]

Establishing the magazine was not accomplished without severe competition and price cutting. No sooner did *McClure's* appear than *Cosmopolitan* cut its price to twelve

[7] Syndicate Scrapbook, "1892-1896," May 29, 1893, McClure Papers; McClure, *Autobiography*, 214.

[8] McClure to Hattie McClure, Jan. 14, 1893, McClure Papers; McClure, *Autobiography*, 215.

[9] Syndicate Scrapbook, "1892-1896," Oct. 12, 1894, McClure Papers.

[10] *Ibid.*

[11] McClure to Hattie McClure, Jan. 14, 1893, *ibid.*; Syndicate Scrapbook, "1892-1896," Oct. 12, 1894, *ibid.*

and a half cents per issue or a dollar and a half per year. A month later *Munsey's* went to ten cents a copy and a dollar for a year's subscription.[12] In May of 1895 McClure learned that *Cosmopolitan* was contemplating another price cut, which would have taken it down to a dime, the price of *Munsey's, Godey's,* and *Peterson's.* McClure, along with Phillips, finally persuaded the reluctant staff into following the move.[13] "I let Munsey demonstrate the success of the ten-cent magazine in two ways," McClure later pointed out half-truthfully, by getting "circulation and getting advertising, before putting the magazine down to ten cents. I am so conservative I am rarely willing to perform experiments myself. To Mr. Munsey's boldness is due the success of the ten cent magazine largely."[14] Regardless of McClure's motives, the price cut inaugurated a revolution in American journalism. With *Munsey's, McClure's,* and *Cosmopolitan* selling at half the rates of the *Century, Harper's* and *Scribner's,* the die was cast—the country was to be the empire of the low-priced, heavily illustrated, advertisement-laden, popular monthlies with their contents emphasizing youthful optimism, self-improvement, and success.

McClure's decrease in price was made possible by Colonel Pope, who gave the magazine two loans, totalling $9,000, in return for the concessions of special advertising rates, twenty-five percent below those announced.[15] As McClure predicted, "You can't get behind ten cents," and circulation, partly spurred by Miss Tarbell's famous series on Napoleon, immediately mounted to record heights.[16] From 60,000 in the fall of 1894, circulation grew phenomenally to 166,000 by July, 1895, and to 250,000 by July, 1896. *McClure's* average circulation during its first year of

[12] Mott, *A History of American Magazines,* IV, 5.
[13] McClure to Hattie McClure, May 26, 1895, McClure Papers.
[14] Office memo to Baker; n.d., Baker Papers.
[15] McClure to Hattie McClure, May 26, 1895, McClure Papers; Phillips to McClure, May 28, 1896, *ibid.*
[16] McClure to Hattie McClure, May 26, 1895, *ibid.*

operation was 27,072, but by 1896 it was 258,374, nine times greater, an unequaled feat.[17] By 1900 *McClure's* and *Cosmopolitan* had exceeded 350,000 and *Munsey's* figures were almost double that. Deserted by their clientele, *Century* and the class monthlies had long since commenced a decline.

McClure's advertising rates swiftly rose from fifty to eighty dollars per hundred thousand circulation, but it was still one of the best buys available.[18] While the first issue of the magazine carried 24½ pages of advertising, twice as much as the literary monthlies, and the next four numbers averaged only 8, by 1895 the net pages of advertising reached 66 and by 1897 over 100. Between 1895 and 1905, Albert Brady was fond of saying, the journal had carried the "largest amount of advertising of any magazine in the world," despite larger circulation by other periodicals.[19] By 1905, with over 450,000 copies printed per issue, *McClure's* carried 200 pages of advertising at $400 per page, the maximum of any American magazine.

As finances improved, both the manufacturing process and the staff underwent rapid change. In the winter of 1895 the largest press ever manufactured by M. B. Cottrell Company was proudly installed in *McClure's* offices in the Lexington Building on 25th Street. Kipling was especially fascinated by it. Oscar W. Brady was brought from Iowa to supervise the printing operations which covered two-thirds of an acre of floor space.[20]

But more important changes were going on in the editorial offices on the sixth floor. In a small, partitioned office, where McClure and Phillips sat side by side, an office

17 "The Story of McClure's," *Profitable Advertising* (Oct. 15, 1897), 140.
18 Syndicate Scrapbook, "1892-1896," July 31, 1895, McClure Papers; Phillips to McClure, May 28, 1896, *ibid.*; Mott, *A History of American Magazines*, IV, 21.
19 "The Story of McClure's," *Profitable Advertising* (Oct. 15, 1897), 143. See Mott, *A History of American Magazines*, IV, 21, for a discussion of *McClure's* trade policies compared to that of other magazines.
20 "The Story of McClure's," *Profitable Advertising* (Oct. 15, 1897), 145.

that differed from others on the floor only in that it had upholstered chairs, the decision was finally made to hire Ida M. Tarbell. No single writer was identified more closely with *McClure's* early success than was Miss Tarbell. She was an outstanding type of that nineteenth century genus, the self-made woman.

Ida Tarbell, born in 1858, was the daughter of ardent Pennsylvania Republicans, her father having voted for Fremont.[21] One of her brothers, an acquaintance of Lincoln, lost an arm at Gettysburg, and another served as a major of colored troops, being appointed by Lincoln.[22] She was raised on stories of the abolitionists and remembered the tragedy of Lincoln's assassination. Her father, Franklin Sumner Tarbell, was an oil producer in the Titusville, Pennsylvania, oil boom, until forced out of business by Rockefeller's Southern Improvement Company. It was in the rugged, rough and tumble boom environment that Miss Tarbell matured, remembering well the lessons of laissez-faire and savoir-faire.

Her section was the same back country that produced Frederick Howe, later a partner of James Garfield, on one hand, and Henry H. Rogers, the Rockefeller partner, on the other, both of whom were her good friends. Another boomer who learned the lesson of the rebate from experience was Samuel "Golden Rule" Jones, who later emerged as a progressive. After selling out to Standard Oil he moved from Titusville to Toledo, Ohio, where he revolutionized municipal politics.[23]

Since the fortunes of the Tarbell family inversely hinged on those of Standard Oil, the end was foreordained by the law of the concentration of wealth. When forced from business in 1882, Ida Tarbell's father and brother, William

[21] Ida Tarbell, *All in the Day's Work* (New York, 1938), 12.

[22] Abraham Lincoln to S. Newton Pettis, April 27, 1864, Tarbell Papers, Allegheny College. Unless otherwise cited this Tarbell collection is referred to.

[23] Samuel Jones, *The New Right* (New York, 1899), 44, 50.

Walter Tarbell, sought to repair the family's lot by taking claims in the Dakota Territory. Seeing little prospect in the territory's free land, both eventually returned to Pennsylvania, where William Tarbell completed his legal training and eventually became a counsel for such independent producers as Pure Oil and Gulf.[24]

Miss Tarbell's mother was a former schoolteacher who insisted that the family remain unreconciled to a "status revolution" in the form of disaster. Her letters to Ida Tarbell ring with revolt: "It seems terrible that in this land of plenty, this land of which we proudly speak as the 'home of the free,' people should be starving; yes actually starving by hundreds and thousands."[25] The Pullman strike and the depression of 1893 convinced her, so she wrote Ida in Paris, that "whisky and monopolies are fearful evils—and growing in their devilish power over the country; no wonder such a woeful state of things exists for us—no wonder that such a terrible problem stands before the country to be solved;—peacible [sic], if possible—by force if it must be— but to be solved and answered by this generation before God and the world. . . ."[26] These were fighting words from a fighting family. Mrs. Tarbell, reduced to selling milk while her husband did manual labor in the oil fields, considered adopting socialism, but felt in the final analysis that it was unable to cure men's avariciousness.[27] Rather, Mrs. Tarbell became a participant in that cluster of reforms connected with the Chautauquan Literary and Scientific Circle.[28] Albert Shaw in the *Review of Reviews* called the Circle, with its hundred thousand members, the "greatest popular educational movement of modern times."[29]

This, then, was Ida Tarbell's intellectual background.

[24] See William Walter Tarbell to William Bayliss, March 30, 1882, Western Americana Papers, Yale University.
[25] Mrs. F. S. Tarbell to Ida Tarbell, Aug. 6, 1893, Tarbell Papers.
[26] *Ibid.*
[27] Esther Tarbell to Ida Tarbell, July 23, 1893, *ibid.*
[28] Mrs. F. S. Tarbell to Ida Tarbell, July, 1896, *ibid.*
[29] Mott, *A History of American Magazines,* IV, 545.

She followed her mother's lead and suffered a loss of faith in revolution as a divine weapon only when she viewed its extremes at work in France in the Boulanger movement.[30]

Ida Tarbell's parents were fiery supporters of the movement for woman's rights as well as for temperance. Frances Willard was often a family guest.[31] This probably explains Ida's determination to obtain an education at Allegheny College in Meadville, Pennsylvania. At Allegheny, as at Knox, congenial abolitionist, temperance, and suffragist sentiments prevailed.[32] She was the defiant, sole female in her class. After obtaining her degree, Miss Tarbell spent a brief stint teaching; then she returned to Meadville to join Dr. Theodore I. Flood's staff on *The Chautauquan*.

Dr. Flood, a minister, edited *The Chautauquan*, gave it a circulation of 40,000, and made it one of the more liberal voices in the country. A bit like Flower's *Arena*, it was mugwump, temperance, feminist, pro-labor, anti-slum, and, not a little like its founder, Methodist.[33] In the midst of the oil region, *The Chautauquan* naturally looked askance upon the rise of the monopolistic trusts.[34]

In addition to writing short home-making articles for the magazine, Miss Tarbell fulfilled a number of editorial chores. Often she annotated the Circle's reading for the magazine. During the summer she aided in publishing the society's newspaper, which usually reprinted lectures given at *The Chautauquan* camp grounds. It was here that she made the acquaintance of Robert and John Finley, young Hopkins graduate students, who, like herself, enjoyed the

---

[30] Tarbell, *All in the Day's Work*, 143.   [31] *Ibid.*, 32.

[32] *Ibid.*, 40. Miss Tarbell refused to support feminine suffrage until much later. In the muckraking era she returned an invitation to join a suffrage committee, saying, "I certainly do not object to belonging to a body which is considering that question . . . ; but I do not want to ally myself with one whose aim is securing suffrage." (Tarbell to Kathrine Mackay, Nov. 15, ?, Tarbell Papers.)

[33] See Mott, *A History of American Magazines*, IV, 545ff.

[34] See *Chautauquan*, X (Feb., 1890), 572.

summer enthusiasm of western New York. John Finley often read her proof for newspaper articles.[35]

Still single and tired of her feminine columns for the magazine, Miss Tarbell decided to go to Paris to study the European technique of writing, particularly of historical research. One of her successors on *The Chautauquan*, it is interesting to note, was the boyish, roly-poly John M. Siddall, who became her protégé at *McClure's* a few years later.[36]

In the salons of the Third Republic, soon to be rocked by the anti-Semitic Dreyfus affair, Miss Tarbell was an occasional wide-eyed visitor. But more of her time, by necessity, was spent absorbing the radicalism of the Left Bank. There she had acquaintances who survived the depression years by living on as little as ten cents a day.[37] The most advanced capital in the world aroused Miss Tarbell's interest in the revolutionary role of women. Soon she was totally absorbed in a history of Madame Roland's participation in the French Revolution.

For two years, the lonely, self-sufficient, always decorous American—somewhat similar to Henry James' caricature of his compatriots—earned her precarious livelihood by writing for various American magazines, such as the new *Scribner's*. In one ambitious foray she attempted the syndication of a foreign news letter.[38] But McClure's Associated Literary Press, with a good European reputation, was a more accessible and remunerative market. After inundating the syndicate with her translated cribbings from French newspapers, as well as suggestions for articles, Miss Tarbell was finally employed to do more extensive work.

In the spring of 1892, seated high in his sixth floor office,

---

[35] Tarbell, *All in the Day's Work*, 76.

[36] When Flood was retiring in 1898, he sought an editor who shared his views, and the position was offered to Ray Stannard Baker, then on McClure's. See Baker to Father, April 14, 1898, Baker Papers.

[37] Ida Tarbell to Mrs. F. S. Tarbell, n.d., Tarbell Papers.

[38] *The Baltimore Sun* to Ida Tarbell, Feb. 8, 1892, *ibid.*

McClure picked a manuscript off Phillips' desk. Upon reading "On the Paving of the Streets of Paris by M. Alphand," he immediately decided to make Miss Tarbell his Paris representative.[39] A resident writer in France was needed. McClure often used French newspaper articles translated by either Harriet or her sister, Mary, in the syndicate. It was an inexpensive, if questionable, way of obtaining material. This was to be Miss Tarbell's first function. She was willing to translate short stories, of which the syndicate needed at least one a day, at less than a dollar a copy, while her other pieces, more lengthy, were worth from two to twelve dollars each.[40] Some of Miss Tarbell's articles, of no value to the syndicate, were sold to editors as a favor to her. By the end of 1892, there was almost weekly correspondence between Paris and the New York editorial offices.[41]

Phillips and McClure were delighted with Miss Tarbell's work, which profited, said McClure, from an imitation of the French historians "then so much in advance of our own."[42] Within the year the editors decided to broaden the scope of her activity. Theodore Stanton, who had served as the syndicate's editorial representative in Paris, joined the growing Associated Press, and in 1892 Miss Tarbell was appointed to his position. Her new responsibility required considerable travel, soliciting and writing manuscripts.[43] Soon she was interviewing such personages as Professor Drummond in Scotland, where she was instructed to write the "autobiography of his soul" as one of the millions of readers interested in him.[44] Such was the pap that made for editorial bliss in the backwaters of the land.

Soon McClure was also using Miss Tarbell to investigate his abiding whim, the inventions of man "that have con-

[39] See McClure *Autobiography*, 218; Tarbell, *All in the Day's Work*, 118.
[40] McClure to Tarbell, Jan. 20, 1893, Tarbell Papers.
[41] McClure to Tarbell, Nov. 5, 1892, *ibid.*
[42] McClure, *Autobiography*, 218.
[43] McClure to Tarbell, Nov. 5, 1892, Tarbell Papers.
[44] McClure to Tarbell, Feb. 6, 1894, *ibid.*

quered space and time."[45] Advances in steamships, railroads, telegraph and cable systems, as well as the Mont Blanc observatory and the Bertillon system for the identification of criminals, received her attention, and, indeed, Miss Tarbell's first article in *McClure's* in July, 1894, was the "Municipal Laboratory," a discussion of the health practices of French cities.[46] McClure and Miss Tarbell, it might be added, like their colleagues, were awed by the marvels of modern science—that is, at the level of Marconi and the Wright brothers. But more of that later.

When *McClure's* commenced publication in 1893, Miss Tarbell was invited to assume the editorship of the syndicate's Youth Department recently vacated by Frances Burnett.[47] Although genial August Jaccaci, who managed *McClure's* art department, added his charm to McClure's enthusiastic persuasiveness, Miss Tarbell preferred the charms of Paris.[48] She stayed. She was always the only employee more firm—or stubborn—than McClure.

An invitation to continue her studies in the French Revolution by writing a biography of Napoleon finally brought Miss Tarbell to *McClure's* in the summer of 1894. McClure knew her weaknesses too. As the centennial of the French Revolution passed in France, the Bonapartists sought to capitalize on the event by creating a sentiment for Napoleon. The mania overflowed to America, where McClure noticed in the fall of 1893 that several magazines proposed articles on the Corsican conqueror. Would not some "fresh, striking, unpublished documents, letters or what not" dealing with Napoleon be a timely venture for the new *McClure's*, he proposed.[49] Having just read that there was one Revolutionary collection of 30,000 portraits in Paris, McClure intended to accompany the article with a "Human Document" series of Napoleonic pictures. Despite her deep

45 McClure to Tarbell, June 19, 1894, *ibid.*   46 *Ibid.*
47 McClure to Tarbell, Jan. 26, 1893, *ibid.*
48 McClure to Tarbell, Feb. 10, 1893, *ibid.*
49 McClure to Tarbell, Dec. 6, 1893, *ibid.*

71

involvement, and it was an emotional involvement, with the volume on Madame Roland, Miss Tarbell found McClure's bait irresistible, though she insisted that the cult of Napoleon would be about as interesting as Napoleon himself.[50]

The article accompanying the Napoleon pictures had already been begun by Robert Sherard, a great-grandson of Wordsworth, who wrote occasional pieces for the syndicate and the magazine.[51] But with his British bias the article became a rather negative, jingoist anti-Napoleon piece of writing. In Miss Tarbell's care the article was to undergo a metamorphosis. Originally intended to be only a text for reproductions of famous paintings of Napoleon—and it should be remembered that *McClure's* was one of the most heavily illustrated magazines in the country—Miss Tarbell made the text into a life history.

The best collection of pictures, it was found, was owned by Gardiner Green Hubbard, of Washington, D.C., the father-in-law of Alexander Graham Bell. Both men were to collaborate with *McClure's* in the publication of the *National Geographic Magazine* a few years later. Working through the collection while writing in the Library of Congress, within six weeks Miss Tarbell had finished the first of seven installments to the satisfaction of both Hubbard and McClure. As her series on Napoleon appeared, *Scribner's* published the long delayed *Madame Roland*.

Her Napoleon was only a modest success when compared with subsequent series. *McClure's* circulation improved slightly. Still McClure exploited her biography in his most showman-like manner. In the spring of 1895 he announced a *McClure's Magazine Library* with *Napoleon* being the "first of a series of books to be issued quarterly."[52] After inviting other publishers to advertise their works on Napoleon in the volume, at a cost of forty dollars a page, he

[50] McClure to Tarbell, Jan. 6, 1894?, *ibid.*
[51] He had an article on Suez in the first issue of the magazine.
[52] Syndicate Scrapbook, "1892-1896," April 27, 1895, McClure Papers.

printed an edition of 30,000 and peddled copies at fifty cents for paper and a dollar for hardback. Thus the Napoleon volume served as an entrée to the book publishing business which McClure was to enter two years later.

Only a few months after the first article on Napoleon appeared, McClure's thoughts turned towards another great hero whose rise to power had also been synonymous with revolutionary change. He decided to have a "series of articles on Lincoln, written by many different men who had known him, and of having Miss Tarbell edit these articles, bring them into scale with one another, and herself write in the portions of Lincoln's life that these articles did not cover."[53]

"Lincoln," wrote Miss Tarbell, "was one of Mr. McClure's steady enthusiasms. I once saw him, in puzzled efforts to find the reason for the continued life of a great American magazine, going through the file from the Civil War on, solely to find out what attention had been given to Lincoln. 'Not a Lincoln article in this volume, nor in this,' he cried. 'It is not a great magazine, it has overlooked the most vital factor in our life since the Civil War, the influence of the life and character of Abraham Lincoln.' "[54]

McClure's instinct to move from Napoleon to Lincoln seemingly was wrong. Nicolay and Hay's biography of ten volumes, published in 1890, appeared to cover the field adequately, and *Century*, which had carried a serial abridgment of these volumes for two and a half years, had preceded them with a lengthy series, "Battles and Leaders of the Civil War," which had been a popular success.[55] With grave trepidations Miss Tarbell applied her historical skills to Lincolniana.

The first installment of what was to become a two-volume work appeared in the summer of 1895, a few months after Miss Tarbell began her research by interviewing Robert

[53] McClure, *Autobiography*, 221.
[54] Tarbell, *All in the Day's Work*, 161.
[55] Mott, *A History of American Magazines*, III, 470.

Lincoln and John Nicolay. Employing the methods of a journalist as well as those of a historian, for four years Miss Tarbell searched for photographs, manuscripts, and eye-witness accounts that would satisfy her heady editor's demands for a popular history. In Galesburg, where the young Carl Sandburg was finishing college, she found the "stirring and picturesque material that I sought" about the great debates, in which she was particularly interested.[56] A number of citizens there, including John Finley, "my old friend on the Chautauqua Assembly Daily Herald," were of aid in the project.[57]

Within ten days of the appearance of Tarbell's life of Lincoln, *McClure's* added 40,000 new subscribers and, within three months, 100,000 subscribers.[58] In a small town on the Middle Border a boy "went out on the street and in less than an hour picked up more than forty subscribers."[59] With such success *McClure's*, at the beginning of its career, associated itself with the Lincoln epic and the abolitionist tradition. While the magazine sponsored Lincoln scholarships at Knox and served as a clearing house for Lincolniana, Miss Tarbell's work went on. Eventually she wrote several other volumes on Lincoln, such as *A Boy's Life of Lincoln*, ghosted Charles A. Dana's memoirs, and edited Carl Schurz's memoirs before she completed McClure's obsession with the Civil War.

McClure's fiction supplemented Miss Tarbell's factual articles. Spiced with heavy helpings from the carefully cultivated English writers, it was no less significant in boosting circulation. That this was true was due principally to another strong-minded woman, Viola Roseboro'. Like Miss Tarbell, Miss Roseboro' worked for the syndicate's literary department but transferred to the magazine when it

[56] Tarbell, *All in the Day's Work*, 171.
[57] *Ibid.*, 171, see 161-178.
[58] Press release dated Nov. 23, 1895, McClure Papers; McClure, *Autobiography*, 221-22.
[59] S. H. Elrod to McClure, April 5, 1914, McClure Papers.

appeared. Also like Miss Tarbell, who was to remain her close friend for forty years, Miss Roseboro' was a believer in the Lincoln mystique. "All of her life," wrote a friend who knew her well, "Viola was to worship Lincoln. In old age, on Staten Island, she pored over Carl Sandburg's physically heavy volumes, not alone because he brought back to her the war days and the momentous day of Lincoln's death."[60] In other ways Miss Roseboro's opinions and experiences were quite different from those of either Miss Tarbell or McClure.

Miss Roseboro' was a hard-smoking ex-actress and writer.[61] She had been born in Tennessee, the daughter of Rev. Samuel Roseboro and Martha Colyar Roseboro. One of her uncles was Arthur S. Colyar, who as owner of the *Nashville Daily American*, president of the Tennessee Coal and Iron Company, and Governor, did much to shape Tennessee's Bourbon politics after Reconstruction. But Miss Roseboro's pious parents were ardent abolitionists, forced before the war to migrate first to Missouri, then, when violence threatened, to Illinois with a price on their heads. The family felt bereaved when John Brown was hanged in Virginia. "What a price to pay for good motives," her mother remarked.[62] When the war finally came, her father served as a chaplain for Union troops in Tennessee.[63]

Miss Roseboro's career as an actress was short and unsuccessful, and so she imitated her friend, Sarah Orne Jewett, and attempted to maintain herself by writing. Even this occupation, despite the influence of her family, presented difficulties. Richard Watson Gilder of *Century* accepted one of her stories only to find innumerable others in the mail.[64] Even this honored patronage did not alleviate

[60] Viola Graham, *Duchess of New Dorp* (2 vols., Danville, Ill., 1955), I, 101.

[61] See Eugene Wood to Brand Whitlock, Oct. 30, 1899, Whitlock Papers, Manuscript Division, Library of Congress.

[62] Graham, *Duchess of New Dorp*, I, 73.

[63] *Ibid.*, I, 49, 68, 73, 79, 204.

[64] Viola Roseboro' to Richard W. Gilder, n.d., Century Papers, New York Public Library.

her acute "anxiety for the struggle of life," and she still occasionally found herself "financially crippled—a state that with all my poverty I don't often get into," and forced to survive by beneficent loans.[65]

By 1886 Miss Roseboro' had made the acquaintance of McClure and was selling her stories to the syndicate as well as to the *Century*.[66] Her second novel, *The Joyous Heart*, published in 1903, was dedicated to McClure. Typical of her work, it was a northern study of the slave question in Tennessee and contained a statement of Negro rights.[67] Many of Miss Roseboro's ideas were quaint, but one of her often-articulated sentiments was that the amalgamation of the races was inevitable.[68] Her favor was ever with the underdog, be it poet, publisher, or politician.

Miss Roseboro' was greatly influenced by Ely and Finley's volume, *Taxation in American Cities*, which "convinced her that, politically, she was a Mugwump, and Independent."[69] Although she was about as unconcerned with politics as with other conventionalities, her feelings were often confused. In a rare moment in 1890, when New York City braced for its perennial bout with Tammany Hall, Miss Roseboro' wrote Gilder that she was "waiting eagerly for news of the triumph of decency" in the election.[70] She wanted the status of women improved, but thought the feminine vote superfluous; she disliked socialism, but read Edward Bellamy and discovered Jack London for *McClure's*.[71]

When *McClure's* was founded, Miss Roseboro' became a reader for the magazine. The informally run office was congenial for her, and in her new patrons she found "her father's philosophy of life."[72] McClure found in Roseboro',

[65] Viola Roseboro' to Richard W. Gilder, March 6, 1891, *ibid.*
[66] Graham, *Duchess of New Dorp*, I, 266, 279; Syndicate Scrapbook, "1892-1896," June 28, 1893, McClure Papers.
[67] Graham, *Duchess of New Dorp*, II, 75.
[68] *Ibid.*, I, 43.   [69] *Ibid.*, I, 283.
[70] Roseboro' to Gilder, Nov. 6, 1890, Century Papers.
[71] Graham, *Duchess of New Dorp*, I, 259, 300; II, 43.
[72] *Ibid.*, II, 8.

Will Irwin later wrote, "a manuscript reader with a mind as original as his own."[73]

Miss Roseboro's major responsibility centered on two barrels located on the sixth floor, filled with thousands of unsolicited manuscripts.[74] The number of manuscripts submitted must have been quite large. As early as 1890 the *Ladies' Home Journal*, which paid considerably less than *McClure's*, was receiving over 15,000 manuscripts a year from which it accepted less than 500.[75] From the barrels Miss Roseboro' tried to pluck the best authors. The unsatisfactory were always placated with an encouraging letter. Many loved her devotedly and conceded, "she is a good fellow and smokes good tobacco."[76]

Several readers were hired by Miss Roseboro'. Molly Best, who became a close comrade, was one. Then, in 1902, a young Harvard graduate destined to become a significant poet, Witter Bynner, or "Bitter Winter," as O. Henry jokingly called him, joined the staff. Bynner later wrote that his first job was to separate the sheep from the goats, to take the promising manuscripts, pack them into an old suitcase, and carry them to Miss Roseboro's apartment on Staten Island for her to read.[77]

In time Miss Roseboro' emptied the barrels and "founded a school of fiction."[78] Rolling her own cigarettes in public and using pointed Anglo-Saxon words, Viola Regina, as the staff called her, had little use for the Victorian attempt to imitate an old imitation of reality. In more perilous times she had fought with Gilder, who insisted on amending one of her short stories to read "good heavens" instead of "good Gawd." To her utter chagrin she lost.[79]

[73] Will Irwin, *Propaganda and the News* (New York, 1936), 69.

[74] *Ibid.*, 69; Will Irwin, "Strictly Personal: Viola Regina," *Saturday Review of Literature*, XVIII (March 3, 1945), 15.

[75] Mott, *A History of American Magazines*, IV, 39.

[76] Eugene Wood to Brand Whitlock, Oct. 30, 1899, Whitlock Papers.

[77] Quoted in Graham, *Duchess of New Dorp*, II, 16, 17.

[78] Will Irwin, "Strictly Personal: Viola Regina," *Saturday Review of Literature*, 15.

[79] Roseboro' to Gilder, Dec. 14, 1889, Century Papers.

77

But basking in the glow of McClure's tolerant editorship, she gave that nebulous American realism being cultivated by William Dean Howells and his disciples a public.

From prison William Sidney Porter submitted a story which appeared in the syndicate's offerings in 1898.[80] And in 1899 Miss Roseboro' picked Porter's "Whistling Dick's Christmas Stocking" for the magazine over McClure's strong objections.[81] It was the first time O. Henry had achieved magazine publication. In subsequent years *McClure's* published several of O. Henry's short stories, including "The Phonograph and the Graft" in 1903, a muckraking piece about an Indian's confidence racket among the Latin Americans.[82]

On another occasion Miss Roseboro' rushed in to inform the astonished McClure that she had a "serial sent by the Lord God Almighty to *McClure's Magazine*," and produced, after much cutting, Booth Tarkington's first novel, *The Gentleman from Indiana*.[83] Other discoveries of Miss Roseboro's were Myra Kelly, creator of "Little Citizens," character studies of East Side Jewish children; and George Madden Martin, author of the famous "Emmie Lou" stories. Harvey O'Higgins, whom she encouraged, used *McClure's* to publish realistic stories about the antics of Tammany Hall. Rex Beach, Edith Wyatt, Jack London, and Willa Cather were other unknown writers whom Miss Roseboro' patronized "as if she had known what the end was to be in each case, and exactly how popular each of these writers was to become."[84] Miss Cather's relationship with Miss Roseboro' and *McClure's* became more intimate in 1905 when she became an editor of the magazine. While Miss Roseboro', more than any other person, was responsi-

---

[80] Graham, *Duchess of New Dorp*, II, 18.

[81] Roseboro' to McClure, n.d., McClure Papers; Irwin, "Strictly Personal: Viola Regina," *Saturday Review of Literature*, 15.

[82] Nine of O. Henry's stories appeared in *McClure's*.

[83] Irwin, "Strictly Personal: Viola Regina," *Saturday Review of Literature*, 15.

[84] McClure, *Autobiography*, 247; see Graham, *Duchess of New Dorp*, II, 43, 80.

ble for the high quality of the magazine's fiction, Witter Bynner supervised the department of poetry.

It would be amiss to neglect Bynner. Coming to *Mc-Clure's* from Harvard, Bynner included among his heroes Thomas Paine, Jefferson, and Wendell Phillips.[85] At Bynner's behest A. E. Housman's poems from *The Shropshire Lad*, already in print as a volume, were given their first American publication. Bynner's first poems, written at the beginning of a distinguished career, also appeared in the magazine with Miss Roseboro's approbation.[86] Little regard was given to the fact that Bynner was a Negro.

Another poet, whose strength was recognized by the *Mc-Clure's* editors long before he became famous, was Edwin Markham, author of "Man with a Hoe."[87] McClure published most of Markham's best work, and the California poet's "Lincoln, Man of the People," which appeared in his third volume of poetry, must have further endeared him to Miss Tarbell, Miss Roseboro', and the other editors at the 25th Street office.

Perhaps it was Markham's poem which moved John Phillips to write his "Lincoln" for Miss Tarbell's *In the Footsteps of Lincoln*. It is a credo of heroic natural forces moving against the evil of bondage, one to which Miss Tarbell and Miss Roseboro' as well as Bynner and Markham could have subscribed:

> In him distilled and potent the choice essence of a race!
> Far back the Puritans—stern and manful visionaries,
> Repressed poets, flushed with dreams of glowing
>   theologies!
> Each new succession, out of border hardship,
> Refined to human use the initial rigor of the breed,

---

[85] See *Twentieth Century Authors*, ed. by Stanley Kunitz and Howard Haycraft (New York, 1942), 231.

[86] See insert dated Nov. 30, 1960 in letters from Willa Cather to Viola Roseboro', Bynner Papers, Harvard University; Graham, *Duchess of New Dorp*, II, 17.

[87] *Ibid.*, II, 40.

Passing to the next the unconscious possession of a
    perfecting soul
Each forest clearing gave something of a neighborly
    grace,
The rude play of cabin-bred natural people something
    of humor,
Each mountain home something of inner daring,
Each long-wandering life something of patience
    and of hope!
In the open, far-seen nature gradually chiseled
The deepening wistful eyes.
Each axman and each plowman added
Another filament of ruggedness;
Unknowing minds dumbly cried for injustice. . . .

At last was ready the alembic, where Nature stored
    and set apart
Each generation's finest residue,
Waiting for the hour of perfect mixture—
And then the Miracle![88]

[88] Ida Tarbell, *He Knew Lincoln* (New York, 1907), i.

Chapter V. A Magazine
of Reporters

AFTER 1897 *McClure's* took on the aspect which became so familiar during the muckraking movement. Well-educated, literate young men were slowly added to the staff, men who would often confer with McClure on one of his hasty proprietary tours of the editorial offices, then race away on one of the zesty editor's assignments. Before either investigating the contents of *McClure's* or following the road to muckraking, we need to see who these new men were and how they fitted into a staff already composed of the "Chief," as McClure was called, restlessly searching for something new to invent; Phillips, more cautious than in his student days and always quietly lying in wait to kill a generalization with a fact; and the Bradys, close-knit, loyal, and capable men of finance and technology.

McClure's intent, as he reveals in his *Autobiography*, was to accumulate a permanent staff of writers, a staff patterned on that of A. F. Walter's *London Times*, which had unequaled foreign correspondents. So the female literati, Tarbell and Roseboro', were soon surrounded in the editorial offices by a reportorial staff that included numerous experienced newspaper journalists. From this reservoir of talented men McClure wanted articles in depth dealing with the crucial events of the day—wars, inventions, and personalities. These men were to exploit the magazine's principal advantage over the daily newspaper: the ability to analyze events and reconstruct them in perspective. Such a permanent staff was employed by a haphazard process of assimilation. It grew as *McClure's* circulation mounted. Most of the writers had served as reporters, an occupation that became a school for American realistic literature. This can be shown by a brief inspection of the men in the editorial rooms following the war with Spain.

Present was John H. Finley, who resigned the Knox presidency in 1899. When Finley was hired, Frank Norris, previously on the *San Francisco Wave*, had been on the staff for a year. They were soon joined by Samuel Hopkins Adams, nine years a reporter for the *New York Sun*. William Henry Irwin worked for both the *Wave* and the *Sun* before turning his reportorial talents towards *McClure's* new journalism. Later, both Mark Sullivan and Willa Cather came to *McClure's* after being reporters, as did Cleveland Moffett, Burton J. Hendrick, and George K. Turner. Finley Peter Dunne, who wrote for *McClure's* and distributed his popular and profitable Dooley essays through the McClure syndicate, had made his reputation first as a writer and editor.[1] But the greatest impact between 1898 and 1906 was made by three men—all former reporters. They were, in order of arrival, William Allen White, Ray Stannard Baker, and Lincoln Steffens. Three more different men could hardly have congregated in the busy, noisy offices on 25th Street.

William Allen White's career was a queer mixture of provincialism and association with the mighty.[2] A denizen of Emporia, Kansas, White was the only son of Dr. Allen White and Mary Hatton White. From his Knox-educated mother he inherited Republicanism. White not only remembered the "stories he was told of the adventures of the army of the border" but also retained "a curious wonder as to why these men had red legs."[3] He remembered the tales of John Brown, having "heard the story of the drama's beginning, rise, and close a dozen times," recalling "that the man wore a buffalo skin overcoat, and that the men said he had dark, piercing eyes."[4] The boy who remembered the tales of the Civil War, "having heard the story a thousand times," liked best the songs "Old Nicodemus," the "Year

[1] Phillips to McClure, June 3, 1904, McClure Papers.
[2] See William Allen White, *Autobiography*.
[3] *Emporia Gazette*, July 4, 1907, quoted in White's *The Editor and His People*, ed. Helen Mahin (New York, 1924), 161-66.
[4] *Ibid.*

of the Jubilee," "We Shall Meet But We Shall Miss Him," "Tramp, Tramp, Tramp," and "Hang Jeff Davis to a Sour Apple Tree."[5] After a few years at Kansas State and employment as a reporter in Kansas City, White bought the *Emporia Gazette* in 1895. His passionate but later regretted blast against the Populists, "What's the Matter with Kansas?" cast him immediately into national fame in August, 1896, as the defender of the high-tariff, yellow-metal McKinley. The phrase "What's the Matter with . . ." was taken from popular slang. All across the western country people "thrilled to William Allen White's ringing editorial," wrote another resident of that region, who felt that "Emporia was just such a place as Galesburg" because it "would have nothing of 'sixteen to one'; it was still Republican, as it had been Liberty, free soil, abolition and Whig."[6]

Shortly after McKinley's election the rotund, ever-jolly editor published his first volume, *The Real Issue*, a collection of regional short stories modeled on the characters created by his friend James Whitcomb Riley.[7] Within a month of its appearance the young Kansan had an urgent letter from *McClure's* requesting the right to republish one story, "The King of Boyville," and ordering a half dozen short stories at five hundred dollars each.[8] The magazine eventually published two of White's pieces, one being the adolescent short story, "Boyville," in March, 1897. That same spring White came to New York, entertained en route by Mark Hanna and Governor Roosevelt, whose friendship had been gained by his famous editorial the previous summer. But the real purpose of his visit was to make the acquaintance of the McClure gang.

"The McClure group," wrote White, "became for ten or fifteen years my New York fortress, spiritual, literary, and because they paid me well, financial."[9] They, like him, were

5 *Ibid.*

6 Calkins, *They Broke the Prairie*, 419.

7 White to James W. Riley, March 2, 1897, Riley Papers, Lilly Library, University of Indiana.

8 White, *Autobiography*, 287.   9 *Ibid.*, 301.

at heart Midwestern and talked the Mississippi Valley vernacular which he and Vernon L. Parrington used in their country store chats in Emporia. There were few New England formalities in the McClure group, White thought, for "they thought as we thought in Emporia about men and things."[10]

White was quickly accepted. His mother, his talent, his constant flow of country talk, of witty *bons mots* were on his side. For his own part, the deep indebtedness for the *Gazette* (a mortgage which Phillips helped carry) and his support of McClure's politics cemented his relationship with the magazine.[11] Since Miss Tarbell was deeply involved with her work on Lincoln, whom White especially admired, "they found common ground there and began a friendship which was to last until her death."[12] After being properly feted, including an introduction to William Dean Howells, then in New York, White was surfeited with ideas for articles by the ebullient McClure. He numbly left New York with a binding arrangement to submit most of his material to the syndicate and the magazine.[13]

White's "Court of Boyville" stories, published as a book by that title in 1899, first appeared in *McClure's*, but his main staple for the magazine consisted of short sketches of major political personalities, such as his friends Hanna and Roosevelt. In his inimitable fashion White delineated the characters of Bryan, Cleveland, McKinley, Croker, Quay, and, in an article that was almost libelous, Senator Thomas Platt, the boss of New York State. When Platt threatened to sue, White chortled, "Don't let that worry you. If he brings suit we can get the New York papers so full of politics that would make the Lexow investment [*sic*] look like sixty cents, for at the end of that time 'McClure's' magazine would be advertised all over the civilized world. No twelve

10 *Ibid.*
11 White to Phillips, May 8, 1901, Baker Papers.
12 David Hinshaw, *A Man from Emporia* (New York, 1945), 82.
13 *Ibid.*, 83; White to Phillips, May 8, 1901, Baker Papers.

human beings could be found who would give Platt a character, and he would have to pay the costs."[14] White's political realism "prefigures much of the muckraking material that was to give *McClure's* its lasting fame."[15]

The same spring of 1897 witnessed the arrival of another young journalist at the offices. Ray Stannard Baker was the oldest son of a Wisconsin family. His father was president of a land company, founded during the depression of 1873, which eventually became a successful family enterprise. It was the same type of business that the senior Tarbell had rejected in North Dakota. At Michigan State College, which Baker attended, he was much impressed by a science professor, Dr. Beal, who was, like Albert Hurd, a former student of Louis Agassiz. Baker married Beal's daughter, Jessie, shortly after graduation. While at East Lansing, Baker had ample opportunity to meet Edward P. Anderson, a contributor to the McClure syndicate and a brother of Melville B. Anderson, who had befriended and advised McClure at Knox. After graduation Baker briefly studied law at the University of Michigan before moving to an overgrown Chicago in 1892. There he became a reporter for Victor Lawson's *Chicago Record*, which boasted a long career of "demanding Sunday observance and battling for civic virtue."[16]

Chicago, from a reporter's perspective, proved to be a university with its own educational powers, convincing Baker that "we were not absolutely perfect."[17] During the depression of 1893 Baker was responsible for reporting on all of the municipal charity work. A sensitive, introspective man, Baker was shocked by what he found. "There are thousands of homeless and starving men in the streets," he

[14] White to August Jaccaci, Dec. 20, 1901, White Papers.
[15] Lyons, *Success Story*, 151; see Phillips to Finley, Oct. 24, 1900, Finley Papers.
[16] George Ade to Finley Peter Dunne, Jan. 6, 1932, Dunne Papers, Manuscript Division, Library of Congress. See Baker, *American Chronicle* (New York, 1945), 33, 288-91.
[17] *Ibid.*, 83.

wrote his father; "I have seen more misery in the last week than I ever saw in my life before."[18] His education went even further. Soon he was marching with Jacob S. Coxey's small "army" assembled at Massillon, Ohio, where, "if we didn't have to work so hard we would be having a glorious time."[19] And in the summer of 1894 he witnessed the Debs rebellion as the American Railway Union fell before the onslaught of Pullman, the railroad owners, and the federal government. "I sincerely hope the men will come out ahead," he wrote.[20] And yet he felt their leaders were often "cheap and for the most part 'nasty'—professional agitators of the worst type."[21] This was an unfair judgment of Debs, but it bespeaks a mind struggling to see both sides. Baker could rarely be a dogmatist about what he saw— even after years of muckraking.

Baker learned of Chicago's considerable political corruption first hand under the tutelage of William T. Stead, the English journalist whom both McClure and Robert Finley patronized. It was Stead, pioneer of the so-called "new journalism," who pictured the Chicago traction magnate Charles T. Yerkes as one of the money-changers being cast from the temple on the cover of his *If Christ Came to Chicago*.[22] Under Stead's stimulus Baker saw the formation of the Chicago Civic Federation, which acted as a clearing house for municipal reform, and yet he was less prepared to cast his lot with the reformers at this time than fellow journalists Brand Whitlock and Finley Peter Dunne. He was not ready to decide which side was right.

A career as a magazine writer opened up for Baker in January, 1895, when Lyman Abbott of *Outlook* accepted one of his articles on police reform in Chicago and solicited another on the nationally famous Jane Addams and her

18 Baker to Father, Dec. 15, 1893, Baker Papers.
19 Baker to Father, April 2, 1894, *ibid.*
20 Baker to Father, June 27, 1894, *ibid.*
21 Baker to Father, Sept. 1, 1894, *ibid.*
22 Baker, *American Chronicle*, 26-33.

Civic Federation.[23] But feeling, as he was always to feel, that fiction was a higher calling, Baker instead turned to the hoary *Youth's Companion*, the country's largest juvenile magazine, which he conquered with a succession of heroic adventure stories. As he looked for other dragons to slay, the young *McClure's Magazine*, which he had followed from its origin, presented itself.

McClure's series on Lincoln was responsible for Baker's first contact with the magazine. "I had been fascinated," he wrote, "by an article in it on Abraham Lincoln by Ida M. Tarbell, and wrote the editor that an uncle of mine, Lieut. L. B. [*sic*] Baker of Michigan, had been in command of the party that pursued and captured J. Wilkes Booth."[24] Baker's irresistible offer to McClure suggested that his uncle had "interesting reminiscences of his experiences, and a number of documents and pictures."[25] Miss Tarbell, immediately interested since the magazine was seeking such an account, commissioned the piece, and McClure wrote soon afterwards that "we are going to publish the Booth article in our May number and we should like very much to publish several articles. . . . Perhaps we could together plan out a series. . . ."[26] McClure always wanted a series, believing that series built circulation. Soon Baker was holding McClure spellbound with fascinating stories about the secret service during the Civil War, in which his father had served and which his father's cousin, General Lafayette C. Baker, had supervised. Tolerating no more suspense, John Phillips sent Baker fare to come to New York for further consultations. The result was that an entire series on the secret service was planned with hopes that it could be made into a book.[27] Like White, Baker's initial articles in *McClure's* only served to lead to a radically different type of endeavor.

23 Baker to Father, Jan. 5, June 22, 1895, Baker Papers.
24 Baker, *American Chronicle*, 73.   25 *Ibid.*
26 Tarbell to Baker, Jan. 6, 1897, Baker Papers; McClure to Baker, March 9, 1897, *ibid.*
27 Phillips to Baker, March 20, 1897, *ibid.*

Back in Chicago Baker's arduous work on the series failed to satisfy John Phillips, who rejected most of the stories because they had the "appearance of fiction," which was his way of saying they lacked authenticity.[28] By January, 1898, Baker had decided to attempt another series suggested offhandedly by McClure to hail the new prosperity, "The Romance of Capital." Once the stories were finished, McClure promised, "we will have found out as to the other," or whether Baker could join the McClure staff.[29] With a great deal of daring, Baker resigned his newspaper job and commenced full-time work on the project. It was a risk, but McKinley's prosperity seemed worthy of investigation as an aftermath of the economically oriented campaign of 1896. Still success evaded him. His first articles on banking and copper mines lacked the "human element of interest," though the magazine finally printed "The Movement of Wheat," in December, 1899, and "The New Prosperity" in May, 1900.[30] In 1900 Baker's miscellaneous articles were finally published as *The New Prosperity* by McClure's book company.

Baker's opportunity to join McClure's staff finally arrived in the summer of 1898 with the precipitation of the Spanish-American War. The market for war news was insatiable, and McClure dispatched every available correspondent to the front. Among these were Stephen Crane and Baker.[31] Finding himself belatedly in Cuba, Baker wrote up his interviews with Leonard Wood about the scandals in the military administration. Then, coming back to New York, he surveyed the disembarkation of the Rough Riders and drew a portrait of Theodore Roosevelt, published in *McClure's* in November, 1898, which pleased the Colonel, "more than any other sketch of my life that has

[28] Phillips to Baker, Sept. 27, Sept. 18, Nov. 16, Nov. 24, 1897, *ibid.*
[29] McClure to Baker, Jan. 15, 1898, *ibid.*
[30] Phillips to Baker, Feb. 25, 1898, *ibid.*; Baker, *American Chronicle*, 88.
[31] Baker to Father, May 21, 1898, Baker Papers; Baker, *American Chronicle*, 94.

been written. . . ."[32] As a journalist Baker had grown. His work had been polished and solid, and his position on *McClure's* was henceforth assured.

After the culmination of the war, McClure sent Baker to Germany with instructions to write up whatever interested him, particularly emphasizing new scientific developments. New factories, dueling societies, and German militarism all intrigued Baker. One of his most successful articles was an interview with Professor Ernst Haeckel, one of the first German academicians to adopt the Darwinian hypothesis. All of his articles, including some which John Phillips excluded from the magazine, appeared in a volume, *Seen in Germany*, published in 1901.

With Miss Tarbell, Miss Roseboro', and McClure often out of the office, it was decided that Phillips needed a sort of executive editor on the sixth floor to help him. When offered an editorial desk, Baker hesitated. He had no desire to remain in the magazine's offices solely in the capacity of an editorial assistant. Finally, in the fall of 1901, he left *McClure's* on a long salaried vacation, hoping to claim his destiny as a man of letters by writing fiction. As his replacement Phillips picked Joseph Lincoln Steffens, city editor of the *New York Commercial Advertiser*.

Lincoln Steffens was born in San Francisco in 1866, the son of naturalized citizens. His father, a Canadian, had migrated to Carroll County, Illinois, north of Galesburg, in 1840, and had lived there for several years. For three years he had worked in Freeport, Illinois, probably witnessing the famous Lincoln-Douglas debate there, before migrating to California during the Civil War.[33] Quickly becoming a successful paint and oil merchant, he named his oldest son for the Republican president whose principles he shared.

Lincoln Steffens grew to adulthood relatively unconscious of the political turmoil about him. Henry George was forg-

[32] Theodore Roosevelt to Baker, Nov. 4, 1898, Baker Papers. See Baker, *American Chronicle*, 102-17, for the following two paragraphs.

[33] Lincoln Steffens, *Autobiography of Lincoln Steffens* (New York, 1931), 35.

ing his single-tax thunderbolt to hurl at the "octopus," E. H. Harriman and the Southern Pacific Railroad, which ran the state's politics. General Kearney, whose intemperate speeches about the "yellow peril" helped produce the Chinese Exclusion Act of 1882, was amassing workers for his sand-lot harangues. But neither event made any impression on Steffens.

In 1885, Steffens matriculated at the University of California. And in 1889, the same year Baker graduated from Michigan State and the year before William Allen White left Kansas State University, Steffens finished his degree and went to Germany, the homeland of his family, to continue his studies in philosophy and psychology. Going to Leipzig, where John Phillips had preceded him four years previously, Steffens commenced work under the esteemed Wilhelm Max Wundt.

Trained in medicine, Wundt had founded the first school for experimental psychology in Germany. While at Leipzig he wrote works on logic and ethics and eventually published *System der Philosophie* in 1899. His belief that the study of ethics lies in the realm of ethnic psychology and a psychological approach to the history of custom was alien to Steffens. In his *Autobiography* Steffens ridiculed a science of ethics based on experimental psychology, and his student years were spent seeking some other way out of the relativistic dilemma.[34] Yet in the end he succumbed to Wundt's ideas, as shall be seen.

Tiring of Leipzig, Steffens crossed the Rhine to the Sorbonne, where Miss Tarbell was studying. After a year with the *faculté des sciences* in 1891, he returned to the United States broke, jobless, and married.[35] Steffens longed for a career in politics, but was repulsed because "our Government is the nastiest and vilest on Earth."[36] Perhaps remembering that Wundt had held elective office,

[34] *Ibid.,* 151.   [35] *Ibid.,* 170.
[36] Steffens to Lou Steffens, May 14, 1891, Steffens Papers, Columbia University; Steffens to Mother, Feb. 4, 1901, *ibid.*

90

he wrote his father, "is it possible for a man to rise high in politics in the present state of politics, and be honorable and moral? . . . I have a foolish idea, you know, that the world of today is far more practical than it is Christian—and, of course, between the Christian ideal and the practical fact there is just about 19 centuries difference."[37]

Forced by circumstances to try the practical, Steffens unsuccessfully advertised in New York papers for employment. Finally, he asked his father for capital to start a subscription service which would clip newspaper articles on politicians, authors, or actors who wanted to follow themselves in the press. Steffens had seen this type of agency succeed in Paris, but his father remained unimpressed, and the lucrative field was left for others.[38]

The year before *McClure's* appeared, Steffens became an employee in the city room of E. L. Godkins's *Evening Post*.[39] After working his way up to the Wall Street financial beat, Steffens published a short story, "Sweet Punch," in *Harpers*, and happily planned to devote himself "to short stories exclusively for awhile, till my work is a bit known, when I will come out more boldly with larger works containing my conclusions and views more unmistakenly [*sic*] expounded."[40] But the conclusions of the self-assured optimist waited. *Yellow Book*, four years later, was the next magazine to buy any of his work.[41]

While William Allen White was wandering along the political labyrinth of Kansas City for the daily *Journal* and Ray Stannard Baker was learning the secrets of Chicago's darker politics from William T. Stead, Steffens and the *Evening Post* were aiding the Rev. Dr. Charles H. Parkhurst in his campaign against gambling, prostitution, and saloons. "He represented our mind," Steffens wrote; "he

[37] Steffens to Father, Nov., 1890, *ibid.*
[38] Steffens to Father, Nov. 23, 1892, *ibid.*
[39] Steffens to Father, Dec. 7, 1892, *ibid.*
[40] Steffens to Fred Willis, Feb. 5, 1893, *ibid.*
[41] Steffens to Fred Willis, Aug. 23, 1896, *ibid.*

and we, the people, took a moral view of politics, government, business—everything."[42]

Earlier than either White or Baker, Steffens had become an acquaintance, supporter, and popularizer of Theodore Roosevelt. As a result of the Lexow Committee revelations in 1895, Roosevelt became a Commissioner of Police. Steffens became his close friend through the good offices of Jacob Riis, the *New York Sun* reporter who wrote *How the Other Half Lives.*[43] With the Lexow police exposures, Steffens became something of a reformer himself. He, Norman Hapgood, and some staff members from the *Evening Post* bought and edited the *Commercial Advertiser* in 1897 and made the city's oldest newspaper into a reform organ filled with public exposures.

While city editor of the *Commercial Advertiser*, Steffens became, by his own somewhat inflated account, almost an alter ego to Governor Roosevelt in Albany. This brought Steffens to the attention of McClure, who wanted to use the ex-Rough Rider as a replacement for Lincoln, copy on whom was petering out. August Jaccaci, *McClure's* art editor, had been impressed with the *Commercial Advertiser's* growth, and Steffens was accorded much of the credit.[44] With this recommendation, in 1898 John Phillips contacted Steffens about the possibility of writing a series of articles on Roosevelt, eventually to appear as a book. The possibility of making a thousand dollars a year writing for such a magazine quickly secured Steffens' approval.[45] Although Roosevelt consented to help, only one article was produced.[46] "The pretense of taking his *Life* was kept up

[42] Steffens, *Autobiography*, 247.

[43] *Ibid.*, 255-65. While at the University of California, Steffens remembered, a professor advised him, "you can get the measure of your country by watching how Theodore Roosevelt does in his public career." Quoted in Steffens' "The Real Roosevelt," *Ainslee's Magazine*, II (Dec., 1898), 484.

[44] Steffens, *Autobiography*, 358.

[45] Phillips to Steffens, Dec. 9, 1898, Steffens Papers.

[46] Phillips to Steffens, March 21, 1899?, *ibid.*

for a few years," Steffens said; "it was a good excuse to be near him when he was a source of news, as governor and as president."[47] Otherwise, the book contract was soon forgotten.[48]

But *McClure's* had a more pressing need than copy, and that was to keep a managing editor in the office. Albert Brady, young and overworked, died in 1900, and was replaced by his equally able brothers as secretary and assistant secretary of the firm. Another poignant loss was John H. Finley, who left in the fall of 1900, at the invitation of Woodrow Wilson, to teach at Princeton. Though Finley continued to read copy and to make editorial suggestions, his energies were slowly siphoned off into academic life. Within a year Baker decided to devote his time to fiction. And so Steffens was hired of necessity to be managing editor. But Phillips warned, "all of us take a broad interest in the operations of the house, contributing what we can to the program and effectiveness of the business in all its branches."[49] In fact, that being a day before the popularity of efficiency experts like Frederick Taylor, Steffens' job, like those of the other staff members, was not defined any more specifically. Yet his salary was the same as Baker's, five thousand dollars.

Steffens was given a short vacation prior to joining the staff in the fall of 1901. In the interim Albert Boyden, Finley's brother-in-law, "temporarily" assumed the managing editorship which, after Steffens proved his own ineptitude, became permanently his.[50] With Baker in the West and Miss Tarbell at work on a history of Standard Oil, Steffens found no one in the home office to supervise. Rather, he helped Miss Roseboro' read manuscripts and correspond with authors. James Hooper, whose early stories of the Philippines were considered too brutal even for *McClure's,*

[47] Steffens, *Autobiography*, 350.
[48] August Jaccaci to Steffens, Jan. 4, 1901, Steffens Papers.
[49] Phillips to Steffens, May 3, 1901, *ibid.*
[50] Steffens, *Autobiography*, 359.

was discovered by the two, Steffens says, and with their connivance he joined the staff.[51]

Otherwise, Steffens was less successful. He became a party to the continual friction that ensued between Robert McClure's London office and New York. The securing of copyrights in both the United States and England, the negotiations and payment of various authors, and the placement of accepted material by deadlines created many problems for Steffens, who could never take his clerical responsibilities seriously.[52] Finally, in the summer of 1902, Robert McClure wrote New York that Steffens should be dismissed, but instead McClure sent him away from New York to search for manuscripts.

Steffens, having worked on top of the roaring presses for hardly a year, left New York for the West in search of a story. In Chicago he called on William C. Boyden, Albert Boyden's lawyer brother, neck deep in municipal reform, and this civil formality quickly exploded into an intense interview. Boyden overflowed with the inside facts of a half dozen political struggles in the Midwest. Much of his information could have come from the Chicago daily papers, the rest from Walter Fisher and the young reform element in the city's Republican party. Why not, Boyden suggested, visit St. Paul, Kansas City, or St. Louis, and see for himself? Steffens did, and what he saw took him permanently out of the editorial room and made him a reporter documenting the *Shame of the Cities.*[53]

McClure's recruitment of Steffens in 1901 completed what was to be his muckraking staff. As long as they produced, McClure, like a grand vizier, delighted in lavishing rewards upon his trained practitioners. For example, in 1902 his salary list totalled $93,800, while the total editorial expenses were almost $150,000, with Tarbell, Baker, and

[51] *Ibid.,* 360.
[52] See Robert McClure to Thomas McClure, Oct. 4, 1900, McClure Papers.
[53] Steffens, *Autobiography,* 364-65.

Steffens among the most highly remunerated writers in the country.[54] Undoubtedly this contributed towards their high morale. In their autobiographies these three writers have all attested to the feeling of cohesiveness sensed by the editorial staff, which enjoyed "the most stimulating, yes intoxicating, editorial atmosphere then existent in America or elsewhere."[55]

McClure was "vibrant, eager, indomitable" to Miss Tarbell, "blond, smiling, enthusiastic, unreliable" to Steffens, and to Will Irwin, the "ebullient" editor who shot forth an "idea a minute."[56] McClure's dominance in the editorial offices was based on at least three factors. First, he was the principal proprietor of the magazine, although Phillips and later Tarbell owned a small percentage of stock. Secondly, he was the most widely traveled and widely read of the staff, having crossed the Atlantic several dozen times, and the United States as many, in his editorial career. Like a traveling salesman moving in a gigantic swath, he interviewed the latest authors and names in the news, put them through his own particular inquisition, filled their ears with din about his plans for their stories, then rushed back to New York with a lead on which his authority could not be challenged. Finally, McClure was enthusiastic and imaginative: he could magnify to many powers the smallest ingredient of what he discovered and then perhaps convince his audience that the projection was the reality.

[54] McClure to Moody B. Gates, Aug. 7, 1922, McClure Papers; Financial Sheet, n.d., Tarbell Papers; Mott, *A History of American Magazines*, IV, 39-40.

[55] Baker, *American Chronicle*, 80.

[56] Tarbell, *All in the Day's Work*, 119; Steffens, *Autobiography*, 361; Irwin, *Propaganda and the News*, 66. McClure's flamboyant personality was literary capital freely drawn upon by many writers who knew him. Fulkerson in Howell's *A Hazard of New Fortunes* and, as mentioned, Pinkerton in Stevenson's *The Wrecker* characterized him. He was Willa Cather's editor in "Ardessa," published in *Century* in May, 1918, "who went in for everything, and got tired of everything; that was why he made a good editor."

But McClure was no administrator. The ordinary tasks of assigning stories, proofreading, and choosing make-up in McClure's absence were handled by John Phillips. The two men knew each other's strengths and there was rarely any friction. Phillips, usually passive, was always the master of McClure's moods. It was he who caught and sifted the idea of the day, turned it over critically or left it to die on the vine as McClure's interest turned in other directions. If McClure persisted, he gave way with grace.

As it has been remarked, McClure was unusually generous towards his staff. Office doors on the sixth floor were usually open, and McClure, when in the Lexington Building, was everywhere at once, asking questions about the work in hand. Yet he was a demanding employer. He wanted the loyalty and approbation of his subordinates.

Although the young staff was free from those "New England repressions" that White speaks of, a great degree of Victorian civility prevailed, such as special concessions to the ladies and the formal use of surnames. Steffens was probably the quickest to evade the formality. At five and a half feet, slight of frame, he was the shortest of the staff, being close to McClure's height. Impeccably dressed, quick of wit, and forward as he was, meeting him was something of a shock to the skittish Boyden and Siddall. His self-sufficiency, hostility to criticism, and irritating skepticism of people's motives disguised a brilliant analytical mind that often burdened the staff's tolerance. The Steffens at *McClure's* does not appear to be the Steffens of the *Autobiography*. He was the bantam sophisticate with the pince-nez who asked his political informants what the hell was *really* going on in municipal politics.

Tall and stately, intent upon being proper, Miss Tarbell was the mother hen who soothed discontent and staunchly opposed giving in to all of McClure's whims. She was as firmly attached to Phillips as Miss Roseboro' was to McClure, and yet the two ladies were delightful friends. Needless to say, Miss Roseboro' and Steffens got along capitally; their long correspondence in subsequent years testifies to this. Though often relying on feminine whims, both ladies were respected as colleagues. And both had a retinue of followers among the younger members of the staff, Boyden, Siddall, Bynner, and Irwin.

At first Baker, like Steffens, was content to let McClure, Phillips, and perhaps Tarbell or the Bradys make staff decisions, but with experience he became a more forceful proponent of his views. Like Miss Tarbell, and unlike Steffens, he had no appetite for discord. Of medium height, brown hair, and bespectacled, he listened to all sides of the argument, and cautiously made up his own mind. Unlike McClure, who was dogmatic, but who under argument could often be reduced to the opposite dogmatism, Baker was hesitant to commit himself, but firm and persevering once it was done. Considering his speed and thoroughness at writing, as well as its quality, he was probably the best journalist at *McClure's*, though the judgment is difficult to make.

There were other writers at *McClure's* who never succeeded in leaving as deep an imprint as these three; such were Samuel Hopkins Adams, Mark Sullivan, Frank Norris, and others. Exceptions might be William Allen White and John Finley. The broad acquaintances of both of these men broadened the scope of possible articles for the magazine, as will be seen. Finley, the scholar, and White, the popularizer, one with a Jacksonian profile, the other with a humpty-dumpty air, rounded out the *McClure's* staff in a rather literal manner.

There was no pattern to staff decisions, except that McClure participated in all of them and the various members of the editorial group, meeting either formally or informally, usually gave their consent. McClure felt no obligation to consult anyone except Phillips, but as a matter of policy he usually wrote or questioned personally editorial members for their opinions, hoping that the given idea would be improved. He urged the entire staff to participate in the making of the magazine by bringing forward their best ideas. But in the final analysis, the leads usually came from Mc-Clure, and Phillips dispatched either the stately Tarbell, the humane, introspective Baker, the cynically witty Steffens, or the professional provincial from Emporia to write them up.

In the background of all staff considerations, there was McClure's talk about founding a second magazine or a newspaper. It gave every act the air of hopeful expectancy. The arbitrary act of Zeus might catapult any of them into an even more eminent position at any moment.[57]

Yet the pre-muckraking years were not without their crises. In February, 1897, McClure founded a jointly-owned publishing house with Frank N. Doubleday. The house had grown naturally out of McClure's quarterly publication of such volumes as Miss Tarbell's Lincoln studies. But in 1899 when the press was handling 100 volumes a year and making almost $80,000 profit, McClure precipitated a

[57] See sources cited above and White, *Autobiography*, 301ff, for information on the preceding paragraphs. Passports and photographs, especially in the McClure, Baker, and Tarbell Papers are helpful, and for a full description of the *McClure's* offices at work see "The Story of McClure's," *Profitable Advertising* (Oct. 15, 1897), 139ff. Miss Tarbell felt Steffens had a "messianic complex" because, "as he wrote in calm life that he was more Christian Science than the C. S.—more Christian than the Christian, more Republican than the R's, more Democratic than the D's, more pacific than the P's—that was what was irritating about him to 'lesser people.' He explained he thought only he loved everybody so much more than anybody loved him. But he wouldn't do it. . . . The rest had integrity and did not whine." ("Steffens" folder, n.d., Tarbell Papers.) Siddall was probably the next most disliked person on the staff, at least to Baker: "Talking with (S.) Siddall one always thinks less of human nature, loves less, jeers more. He makes you laugh, that in a dry & solemn world is a blessing. Scratch him a little—break the surface—& you come to the Oberlin [Harvard] in him. His actions are Oberlin, his talk the last N.Y. sophistication. Round . . . like Voltaire. . . . There is scant prospect of comfort in age in jeering at human nature." (Notebook, "VII," Sept., 1915, 106-107.) A dozen years later Baker still dreamed of Siddall, "with his round face, his round mouth, & his round eyes, spoofing at human nature. . . ." (Baker to Phillips, Jan., 1929?, Baker Papers.) Otherwise there seems to have been little hostility among the staff.

rupture as he forced Doubleday either to amalgamate the book concern with the magazine or to separate. The ambitious Doubleday was naturally unwilling to surrender interest in a firm where he was an equal partner to become a minor stockholder in another.[58] McClure promptly formed a publishing house with Phillips, and offered Walter Hines Page, who had been working on an encyclopaedia for the McClure-Doubleday company, its management. But Page allied with Doubleday instead, and together they founded a publishing firm that long outlived *McClure's*. The book list and assets were divided (Doubleday got Kipling), and several employees, including Frank Norris, joined Doubleday. Norris, frightened by McClure's impetuosity, made his decision, then wrote Phillips, "From the time of your first letter to me in St. Louis asking me to come on to N.Y. and try it with you, to the time of your last conversation in your office . . . you have been the best friend I've had outside California."[59] While Miss Tarbell lamented the loss of these "strong men," McClure rejoiced over ridding himself of the "foreign and alien association. . . ."[60] Like the controversy which had surrounded his editorship of the *Knox Student,* McClure's separation from Doubleday portended ill for the future.

Within the year McClure came dangerously close to a second disaster. Harper's publishing house, with four magazines and a book company, unable to compete with the new cheap monthlies, was failing under an indebtedness of $692,000, and McClure attempted to purchase the entire concern.[61] McClure's vision included founding a *Harper-McClure Review*, making Baker editor of *Harper's Round*

58 McClure to Tarbell, Dec. 11, 1899, Phillips Papers; Curtis P. Brady, "The High Cost of Impatience," 44-45, 51.

59 Frank Norris to Phillips, Jan. 9, 1900, Phillips Papers.

60 Tarbell to McClure, Dec. 13, 1899, McClure Papers; McClure to Tarbell, Dec. 11, 1899, Phillips Papers.

61 McClure to Hattie McClure, June 2, 1899, McClure Papers; McClure to Tarbell, Nov. 21, 1899, Phillips Papers.

Table, and installing John Finley as editor of *Harper's*.[62]
But *McClure's* proved incapable of supporting the totter-
ing structure. In 1898 *McClure's* declared a profit of
$83,166. But in 1899, the year Harper's was purchased, *Mc-
Clure's* lost $16,618. In unrealized profits, the loss was con-
siderable.[63] By virtue of Brady's perspicacity the whole venture was ended six months later in a "very extraordinary
fashion."[64] Brady had written into the original contract
that the terms of payment might be altered by the option
of the purchaser, and, feeling the impossibility of the situation, McClure elected to return the 13,500 shares he had
purchased.[65] More than one person, not knowing Mc-
Clure's precarious state of finances, thought he had separated from Henry Mills Alden over political differences.[66]

McClure's break with Doubleday and the Harper's people was followed in 1901 by an even more emotional sever-
ance with August Jaccaci, the gentle art editor who on Will
H. Low's recommendation had been with the magazine
since its founding.[67] Thinking that Jaccaci "was planning
to be the whole thing and Mr. Phillips was blind," McClure
tried to oust him, but found Miss Tarbell and part of the
staff adamantly against it.[68] Yet Jaccaci soon left of his own
accord to found an art agency; it was several years, however, before he was paid for his stock.[69] He eventually received $100,000 for stock that had been originally given
to him. Although Jaccaci was popular with both writers
and staff members, perhaps in McClure's eyes too popular,
a logical complaint against him was the excessive expenses

[62] Baker to Father, Aug. 17, 1899, Baker Papers; Tarbell to Baker,
Sept. 14, 1899, *ibid.*

[63] Financial Report, n.d., Tarbell Papers.

[64] McClure to Tarbell, Nov. 21, 1899, Phillips Papers.

[65] See Lyons, *Success Story*, 162-64; McClure to Hattie McClure, June
2, 1899, McClure Papers.

[66] Mary C. Hurd to McClure, Nov. 23, 1899, *ibid.*

[67] Jaccaci's obituary is found in the *American Art Annual* (31 vols.,
Washington, D. C., 1898-1934), XXVII, 412.

[68] McClure to Hattie McClure, March 22, 1930?, McClure Papers.

[69] Jaccaci to Tarbell, Dec. 20, 1901, Tarbell Papers.

which his department was incurring. Between 1897 and 1902 art expenses mounted from $12,449 to $50,247, while profits were falling by almost twenty-five percent. Upon his departure such expenses fell sharply, as money was transferred to the circulation and advertising departments which direly needed it.[70]

By 1900 *McClure's* was successfully nationalizing political and financial news through the efforts of its brilliant reportorial staff. Circulation was nearly 400,000, making the "widest appeal to people of intelligence in this country. . . ."[71] Even the trade magazine *Printer's Ink* noted that between 1895 and 1900 *McClure's* carried the greatest quantity of advertising of any magazine in the world, averaging in 1899 a circulation of 360,000 with 216 pages of advertising.[72]

Revenue from advertising was averaging almost a half million dollars annually, while circulation produced another $400,000. Out of this net income of almost a million dollars, the magazine paid its expenses of $810,000 in 1899 and $933,000 in 1900, but still earned a considerable profit. The *Harper's* fiasco meant a loss in 1899, but the magazine, only seven years old in 1900, earned profits of $126,000. Subsequently, through the years of muckraking, expenses, particularly in circulation and advertising, quickly mounted, until by 1905 total outlays amounted to $1,199,000, and total profits diminished to $64,000 (1901), $68,000 (1902), $61,000 (1903), $8,000 loss (1904), and $55,000 (1905). Although the magazine paid out $87,000 in dividends during this period, the wolf was ever puffing at the door.[73] Part of the magazine's dilemma was that, by 1904, it was printing "forty, fifty, or sixty thousand more than we need" just "to get the same amount of money for adver-

---

[70] Financial Records, n.d., *ibid.*

[71] Phillips to Baker, May 22, 1900, Baker Papers.

[72] Lyons, *Success Story*, 171; see *Profitable Advertising* (Oct. 15, 1897), 143.

[73] This paragraph based on Financial Reports, n.d., Tarbell Papers.

tising."[74] By 1907 advertising revenues were in a general decline, until by 1915 they were about half the 1900 high.[75]

The muckraking movement was less influential than larger economic forces in determining the financial status of *McClure's*. The exceptional quality of *McClure's* timely, well-written articles gained the magazine an entrance into the upper middle class homes where there was an increasing concern with the country's ills. But the brilliant, famous staff of writers did little to improve circulation and nothing to improve revenues. Increased competition for the middle class reader, increased cost of production and circulation, and limited advertising revenues resulted in a general price increase of magazines after 1905 which improved their status only temporarily.[76]

McClure's ability to accumulate the best journalistic staff in the country contrasted sharply with his financial ineptitude. Certainly one was a contributing factor to the other. His restless nature was constantly overshadowed by Frank Munsey's caution. Munsey did less, published inferior material, but still had a greater circulation and made far more money, forty million, in fact. Like Munsey, McClure was filled with plans for expansion. He would found the *London Times* of America, or a literary magazine, or the mirror image of *McClure's*, the *American*, to be edited by Mark Twain.[77] These plans, like the book reprinting project, the Doubleday business, and the *Harper's* scheme were destined to failure. Though McClure assumed publication of the *Popular Science Monthly* and *National Geographic Magazine* in 1900, he yearned for a larger empire and a better magazine.[78] During his first decade of operation, from 1893 to 1903, he had succeeded in publishing an extraordi-

[74] Phillips to Hattie McClure, June 29, 1904, McClure Papers.
[75] See *Printer's Ink* (March 14, 1918), item in *ibid.*
[76] Mott, *A History of American Magazines*, IV, 5, 33.
[77] McClure to Samuel L. Clemens, Feb. 6, 1900, copy in Phillips Papers.
[78] See Phillips to Baker, May 22, 1900, Baker Papers.

nary magazine, but far greater successes—and failures—lay ahead.

It is time now to inspect in detail the contents of the magazine for this early period, and see how the course towards muckraking was charted.

Chapter VI. *"McClure's* Is Edited with Clairvoyance"

FROM ITS first issue in May, 1893, *McClure's* was as poised as a weather cock for the advent of the future. From then until its famous muckraking issue a decade later, in January, 1903, *McClure's* deviated very little from its announced plan to present "articles of timely interest," which included "the newest book, the latest important political event, the most recent discovery or invention—in fact, what is newest or most important in every department of human activity."[1] "I will have," McClure correctly prophesied, "History, Politics, Finance, Invention, Education, *National* Health, Science, etc. etc. treated say one topic a month by great thinkers."[2] While the content was intended to be encyclopaedic, McClure's editorial purpose was confused.

"As a matter of fact," McClure told a baffled reporter, "I don't think of my readers at all. The original, the distinctive aim, is much broader and higher."[3] Yet shortly he insisted, "I edit *McClure's* for its readers. . . ."[4] The editorial staff was told that *McClure's* was "performing a certain mission," but that it did not exist "for the sake of doing good or furthering a cause. . . ."[5] Thus the editorial policy was, and is, confusing to map out for these years. One newspaper insisted that *McClure's* was edited by instinct, perhaps even by "clairvoyance," as much as by design.[6] McClure admitted as much; "in editing McClure's Magazine, I do the thing that is really in me, precisely as a painter

[1] *McClure's*, I (June, 1893), 96.
[2] McClure to Hattie McClure, Jan. 10, 1893, McClure Papers.
[3] *Profitable Advertising* (Oct. 15, 1897), 140, 142.
[4] *Ibid.*
[5] McClure, Staff speech, fall, 1904, McClure Papers.
[6] *Cleveland Plain Dealer*, Jan. ?, 1903, clipping in *ibid.*

does. . . ."[7] At other times McClure spoke of the need to be interesting, to achieve an unconscious unity of materials, to popularize the more optimistic tendencies of "the world's progress."[8] This is probably as close as one can come to discovering any metaphysical purpose behind the multicolored monthly that came out of the 25th Street factory.

Most of the fifteen hundred articles published during the first decade sprang from McClure's creativity. Years later, as if they had been children, he could name them and recall the history of each. Whenever *McClure's* published Civil War memoirs, portraits of famous Americans, a study of the latest scientific discovery with hints of its future applicability, or episodes in the industrial struggle, the articles reflected the mind and interests of McClure and conformed to his intuitive genie. And so the contents are pluralistic, each article shaped by a different set of hands, by different circumstances. Until 1898 the magazine operated relatively free of any ideological matrix, except that it carried articles pointed towards special groups such as women, workers, and children. In other words, in content it strongly resembled the syndicate from which it got much of its material. The Spanish-American War was a shock which perceptibly turned the contents of the magazine towards current events and, finally, political reform.

Before an analysis of the types of articles which the magazine carried, it might be well to see the editorial method at work. When not loping across his giant bailiwick sniffing for a story at court trials, conventions and exhibitions, and homes of famous authors, McClure scanned the newspapers and periodicals, collecting clippings on topics that interested him. The London and New York offices both collected leading daily papers for him, and frequently staff members sent him clippings from their travels. All of the leading newspapers, along with the *North American Review, Forum, Harper's, Cosmopolitan, Century, Review of Re-*

[7] McClure, Staff speech, fall, 1904, *ibid.*
[8] *Profitable Advertising* (Oct. 15, 1897), 140.

105

views, and *Munsey's,* composed his literary diet. From these McClure gleaned leads. He and Phillips usually selected some clippings for the staff to work into articles.

A characteristic letter which shows this procedure was written by McClure to the home office while vacationing in Beuzeval, France, in 1897. First, there was a clipping about an exciting railway man, whose life Moffett could write up, "It would delight every boy & girl & their parents." A second clipping dealt with the bubonic plague, which he remembered Albert Hurd speaking on at Knox, attributing to it the "downfall of past European civilizations." Would John Phillips write Hurd about this because it would make "a timely paper"? Another clipping, on wood pulp silks, "I am planning to have Moffett do this when he comes. I have the impression that they are utterly inferior as to wearing capacity & are really frauds." Unsurprisingly, Moffett published almost an article a quarter in *McClure's* during its first decade on such subjects as this.

McClure thought a piece on Tiffany's fine tableware "would make a capital article for either the advertising or magazine pages." Dwight L. Moody "should be interviewed for the magazine," and "you & Jaccaci should see" Captain Albert Mahan because *"Mahan and Roosevelt are just our size."* The horseless carriage was the "great subject of the future." Colonel Albert Pope was on the inside of this subject, and someone should see him about it. " 'Light on Wine Labels.'—I call this a bully *temperance* subject. It would make good reading," he felt. Robert Barr's new novel should be serialized; "I advise the frequent use of his short stories." And indeed Barr's by-line appeared almost as frequently in *McClure's* as Cleveland Moffett's.[9] Several

[9] Last two paragraphs from McClure to Phillips, April 21, 1897, Phillips Papers. Another illustrative letter came from Divonne, France, at a later date. McClure suggested that Baker was to emphasize human freedom and the open shop in his union series, Steffens was to keep a "very open mind" evaluating New York politics, while the "Aldrich article will be very sensational, it must be very moderate & accurate," and the self-applauding advertisements in the newspapers were "worse

of these "ideas," as McClure called them, were eventually worked into articles. Alfred Thayer Mahan's series on "War on the Seas and Its Lessons," a study of the naval battles of the Spanish-American War, appeared the next year.

Although McClure's articles can generally be arranged topically, as dealing with either the Civil War, science, industry, or fiction, his interest in all of these was directed towards discovering the great personality that Emerson and Carlyle had described. In every story McClure wanted a realistic portrayal of the human personalities involved. He proudly quoted the *Augusta Chronicle* that, "there is a living personal interest in the character of literature furnished by McClure's Magazine that differentiates it from any other of the monthly publications. . . ."[10] Before considering the other categories, let the truth of this be demonstrated.

The very first issue inaugurated a "Human Documents" series, with elaborate illustrations. Miss Tarbell's Napoleon series had seventy-five pages of photographs alone. The "Human Documents" contained photographs of famous persons, taken at various moments during their lives. For example, during its early years, the magazine ran lengthy pictorial sketches of Henry Drummond, Stevenson, Hamlin Garland, Andrew Lang, Doyle, Frances Elizabeth Willard, and William T. Stead. Stead was commended for being "especially effective in the exposure of political and social abuses."[11]

A second McClure project was "a new style of interview which he patented under the title of 'Real Conversations.' "[12] It was likened to getting two mean dogs together

---

than Munsey" and should be stopped. (McClure to Tarbell, June 22, 1904.)

[10] Quoted in *McClure's,* IV (Jan., 1895), 196.

[11] *McClure's,* II (Dec., 1893), 17. The compliment was returned when Stead's *American Review of Reviews* predicted the instant national success of the McClure brand of the new journalism. (*American Review of Reviews,* VIII [July, 1893], 99.)

[12] *McClure's,* III (Nov., 1894), 504.

for a social discussion. The articles were verbatim conversations between famous authors. When interviewed by Robert Barr, Doyle quietly agreed that McClure was crazy and "would have no hesitation in asking Gabriel to write an article on the latest thing in trumpets. . . ."[13] Hjalmar Boyesen, William Dean Howells, Eugene Field, Hamlin Garland, James Whitcomb Riley, Oliver W. Holmes, and Edward E. Hale interviewed each other before this successful series ended.

McClure soon adopted another type of conversational interview. Miss Tarbell's "Pasteur at Home," supplemented Robert H. Sherard's "Jules Verne at Home" and "Alphonse Daudet at Home." It was fitting that Daudet should be interviewed, since the term "Human Document" was of his coinage. Even an "Andrew Jackson at Home" appeared, written by Old Hickory's granddaughter.

The magazine's earliest political writings were constructed on this same format. Elisha Jay Edwards, writer on politics for the syndicate, wrote articles on both Cleveland and McKinley, but his most popular work treated the struggle against New York machine politics. Edwards, who eventually prepared a history of Tammany Hall for *McClure's,* published in 1894 a laudatory portrait of the Rev. Dr. Charles Parkhurst, the organizer of New York's Society for the Prevention of Crime. Parkhurst's message, the magazine asserted, was "such as no pulpit in this country had delivered since the days when Theodore Parker and Henry Ward Beecher inveighed against the slave power."[14]

The early political sketches of William Allen White, based on personal interviews, were modeled on Edwards' work. Writing prior to the election of 1900, White showed mature political judgment. Bryan was only "a voice," he concluded, and Hanna, whose "solicitude for the people is as tender as that of the late William H. Vanderbilt," was a man who "converted dollars into patriotism."[15] In time

13 *Ibid.*   14 *Ibid.,* II (April, 1894), 477.
15 *Ibid.,* XV (July, 1900), 232; XVI (Nov., 1900), 62, 57, 64.

White's party line eroded. He found little to admire in either Boss Platt or Boss Croker, and much to commend in both ex-President Cleveland and the youthful Theodore Roosevelt. These subjective appraisals were later supplemented by the personal sketches of Baker and Steffens.

In no field was personality more thoroughly explored and exploited than in articles dealing with Civil War heroes. Almost ten percent of all *McClure's* articles between 1893 and 1903 dealt with this theme. One of McClure's editorials explained, "Following an instinct which we have good reason to believe is shared by all of our readers, we have had as one of our foremost interests, in editing the magazine, the inspiring history of our country."[16] In truth *McClure's* claimed to be practically a "magazine of American History and Biography."[17] Its intent, evidently, was to teach by example. Miss Tarbell's announcement of her series on Lincoln in 1895 extolled "the man," "the noblest character of our history," and "the greatest man of the Christian era."[18] "No other story in American history," the magazine insisted, "impressed one more deeply with the solemn duties of citizenship, with the necessity of abiding like a rock by what is lawful and just."[19] As with *Century* in the preceding decade, no contemporary magazine rivaled *McClure's* in the field of Civil War literature.

During its first decade *McClure's* published thirty articles on Lincoln, including Miss Tarbell's "Life of Lincoln," twenty-six articles on General Grant, many written by Hamlin Garland, as many again on the Civil War itself, and dozens of memoirs, including those of Charles A. Dana, who ran the secret service, and Carl Schurz.[20] These articles attempted to discover unknown aspects of popular battles or events. They were obviously aimed at the populous Grand Army of the Republic and its families. Blatantly

[16] *Ibid.*, IX (Oct., 1897), 1101.   [17] *Ibid.*, VIII (Dec., 1896), 192.
[18] *Ibid.*, IV (Jan., 1895), 195; V (Oct., 1895), 480.
[19] *Ibid.*
[20] See *Index to McClure's Magazine, Volume I to XVIII* (New York, 1903), especially 26-27.

pro-northern, they were partisan extolments of their fathers' war.

Miss Tarbell's *Lincoln* may be taken as a case in point. Her method, one which Ray Stannard Baker was to employ later in his multi-volumed life of Woodrow Wilson, involved interviewing every available living man who had known Lincoln. Charles Dana, whose memoirs she shortly wrote, was one of her better sources, but the list included former law partners, party colleagues, and governmental officials. Then she weighed the spoken word with the written. For those familiar with the "complete" Nicolay and Hay volumes, her considerable work produced no significant surprises.[21] Extensively illustrated with practically every extant photograph of Lincoln, the biography, which was run intermittently from the fall of 1896 to the fall of 1899, was a popularized morality play with its heroes and villains. Knox College, already the subject of one article, was given a conspicuous place in the Lincoln-Douglas debates.[22] Since Miss Tarbell had written an entire chapter on the funeral of Napoleon, no less could be done for Lincoln. Such chapters hardly gave new penetrating insights into presidential affairs, but they met the demands of the market.

The ovation was tremendous. More letters on Lincoln arrived than all other editorial correspondence.[23] Even historians Woodrow Wilson and Herbert Baxter Adams were commendatory. Adams was delighted to read another volume about "The Saviour of his Country."[24]

Ray Stannard Baker, as already mentioned, contributed his father's reminiscences of the secret service. Commencing with the "Capture, Death, and Burial of J. Wilkes Booth," the first accurate account of his uncle's exploits, Baker wrote several stories reciting successful Union acts of may-

[21] *McClure's*, VIII (Sept., 1896), 384.
[22] *Ibid.*, VII (Oct., 1896), 401.
[23] *Profitable Advertising* (Oct. 15, 1897), 140; see *McClure's*, VI (Dec., 1895), 109.
[24] *Ibid.*, 109, 111, VI (Jan., 1896), 206.

hem against Rebels.[25] In vain one searches *McClure's* files for evidence of that sectional rapprochement which Paul Buck maintains was transpiring during this decade.[26]

No less engaging than the Civil War were articles based on new scientific advancements, many written by Alexander Graham Bell and Thomas Edison. The generation that linked Pasteur and Einstein acquired an awesome respect for the fructifications of the empirical creed. On the average there was an article in every other issue on such subjects as wild animals, their habits, capture, and taming; aerial navigation, especially gliders, airplanes, and balloons; telegraphy, particularly Marconi's wireless; and attempts to reach the pole.[27] Industry with its sprawling mines and factories was the essence of scientific inventiveness; thus no field to be ignored.

McClure's views on industrialism are of particular importance, since they culminated in muckraking in 1902. A few generalizations may explain this metamorphosis. First, McClure and Phillips were rather ambivalent towards economic ideology—the depression of 1893 had not befriended their private enterprise. And so stories of the Horatio Alger type—then being popularized by Frank Munsey—appeared alongside others full of social discontent. The magazine's ideological pluralism might be explained as an attempt at balance, a toleration of the more radical writings of highly patronized writers like Crane and Garland, and an attempt to secure readers among the laboring classes. But growing concern over the centralization of the nation's industry after the war with Spain created pres-

25 *Ibid.*, IX (May, 1897), 574-85; XIII (Aug., 1899), 355-63; XIV (Jan., 1900), 241-47; XII (Dec., 1898), 179-85. See White's "A Recent Confederate Victory," in *ibid.*, IX (June, 1897), 701; and Roseboro's "In Missouri," in *ibid.*, XIII (May, 1899), 68; both probably autobiographical accounts about the war.

26 Articles on the Union Army competed with reports on the Spanish-American War and the Dreyfus trial; see *ibid.*, XI (June, 1898), and Tarbell to Edgar Bancroft, Aug. 6, 1899, Bancroft Papers.

27 For example see *McClure's*, IX (June, 1897), 647; XIII (June, 1899), 99; III (June, 1894), 39.

sures that moved the magazine towards social concern. And, as will be seen, fictional writing was the first to be conscientiously directed towards these ends; from then on the more radical leanings of the younger staff members began to make themselves felt.

McClure's visit to the ill-timed Chicago World's Fair in the summer of 1893 stimulated his creative urges. He was impressed with the Armour Institute, and dispatched a reporter to write it up as representative of the new Chicago.[28] The article which finally evolved was a benevolent portrait of Philip D. Armour, the beef trust king. Though it served as a prototype for later pieces, including Miss Tarbell's Standard Oil series, the reporter, Arthur Warren, had little but praise for his subject, who supposedly differed from the competitors he had successfully fought off and destroyed: "On one side stands the millionaire of the relentless, grasping sort, unmindful of the interests of his country or his race; and on the other is the millionaire of the Armour sort, a man whose composition is well mixed with the milk of human kindness."[29] Facing bankruptcy, McClure probably felt a tinge of envy.

This piece was shortly balanced by its opposite, Hamlin Garland's "Homestead and its Perilous Trades," an indictment of industrialism worthy of the Fabians. Garland, preparing McClure's Life of Grant, had just published his progressive "A Spoil of Office." Instead of holding a confidential tête-à-tête with Andrew Carnegie, Warren-style, he visited the Homestead factories at Pittsburgh and fraternized with the steel mill hands who had struck and fought with Pinkerton guards two years earlier. The difficulty of getting into the mills was overcome with help from a relative of John Phillips who worked at a blast furnace. It was more than a rustic's repugnance to Pittsburgh that made Garland feel the factory "an inhuman place to spend four-fifth's of one's waking hours" and conclude that the work of the

[28] Ibid., II (Feb., 1894), 260.   [29] Ibid.

112

twelve-hour shifts "was of the inhuman sort that hardens and coarsens."[30] The searing heat, boots literally filled with sweat, bodies maimed and scarred by the scalding molten metal, the deafening roar, and the ubiquitous dirt and soot left Garland with one impression: "the town and its industries lay like a cancer on the breast of the human body."[31] "While capital wastes, labor starves," he concluded; "they probably don't care whether the hands live or die . . . provided they do every ounce they can while they do live."[32]

Garland's view was that of an itinerant journalist. "Homestead As Seen by One of Its Workmen," in a subsequent issue, was a personal chronicle of the lengthy apprenticeship in drudgery served by one of the 27,000 men who ran the mills. The anonymous author explained the exact science of how a muscle adapted to a twelve-hour work day, rested on a boarding-house bed, and dodged the ever-present dangers in the unsafe factory; this article established a level of realism that even the muckrakers did not exceed.[33]

When the Pullman disorders erupted into the American Railroad Union's strike against all major operators, and when Coxey's army marched, *McClure's*, albeit in a subdued vein, continued to show the position of labor in modern capitalistic conditions. In the summer of 1894 Stephen Crane's "In the Depths of a Coal Mine," his first contribution to *McClure's*, was a study of the miner's physical hardship and the enormous cost of the struggle in terms of health and well-being.[34] In fact Crane's article adhered quite closely to the instructions given Baker a few years later when he was writing up a Calumet and Hecla copper mine: "It is of course of great importance that you should go and visit the mine thoroughly . . . it will be necessary to . . . work on the ground from Nature and from life, in order

30 *Ibid.*, III (June, 1894), 19, 10.   31 *Ibid.*, 20.
32 *Ibid.*, 17.   33 *Ibid.*, III (July, 1894), 164.
34 *Ibid.*, III (Aug., 1894), 195.

to get it absolutely true to facts and full of that dramatic weird spirit or whatever spirit the work conveys. . . . The works or the machinery which while not being particularly artistic are yet necessary to the story."[35]

Less artistic and pointed was Cleveland Moffett's "Life and Works in the DuPont Powder Mills."[36] Moffett, who had written with exaggeration of the Pinkerton detectives and their overthrow of the Molly Maguires in the Pennsylvania coal fields, was hardly inclined to be as anticapitalist as Garland and Crane.[37] He thought the dangers of making DuPont powder equally shared by employer and employee, though parts of a worker's torso were often discovered after an accidental blast.

Henry J. W. Dam's "The Great Dynamite Factory at Ardeer" was another romance of capital, but Robert H. Sherard in his "The Deep Mines at Cornwall: A Life of Poverty, Toil, and Tragedy, Supported by Rare Piety" struck a chord in unison with the English protest movement of Wells, Shaw, and the Webbs. Two years earlier, in 1897, Sherard, from whose hands Miss Tarbell had snatched the Napoleon series, had published *The White Slaves of England*, and his *McClure's* articles evidence his realism.[38]

The tin mines at Cornwall, one-half mile deep and projecting out under the sea, were manned by ancient pumps. The mechanism for descending was so crude and unsafe that it had killed the man who invented it, and yet— though many others were subsequently injured—it remained unimproved because of the cost involved. Sherard's piece, which resembled a Fabian pamphlet, was as much an indictment of capitalistic methods as Garland's article on Homestead. By contrast, Lincoln Steffens' first article for *McClure's* on the Klondike gold mines was more concerned with adventure than economic principles of profits and ex-

[35] Jaccaci to Baker, Feb. 10, 1898, Baker Papers.
[36] *McClure's*, v (June, 1895), 3.   [37] *Ibid.*, iv (Dec., 1894), 90.
[38] *Ibid.*, xiii (June, 1899), 184.

ploitation.[39] At the time Steffens was probably closer to McClure's mind than Sherard.

A subsequent contribution of Garland, with a favorite McClure title, "A Romance of Wall Street," dealt with the Grant and Ward failure which contributed to the panic of 1873. It was *McClure's* first article on the chicanery of the market. Garland's blows at business were softened when Ray Stannard Baker assumed responsibility for most of *McClure's* labor and industrial writing. Baker's first volume, *Our New Prosperity*, was considered as a McKinley campaign tract in 1900.[40] "The Movement of Wheat" heralded the new prosperity in 1899, although Baker did not dwell on the fact that the farmer earned slightly more than a dollar per acre of wheat sown.[41] The second article of this series, "The New Prosperity," was published a few months later and concluded with William Allen White's comment that every farm in "Kansas and Nebraska has a new coat of paint."[42] But thousands, bankrupted in the depression, did not have farms, of course.

Most of Baker's articles on the "Romance of Capital" were unpopular with Phillips and McClure for one reason or another. Not all of the defects were literary. John Phillips, perhaps attempting to preserve a balanced view, rejected an effort on banking "on the ground that it tends to weaken the public confidence in these public institutions."[43] Baker, properly chastized by his superior, turned to rather harmless studies of Wall Street. Subjects of his benign sketches included J. P. Morgan and U.S. Steel, the

[39] *Ibid.*, IX (Sept., 1897), 956.

[40] See Baker, *American Chronicle*, 88; John Erwin Semonche, "Progressive Journalist: Ray Stannard Baker, 1870-1914," doctoral dissertation, Northwestern University, Evanston, 1962, 51. Senator Lodge was originally to write the introduction. One paper called the work the "strongest endorsement of the McKinley administration that has appeared in print." (*Riverside* [California] *Press*, May 24, 1900.)

[41] *McClure's*, XIV (Dec., 1899), 124.

[42] Baker, *American Chronicle*, 89; *McClure's*, XV (May, 1900), 86.

[43] Joseph Rogers to Tarbell, April 12, 1900, Phillips Papers.

world's largest trust, which controlled a sum greater than that of Imperial Germany.[44] Nothing better illustrates Baker's departure from the approach of Garland and Crane than the fact that when the American Association of Exporters, composed of Standard Oil, Armour, Pillsbury, and others, decided to publish a magazine, he was considered safe enough to be offered the editorship. His refusal was based on the fact that *McClure's* was a "concern which is making lots of money and which will soon make lots more."[45] Baker's concern about the newly emerging trusts, to which he devoted a chapter in *Our New Prosperity*, soon led him to a more progressive attitude. A pluralistic approach in factual articles on industry contrasts with the sharply defined reform character of *McClure's* fiction. It is time, then, to turn to an analysis of the magazine's fiction and see how it led to muckraking.

Although much of *McClure's* fiction paralleled in topic factual articles, neither Phillips nor McClure exercised the same fine sense of control in this area. McClure's basic criterion for good fiction was readability: "The story is the thing, it must be an interesting, absorbing narrative."[46] Every piece had to be "so interesting that I, personally, shall be ready to read it over again after having read it several times."[47] A story benefited in McClure's eyes if it were "of incident and rapid movement" with "no description or elaboration of character."[48] The best plot "cleverly baffles all attempts at a solution" and does "not disclose itself in the narrative until the proper time."[49] These standards, adhered to by the syndicate, were adequate for juvenile literature, but they were certainly inadequate for sophisticated writing. They were well articulated in a broadside an-

[44] Baker to Father, Sept. 1, 1901, Baker Papers; *McClure's*, XVII (April, 1901), 507; XVIII (Nov., 1901), 3; XVII (Oct., 1901), 507.
[45] Baker to Father, March 15, 1899, Baker Papers.
[46] McClure, Staff speech, fall, 1904, McClure Papers.
[47] *Profitable Advertising* (Oct. 15, 1897), 142.
[48] Syndicate scrapbook, "1888-1892," Feb., 1889, McClure Papers.
[49] *Ibid.*, Aug. 1889; Phillips to Hattie McClure, June 29, 1904, *ibid.*

nouncing a Bret Harte short story: "This is a very interesting and powerful story of pioneer life in California. The hero of the story teaches the village school. The plot is full of exciting incidents involving the claims of a squatter settler, whose daughter is the heroine of the story. The same elements of rude life, courage, deeds, heroism and adventure, that have made Bret Harte's stories so famous and popular, appear in this story."[50]

The novels of Stevenson, Kipling, and Anthony Hope, serialized in *McClure's*, conformed to these standards. Short stories full of dash and excitement were supplied by Doyle and Robert Barr. *McClure's* fiction was written for an audience whose taste for swashbuckling episodes was nigh insatiable. Stories of firemen and train engineers were perhaps the most important category of this type of fiction, eventually replaced by detective stories and westerns. Cy Warman, who sold *McClure's* over a dozen railroad stories, reveled in such titles as "Railroading Over an Earthquake" and "A Thousand Mile Ride on the Engine of the Swiftest Train in the World."[51] Cleveland Moffett also wrote a number of railroad stories, and both Baker and Steffens attempted fictional pieces on fire fighting.[52] Steffens also wrote one melodramatic police story, "Dan McCarthy; Captain of Police," which seems to be modeled on Captain Max Schmittberger, the Tammany policeman who turned state's witness in the Lexow investigations.[53]

Despite such an imposing list of authors, McClure bought fiction more on the strength of reputation or recommendation, as in the days of the syndicate, than on an innate sense of worth. Of brilliant literary talent at *McClure's*, Viola

---

[50] Syndicate circular, Aug., 1888, *ibid.*

[51] See *Index to McClure's Magazine*, 23.

[52] *McClure's*, XII (Nov., 1898), 19; XV (May, 1900), 32. Steffens also used this, it seems, for "Senator Terry Watkins," *Ainslee's*, VI (Nov., 1900).

[53] See Steffens, *Autobiography*, 253-84.

Roseboro' wrote, "I saw it more than once snubbed and never try again."[54]

Miss Roseboro' thought that John Phillips "was the first person I ever heard enunciate the principle that you must not read to guess what other people would like; also I have heard him say how when preoccupied it was natural to do that."[55] Roseboro' read everything and therefore was a more capable judge of literature than the editors.

A case in point was O. Henry's first published story, "Whistling Dick's Christmas Stocking," a holiday story of a trespassing tramp's chicanery and the good humor of a New Orleans policeman who preferred whistling duets to making an arrest.[56] Good Christmas stories were always difficult to get. Since McClure was in Europe during the winter of 1899 and Phillips was away ill, Miss Tarbell made up the holiday number of the magazine, allowing Miss Roseboro' to print whatever fiction she liked. Having written critical and encouraging letters to O. Henry since his first story had appeared in the syndicate the year before, Miss Roseboro' felt the Christmas story which he produced poor but "publishable, and I felt anxious to encourage a mind of that quality."[57] McClure returned with but one comment, "that story about the tramp you put in was not good enough for the Xmas number."[58] And when O. Henry subsequently submitted "Tobin's Palm," "one of the best O. H. ever wrote," McClure rejected it.[59] When Miss Roseboro's tears flowed over the matter, McClure reneged. "Now, now," Miss Roseboro' remembered his saying, "we'll get it back—don't cry! You! send an office boy—no send Bynner; now it's going to be all right. Bynner you know O. Henry, don't you? He lives on 27th Street, doesn't he—get your hat and run right around there and get that story I sent back yesterday."[60] "There came out

[54] Roseboro' to Tarbell, Aug. 12, 1936, Tarbell Papers.
[55] *Ibid.*   [56] *McClure's,* XIV (Dec., 1899), 138.
[57] Roseboro' to Tarbell, Aug. 12, 1936, Tarbell Papers.
[58] *Ibid.*   [59] *Ibid.*   [60] *Ibid.*

one of the Chief's great qualities as an editor," conceded Miss Roseboro'; "he never could stand analysis, talky-talk about qualities in any writing, but he would bet on effects, human emotion, aroused in such a case as this."[61]

It was also Miss Roseboro's tears, it seems, that made Phillips and McClure buy Tarkington's "The Gentleman From Indiana," reconsider "Pigs is Pigs," a popular seller eventually, and print Willa Cather and Eugene Wood. Jack London, Rex Beach, Edith Wyatt, and George Madden Martin, to reiterate, Miss Roseboro' also considered her protégés.[62] "What a devilish hard row," Miss Roseboro' felt, "talent had to hoe," because the editors "never *really* read the things."[63]

Miss Roseboro's assessment of the aesthetic tastes of the magazine's editors had some validity. Yet, it was principally by means of fiction that *McClure's* made the transition to muckraking. Although influenced by the Spanish-American War, the movement towards a politically oriented fiction had begun much earlier.

Early in its career the magazine contained stories by Israel Zangwill, the Jewish writer of London ghetto life. He proved a powerful reform influence in England, and "Incurable" and "Sabbath-breaker" in *McClure's* were as poignant as any of Jacob Riis' writings about the slums.[64] Another writer who seems to have played a significant role in moving *McClure's* towards political fiction was Brand

[61] *Ibid.*

[62] Graham, *Duchess of New Dorp*, II, 43, 70-71.

[63] Roseboro' to Tarbell, Aug. 12, 1936, Tarbell Papers. Willa Cather's experience does not entirely agree with Miss Roseboro's memory. It was McClure, on another's recommendation, who invited her to New York and immediately commissioned all the writing she should do. "Several of these same stories," Miss Cather wrote, "had been sent back to me by Mr. McClure's readers without having ever reached him at all. During my first interview with him he rang for the boy and had the two readers sent in and asked them to give an account of their stewardship. Surely I sat and held my chin high and thought my hour had struck." (Willa Cather to Will Jones, May 7, 1903, Cather Papers, University of Virginia.)

[64] *McClure's*, I (Nov., 1893), 478; II (Jan., 1894), 59.

Whitlock. While working as a clerk in the Governor's office in Illinois, Whitlock approached *McClure's* about writing realistic fiction. One of his stories, written in 1896, suggested to John Phillips "a capital plan for a series of short stories that would deal with the incidents and characters of political life, from the ward caucuses and ward managers up to the chairmen of important political committees and men elected to important offices."[65] With the election campaign of that year afoot, the magazine was in the market for stories "that would have the ring of truth and the stamp of obvious knowledge of political life."[66] "We find," Phillips confided to Whitlock, "we cannot depend upon the old established writers of fiction for the stuff we want; some of their stories suit us and some do not, and we are looking for new blood, and we believe that there is the right stuff here in America for a magazine like *McClure's*."[67]

Whitlock's first contribution to this "curiously enough, unoccupied field of American life" was a short story, "The Pardon of Thomas Whalen," which was based upon his experience of handling Governor Altgeld's pardons, including those for the Haymarket anarchists.[68] But *McClure's* rejected the story, which later appeared in *Ainslee's*.[69] Although it was conceded that his stories were "well written," subsequent ones were also rejected, possibly in accordance with Miss Roseboro's thesis.[70]

With the expert criticism of William Dean Howells, Whitlock's skill improved.[71] While *McClure's*, stimulated by his whole program, was searching elsewhere, *Ainslee's* bought his series on "modern political life," and soon even *Youth's Companion* was buying "stories on municipal poli-

---

[65] Phillips to Brand Whitlock, Sept. 11, 1896, Whitlock Papers.
[66] *Ibid.*   [67] *Ibid.*
[68] Whitlock to Phillips, Oct. 14, 1896, *ibid.*
[69] Phillips to Whitlock, Oct. 17, 1896, *ibid.*
[70] McClure to Whitlock, Oct. 4, 1899, *ibid.*
[71] Whitlock to Octavia Roberts, Aug. 2, 1898, *ibid.* Miss Roberts, incidentally, did publish in *McClure's*.

tics."[72] Although he never published in *McClure's*, Whitlock's flirtation with the magazine was not at an end.

By 1901 Whitlock had finished *The Thirteenth District*, a dull novel which traced the erosion of morality in congressional politics. Howells thought it "easily the best political story I know," despite the superiority of his own *A Hazard of New Fortunes*.[73] McClure seized upon the novel, and, unconscious that he had been rejected for years, badgered Whitlock for any "McClure stories" he might do.[74] Whitlock had no desire to try. Within a season he was to become valuable to *McClure's*, not as a writer, but as an informant to Lincoln Steffens, helping him to understand the clandestine world of Ohio politics.

Only a few stories, dealing realistically with politics, stand out before the Spanish-American War. "Silent Witness," published in 1896, was the story of ward politics in which a saloon-keeper killed an innocent man and went unpunished.[75] Several readers testified to its veracity, but two years elapsed before the magazine began to exploit the field with the stories of Octave Thanet.

Miss Thanet, a very popular, though mediocre, novelist of the 1890's, was much interested in the problems of labor reform. She championed cooperatives and political righteousness. "The Conscience of Alderman McGinnis," published in 1898, concerned a boodling alderman who left his saloon one Sunday morning long enough to "lose a good office, avert a strike, and unconsciously plant the seed that was to convert the brightest of his machine politicians, slowly but surely, into a reformer."[76] The climax of the

[72] Richard Duffy to Whitlock, May 24, 1899, *ibid.*; Corresponding Editor, *Youth's Companion*, to Whitlock, Feb. 12, 1900, *ibid.*

[73] Howells to Whitlock, June 19, 1901, *ibid.*

[74] McClure to Whitlock, May 27, 1902, *ibid.*; Florence Bates to Whitlock, June 5, 1902, *ibid.*

[75] *McClure's*, VI (March, 1896), 399.

[76] *Ibid.*, XI (June, 1898), 296. See George McMichael, *Journey to Obscurity: The Life of Octave Thanet* (Lincoln, Nebraska, 1965), 131, 142-43, 169, 171.

story was not so much the politician's newly found conscience as the insight of a labor leader who thought, "if we fellows would study some of the machine methods, without dropping any of our principles, either, we mightn't find election such a blamed cold day."[77]

Another author, Walter Barr, used his stories to mix machine politics with romance. "In the Third House" reveals the activities of a lobbyist in the Illinois legislature, who, in collusion with a Chicago gang, attempts to sell a traction franchise. The lobbyist's fiancée, like the Victorian ideal, stood opposed to such chicanery. Barr's style was often pedantic, but as he explained that was "for the satisfaction of the good people who cannot make the distinction between buying votes in the legislature and equally illegal methods of obtaining things."[78] The demand of *McClure's* for a happy ending was finally facilitated when the hero reneged on the bribery scheme and, in the next episode, maneuvered himself towards the U.S. Senate and prepared to marry.[79]

The stories of Walter Barr and Octave Thanet, although stock in their format of quick, happy endings, lacked little, save authentication, from being political tracts. The writings of other authors supplemented these deficiencies. Charles Warren, a Harvard-trained lawyer who served as private secretary to Governor William E. Russell of Massachusetts, was such a contributor. Like Whitlock, Warren's deep interest in reform eventually led him to political office, chairman of the Massachusetts Civil Service Commission and a United States attorney under Woodrow Wilson. Warren did three pieces for *McClure's*, including "The Governor's Rehearsal," a study of the political aspects of labor problems.[80]

[77] *Ibid.*, 296. See also *ibid.*, XI (Sept., 1898), 458; IX (Oct., 1897), 1089.

[78] *Ibid.*, XII (Feb., 1899), 365.

[79] *Ibid.*, 362, XII (April, 1899), 535.

[80] *Ibid.*, XV (May, 1900), 76. For other stories of this type see *ibid.*, XIV (Dec., 1899), 189; XV (June, 1900), 151.

These stories by Miss Thanet, Barr, and others gave *McClure's* fiction an economic, social, and political content far more significant than any literary quality they might possess. The capstone was a series commenced by Josiah Flynt, a nephew of Frances Willard. Flynt was a thirty-one-year-old ex-convict who had learned the ways and language of the hobo and criminal. He counted Arthur Symons and several of the English realists among his literary friends. Like Richard Harding Davis, who occasionally disguised himself and submerged into the underworld, Flynt, incognito, as "Cigarette" gathered material for a *McClure's* series, "True Stories From the Under-world," inaugurated in 1900. "These stories," warned the magazine, "are not fiction in the ordinary sense . . . the characters are real and the incidents have all occurred. . . . The stories are intended to point a moral as well as adorn a tale."[81]

Flynt's stories, published as *The World of Graft*, "were as educational as any treatise on municipal government since James Bryce's *American Commonwealth*."[82] Louis Filler has called *The World of Graft* the "first genuine muckraking book."[83] Of course this genre had already been pioneered by various *McClure's* writers, and Alfred Henry Lewis's *The Boss*, published in the same year, employed much the same technique.

Although earlier writers had written accurately enough of labor and politics, none had adequately worked beyond the saloon keeper to the criminal class and shown in detail its relationship to the elite power structure. This was a surprising omission considering McClure's abiding interest in lawlessness and its causes. The magazine had published many articles on criminals and their apprehension, but

[81] *Ibid.*, xv (Aug., 1900) 356. Arthur Symons thought Flynt's "mind was stubborn. . . . I never saw him conscious of the beauty of anything; I do not think he read much or cared for books," but Flynt's writings made the word "graft" standard English. See Josiah Flynt, *My Life* (N.Y., 1908), xiii.

[82] Louis Filler, *Crusaders for American Liberalism*, Collier edition (New York, 1961), 90, see 83-92.

[83] *Ibid.*, 90.

nothing had equaled Flynt's conversation with "guns," the full-time thieves, who seem to have been better informed about the "system" than many in public office. Not a few pulpits and newspapers, just as the earlier *McClure's* articles had shown, knew of the type of boodling prevalent in the city machine. But specifics on corruption from the pariah criminal class itself were new to popular journalism. From Galesburg to Emporia, from New York to Chicago, news reporters knew where the houses were, knew why they were not closed, along with the unlicensed saloons, and yet Flynt's stories proved popular and startling to vast numbers of the American bourgeoisie. The fact that reform movements existed in New York, Chicago, and scores of other cities prior to Flynt's revelations is proof that his accounts were hardly new. Indeed, the purpose, so *McClure's* said, of the studies was "not to gratify an idle curiosity, but in the hope that they will aid the movement now in progress to better the government of our cities. . . . It is a mere coincidence that these articles are published just as Chicago and New York are arousing to the need of reform."[84]

Flynt's method was to submerge briefly, then emerge with an article full of evidence from the testimony of his friends. During three months of 1900 he interviewed underworld figures, many of whom were personal friends, in regard to the police management of criminals in Chicago, Philadelphia, New York, Boston, Allegheny, Pittsburgh, and parts of Ohio; he came back with the conclusion that "Chi" was, in Boss Plunkitt's terms, the only honest city. But because he wrote anonymously, swiftly, and under the guise of fiction, his articles were denied the power and influence which the writings of Steffens, his successor, enjoyed. It was the *Chicago Press* which noted that the exposures were not being followed up, partly, it seems, because nothing Flynt wrote really constituted news.[85] Nonetheless, Mc-

[84] *McClure's*, XVI (Feb., 1901), 327.
[85] *Ibid.*, 334.

Clure was satisfied with the project, and undoubtedly so was Miss Roseboro'. In March, 1901, with an issue that contained studies of New York's infant reform effort written by Steffens and Roosevelt, the magazine explained, "Before conditions can be cured they must be understood; and Josiah Flynt's papers bring to life views, motives, attitudes, that but for him the reformers would guess at. . . . They are calculated to win readers that scorn preachments, to make men ponder our parlous state who never condescended to reflect seriously on it before, and to awaken to action these who hitherto only reflected."[86]

Flynt's "Human Documents" were of a new sort of realism, a vivid closeness to action, a portrayal of the human element in a manner that differentiated them from *McClure's* other material on politics principally because they made "abstractions real."[87] Whether Flynt was a good reporter or not is difficult to determine. Some of his cronies felt, "a reform party is a disorder, but a reform party that has elected its candidate becomes a lingering disease," and Flynt himself was convinced that Seth Low's administration, usually regarded an exemplary, left corruption unchanged and Tammany unfettered.[88] But by the time Boston was written up, Flynt was quoting hearings and newspapers and writing with a greater sense of evidence.[89] From his interviews Flynt attempted to describe the tribute system presided over by the New York machine in "The Tammany Commandment."[90] His analysis of the system revealed how much was paid, to whom, and when. The article was so bold, the magazine later asserted, that the chief of the New York detectives warned Flynt to leave town or get the third degree because his work constituted "an exposure such as cannot but open the eyes of the great American cities to the perils of the alliance which to-day governs most of them

[86] *Ibid.*, XVI (March, 1901), 480.   [87] *Ibid.*
[88] *Ibid.*, XVI (Jan., 1901), 232; XVI (Aug., 1901), 570.
[89] *Ibid.*, XVII (June, 1901), 115.   [90] *Ibid.*, XVII (Oct., 1901), 543.

125

and is daily extending its rule."[91] Although the great impact of exposure came later, with Flynt the interest in reform was considerably broadened from the years when Baker had been reined in and Whitlock had been rejected.

Two writers on the *McClure's* staff applied Flynt's approach to the temperance problem, interest in which was also renewed after the Spanish-American War. George K. Turner's "A Temperance Campaign" exposed the subtle way in which a district political machine started and abetted a temperance movement—in order to get more graft from the local saloons. The people in Turner's fictional Meadeville "fondly imagined that they settled their own questions by popular vote, but in the last analysis" everything revolved around ward politics.[92] Joseph M. Rogers, who, like Turner, became a McClure editor after the war, did a poignant study of the Irish saloon keeper who doubled as a boss in politics, and was, by then, a stock character in *McClure's* as in reality. But it was in the literature of stock market manipulation, a field later preempted by Tom Lawson's famous *Frenzied Finance*, that the Flynt method was most successfully pursued. The writer was Edwin Lefevre.

Lefevre was a thirty-year-old former school teacher who briefly served as the financial editor of the *Commercial Advertiser*, where Steffens managed the city room. In his autobiography Steffens credits the taunts of the newspaper staff with driving Lefevre to write fictional accounts of the market manipulations which he saw on Wall Street, but the young author was desperately searching for capital to pursue his speculative ventures. *McClure's* not only paid him well, but evidently polished Lefevre's rather plodding style. His series, *Stories of Wall Street*, was a popularization of the standard financial crimes of those whom Frederick Lewis Allen called the lords of creation. "The Break in 'Turpentine,'" story of "dumping from the inside" and "catching

[91] *Ibid.*, XVII (Jan., 1901), 201; see Josiah Flynt, *My Life*, 358.
[92] *Ibid.*, XVI (Nov., 1900), 20.

the shorts," could have been true of any trust in the market but was evidently modeled on Havemeyer and the sugar trust.[93] Another story, "The Man Who Won," was seemingly based on the James J. Hill-E. H. Harriman battle over the Northern Pacific Railroad, an event that almost broke the market in 1901 and led to the creation of the Northern Securities Company.[94] Lefevre often dwelt upon the individual, rather than the institutional, criminality permitted in the easy-going, speculative atmosphere of New York banking society. In "The Tipster" a plunger finally got his due after ruining several men, and "A Woman and Her Bonds" served as a sort of satyr play to the other tales of tragedy and degeneration, as the feminine mystique confronted the intricacies of the gyrating bond market.[95] When Lefevre's series was completed, *McClure's* solicited similar material from David Graham Phillips, whose *Treason of the Senate* later cast him into notoriety. His "Thursday at Three," which appeared in December, 1902, was another vignette on Wall Street, but by then more academic, documented studies were being undertaken for the magazine.[96] Miss Tarbell had already commenced her work on the history of Standard Oil.

After this inspection of the contents of *McClure's* during its first decade, a few generalizations seem possible. The magazine's contents were clearly popular, gauged to reveal and appeal to human personality. The heroic qualities of Civil War figures were thoroughly exploited, and to a considerable extent the whole complex of abolitionist reforms found expression through the magazine. Although *McClure's* was hardly as vocal as the *Arena*, or perhaps others, with one of the largest circulations in the country,

[93] *Ibid.*, xvi (April, 1901), 538. See Edwin Lefevre, *Reminiscences of a Stock Operator* (Garden City, N.Y., 1923, 1938), 85 for an account of these years. Lefevre later made a million dollars in one day's trading in the stock market break of 1907.

[94] *Ibid.*, xvii (Aug., 1901), 360.

[95] *Ibid.*, xiii (Nov., 1901), 71; xvi (Feb., 1901), 339.

[96] *Ibid.*, xx (Dec., 1902), 143.

it opened its pages to men who were filled with discontent and hope for a new era.

As the first issue of *McClure's* reached the newsstands, Theodore Roosevelt wrote complimenting McClure on James Parton's published letter championing civil service reform: "I wish to congratulate you on behalf of all civil service reformers for the vigorous letter. . . . You have rendered a real service to the cause of good government by publishing such a letter."[97] And Brooks Adams could explain in *McClure's* that "in America there is no administration in the modern sense of the word. Every progressive nation is superior to us. . . ."[98] Thus *McClure's* closed its first decade with discontent, often disguised and ambiguous, directed at the country's conditions. How else should it commence the second decade but with the same themes highly accentuated, maintaining with Edwin Markham

I come to break the chain of infamy
That Greed's blind hammers forge about the Earth.[99]

In the editorial offices forces were already at work destined to shove *McClure's* foursquare in the direction of reform.

[97] Roosevelt to McClure, May 29, 1893, McClure Papers.
[98] *McClure's*, XII (April, 1899), 563.
[99] *Ibid.*, XIV (Dec., 1899), 123.

128

Chapter VII. The Genesis of Muckraking

IT IS difficult to maintain either that reform journalism came "suddenly, unexpectedly, upon the American scene," or that sole "credit for the sponsorship of muckraking does undoubtedly belong to McClure and *McClure's*."[1] The magazine only played in symphonic form what was already by 1903 a lively melody. The country at large, the press in general, and the national government were already preparing for battle with the two hundred odd trusts that had arisen behind the Dingley Tariff of 1897.[2] In the cities the National Municipal Reform League, the Civil Service Reform League, the Woman's Christian Temperance Union, the Anti-Saloon League, and even the Christian Endeavor, to name a few organizations, were arousing the middle class against political machines. Although their aims were far more modest than those of Bryan, Debs, or Henry George, these groups wanted the abolition of the liquor traffic, the gambling dens, and the houses of ill fame.[3]

This public sentiment between 1899 and 1903 must be accounted as the greatest force shoving *McClure's* towards radical journalism. But other public forces were at work. The editorial staffs pouring out of the Manhattan office buildings in the publishing district were abuzz over the clarity with which Governor Theodore Roosevelt and Mayor Seth Low spoke for the public interest. Josiah Flynt had shown vast new areas for the application of their methods. Daily the Wall Street situation was becoming more ominous. In the wind, all of the writers attest, was

[1] Louis Filler, *Crusaders for American Liberalism*, 31, 95.

[2] See *ibid.*, 6off; C. C. Regier, *The Era of the Muckraker* (Chapel Hill, 1932), 47ff, 53-55; Mark Sullivan, *Our Times* (6 vols., New York, 1926-35), II, 253; Elmo Ellis, *Mr. Dooley's America*, 224, 401.

[3] *Galesburg Daily Mail*, June 1, 1895; see *Emporia Gazette* (w), Sept. 21, 1899; *Chicago Inter-Ocean*, Sept. 16, 1899.

the expectancy of reform.[4] In the *McClure's* office a profound change was taking place between 1900 and 1903, and to understand that development these external forces must be kept in mind.

Two men are especially significant in McClure's editorial decision to move from the high grade fictional realism of Flynt and Lefevre to the authenticated exposures so characteristic of the magazine's muckraking. Their roles are worth considering at length. Both John Finley and Alfred Maurice Low, a Washington journalist, helped McClure and his band of ex-reporters solidify their thinking on the questions before the country.

John Finley came to McClure's office in 1899 as a thirty-four-year-old, tall, polished academician, who was to manage one of the magazines acquired from *Harper's*. When that position did not materialize, Finley stayed in the editorial offices for over a year, helping his brother-in-law, Albert Boyden, as well as Phillips and Miss Tarbell. Although at first resented as something of an intruder by his friend Miss Tarbell, Finley soon showed the capabilities which were to make him a masterful editor of the *New York Times* at a later date, and won warm acceptance.[5]

Finley, because of his connections with the *Charities Review*, brought the entire *McClure's* staff into contact with the powerful Charity Organization Society of New York. Robert Weeks DeForest, president of the Society and Finley's long-time friend, became Seth Low's first tenement house commissioner. As such, DeForest relied upon the advice of the new *McClure's* editor to the extent of letting him recommend housing inspectors.[6]

Because of his academic training and experience in the administration of charities, Finley's advice and friendship were sought by other reformers across the country. He was

[4] See Mark Sullivan, *The Education of An American* (New York, 1938), 200.
[5] See Tarbell to Finley, May 3, 1900, Phillips Papers.
[6] Robert W. DeForest to Finley, Dec. 21, 1901, Finley Papers.

the first to introduce the *McClure's* staff to Jane Addams, Albert Beveridge, Robert La Follette, Woodrow Wilson, and Frederick Howe.[7] Howe particularly served as the staff's window upon the progressive battle in state and municipal politics.

Undoubtedly Finley explained to his colleagues how Frederick Howe and Tom Johnson were having their reform efforts in Cleveland undermined by "Boss" Cox of Cincinnati, how Cox used the Ohio legislature to pass special local legislation to control Cleveland and Toledo—where Brand Whitlock and Mayor Sam Jones were also making a reform fight.[8] *McClure's* staff was probably informed when Whitlock argued a case before the Ohio Supreme Court that resulted in Cox's elaborate machinery being declared unconstitutional.[9] But Cox, with other methods, soon voided the court's decision.

At this point the Ohio reformers turned to *McClure's* for aid. Whitlock's early stories might be viewed as an attempt in this direction. Although the *Atlantic Monthly* published one "blow for municipal reform," Howe and Finley were unable to enlist *McClure's* help in raising "such a storm throughout the state as may compel proper action by the legislature."[10] Finley proved unable to get Howe's brilliant writing into the magazine, but the seed must have been well planted in McClure's mind as to the role he could play.[11] It was rather with the *North American Review* that Finley got Howe a commission to write on "Municipal Legislation."[12]

In other ways Finley was more successful in influencing the magazine. He was probably responsible for an article in March, 1901, "Reform through Social Work," by Theodore

[7] Jane Addams to Finley, June 12, 1902, *ibid.*; Albert Beveridge to Finley, Sept. 18, 1899, *ibid.*; Robert La Follette to Finley, n.d., *ibid.*
[8] Frederick Howe to Finley, Oct. 27, 1902, *ibid.*
[9] Whitlock to Octavia Roberts, Jan. 2, 1903, Whitlock Papers.
[10] Edwin B. Smith to Whitlock, July 9, 1902, *ibid.*
[11] Tarbell to Phillips, April 9, 1900, Phillips Papers.
[12] Howe to Finley, Dec. 3, 1902, Finley Papers.

Roosevelt, who was within six months to become president. But, more important, Finley used his standing as a professional economist to interest McClure in the trust question.

With Miss Tarbell finishing her work on Lincoln and Baker his on prosperity, Finley saw a great new feature in the Trust Convention called by Miss Addams' Chicago Civic Federation in September, 1899. Well known among the 500 delegates who came to Chicago were Richard Ely, Congressman George W. Prince from Galesburg, John Bates Clark, and Jeremiah Jenks, all of whom were Finley's acquaintances.[13] Jenks, formerly at Knox, represented McKinley's United States Industrial Commission and was one of the first speakers. When a subsequent speaker, William Jennings Bryan, took the podium and called for new national legislation against the trusts, Finley, like his teacher Ely, probably felt elated. William Allen White, still clinging to the old order, went away from the convention stunned. "Now the Trust is a bad thing only on one side —that it gives its manipulators a chance to play the hog," the young editor temporized.[14]

McClure, on the other hand, was delighted at Finley's suggestion to investigate this field: "I think you will find in the trusts a great theme," McClure wrote, "and hope that you have been in Chicago this week, attending that great Convention. There is plenty of material there, which . . . will command great attention."[15] Within a year McClure was to commission Lefevre's stories on Wall Street. Having thrown down the gauntlet, Finley accepted Woodrow Wilson's invitation to teach at Princeton in 1900. But for several years he continued as one of *McClure's* most pro-

[13] See *New York Times*, Sept. 13, 14, 1899; *Chicago Inter-Ocean*, Sept. 13, 15, 16, 17, 1899. Also present were Ignatius Donnelly, James B. Weaver, Champ Clark, John P. Altgeld, James Vardaman, Henry Wallace, Sr., Samuel Jones, and J. Allen Smith. See *Official Report of the National Anti-trust Conference* (Chicago, 1900).

[14] *Emporia Gazette* (w), Sept. 14, 1899.

[15] McClure to Finley, Sept. 14, 1899, Finley Papers.

gressive and informed editors. The man who supplemented Finley's work and laid the blueprint for *McClure's* final onslaught against the trusts was an English-born journalist, thirty-nine years of age in 1899, Alfred Maurice Low.

Low was the son of a well-known Jewish family in London. Educated at King's College, he took an M.A. at Dartmouth, and, like Finley, was a professional political economist as well as a journalist. Having been in the United States for ten years in 1899 (and staying for thirty more), Low had given particular attention to the ineffective use of the Sherman Act against the sugar trust in 1895. He was a vitriolic, probably an egregious, journalist, and his correspondence from Washington to Charles Taylor's *Boston Globe* and the *London Morning Post* was often sensational reading. It was probably as a result of McClure's long association with Charles Taylor that he first met the impulsive Low. The English journalist had impressive credentials, which McClure must have weighed. A friend of Theodore Roosevelt, Low had investigated English labor legislation for the United States Department of Labor. In time he was knighted for his authorship of such volumes as *The Supreme Surrender* (1901), *Protection in the United States* (1904), and *A Short History of Labor Legislation in Great Britain* (1907).

Low's views on economics were similar to those eventually adopted by President Roosevelt. The sudden development of the trusts, he felt, was a peculiar American phenomenon which "gave rise to more discussions and more conclusions predicated on false premises than perhaps any other one branch of economics."[16] "The outcry against the trusts, or more properly speaking, combinations, is illogical and hysterical," he wrote in 1904; "in themselves combinations are a good thing and an evidence of progress, but as with many other agencies intended to be the servant

[16] Alfred Maurice Low, *Protection in the United States* (London, 1904), 119.

133

they have become the masters. . . ."[17] Like Herbert Croly later he believed the trusts beneficial in that they eliminated "ruinous competition," but they should be carefully watched, and if deleterious, "the power of monopoly and oppression can always be curbed."[18]

In the spring of 1899, as the Chicago Trust Convention was being called, Low suggested to McClure a magazine series on the trusts. Having occasionally written articles for *McClure's*, perhaps he hoped that McClure would assign him the series. To ensure that the project be considered, Low also wrote Miss Tarbell, whom he knew.

When Low's long letter intercepted Miss Tarbell in Boston, it must have made breathless reading. McClure never seems to have received his. Low posed the same question as Finley: "Can an investigation of the Trusts be made of sufficient interest to the readers of a popular magazine?"[19] Could it be settled for the first time whether a trust "is a good or a bad thing," thus making an appeal to the masses as well as to the political economists and students of sociological problems? "I think it can," he wrote, remembering the McClure method, "because the question is full of intense human interest."

Why not take the controversial sugar trust controlled by Havemeyer, suggested Low, and discuss "who were the earliest sugar refiners in this country; the gradual rise and growth of the business; . . . the refiners as men—personal and descriptive." The "origin of the Trust" should be inspected. One should answer "how it was formed; how the refineries were brought into the Trust; the measures employed—coercion or hope of profit; how payment was made; the price for properties compared with their true value."

What was the effect of the trust on workers? "Assuming, which is the popular belief, that wages have been reduced

---

[17] *Ibid.*, 127, 128   [18] *Ibid.*, 120, 127.

[19] A. Maurice Low to Tarbell, March 27, 1899, Phillips Papers. The next four paragraphs, unless otherwise noted, are from this same source.

from time to time when the Trust obtained control, that factories have been closed and men thrown out of employment, it is easy enough to see here the material for a chapter to arouse popular sympathy and excite interest." If the unlikely opposite proved the case and "wages have been increased and additional opportunities afforded for labor, certainly not less interesting is it to see the trust presented in the new and unexpected *role* of commercial philanthropists [sic]."

Low was interested in the political role of the trust. "Has it contributed to Presidential campaign funds; has it had any influence in shaping the sugar schedules of tariff bills; has it kept a watchful eye on the law makers in Albany, Trenton, etc." Low was knowledgeable about such things, and he eventually broke with the President over the question of campaign contributions from corporations.[20]

Then there was the Wall Street face of the trust. Why did sugar stock "advance 30 points one day and drop back 20 the next?" If one could take this theme and "clothe the statistical skeletons with the living expressions of men on both sides whose opinions carry weight," Low was convinced, a readable and universally popular series could be created.

With scores of books coming out annually on trusts and with some magazines hesitatingly entering this field, there could be no doubt about the timeliness of Low's proposition. But John Phillips and Miss Tarbell, supervising the magazine while McClure was abroad for a year, were hesitant to commission Low. They felt him a "man of prejudice," "indiscreet," and lacking "discernment."[21] Low, like David Graham Phillips and Hearst, soon found even Roosevelt sharing this assessment. "Maurice Low is a circumcised skunk," the President said; "he knows nothing whatever and would misrepresent anything he did know. He is a

---

[20] See *The Letters of Theodore Roosevelt*, ed. by Elting Morrison (6 vols., Cambridge, Mass., 1951-1952), V, 250.

[21] Joseph Rogers to Tarbell, May 1, 1900, Phillips Papers.

liar of bad character."[22] While entertaining the proposal on trusts, John Phillips felt "Mr. Low is not aware of the fact that the best writers for *McClure's* have been those who have been educated under the tuitlage [sic] of its editorial staff and that this has taken in many cases a great deal of time and required many changes and much re-writing. . . ."[23]

Within a few months Phillips had sent Miss Tarbell to France, evidently with Low's letter on the sugar trust, instructing her to "show the outline to Sam, get his decision."[24] McClure, convalescing from over-exertion, responded, "don't worry about it . . . I want to think it over."[25]

McClure returned to the New York offices in the spring of 1901, ablaze. First, the articles of Flynt and Lefevre had struck a popular chord exposing corruption that even the neighborhood newsboy knew existed, and, secondly, in his absence hundreds of trusts, headed by Morgan's U.S. Steel, had arisen. Even Colonel Pope was an officer in the bicycle trust.[26] McClure vitalized the office staff with his excited assertion that the trusts were "the only side of present day interests that we did not seem to be grappling with in the magazine. It ought to be one of our great features for next year. . . ."[27] The seed planted by Finley and Low had finally borne fruit. But undoubtedly McClure made his decision with the encouragement of Phillips and Miss Tarbell.

When Baker, who was on the West Coast working on his fiction, wrote that the natural resources of that area might make a good article, Miss Tarbell immediately responded with an account of the staff discussions.[28] "You speak of something on the part the discovery of oil is playing in

[22] Elting Morrison, ed., *The Letters of Theodore Roosevelt*, VI, 908; V, 250.

[23] Rogers to Tarbell, May 1, 1900, Phillips Papers.

[24] Tarbell, *All in the Day's Work*, 205.   [25] *Ibid.*

[26] *New York Times*, Sept. 1, 1899. His son, George Pope, soon became president of the National Association of Manufacturers.

[27] Tarbell to Baker, April 29, 1901, Baker Papers.

[28] Baker to McClure, June 12, 1902, McClure Papers.

California," she wrote; "I shy a little at the subject."[29] Going beyond the "describing the discovery and opening of the great natural resources," the magazine needed to show clearly "the great principles by which industrial leaders are combining and controlling these resources."[30]

The staff's "new plan of attack" as revealed by Miss Tarbell was basically that suggested by Maurice Low. Why not tell the life history of a great collier or steel plant, its small beginnings and growth, its forced alliances to get transportation, its combinations, "and so on, until it is finally absorbed into a great Trust."[31] One could treat the company as an organism, "give it an individuality, a human quality."[32] Many questions remained to be answered satisfactorily. The questions were those posed by Low: "How do these aggregations obtain their control? Is it by greater acumen, persistency, and energy of their promoters, or is it by seizing special privileges, by criminal underselling, by manipulating the stock market? How do they keep their power? . . . Have prices fallen under trust management as rapidly as they naturally would have fallen under free competition? Is the public getting a share of the vast savings . . . ?"[33] Baker was quickly persuaded that the series should be done.

Although Baker shared the enthusiasm of the New York office, he steadfastly preferred that Miss Tarbell do the writing rather than himself.[34] Miss Tarbell, having finished with Lincoln, finally shouldered the responsibility for the series.

The logic by which Standard Oil was chosen as Miss Tarbell's subject appears to be substantially that given by her and McClure in their autobiographies.[35] There was, Miss

[29] Tarbell to Baker, April 29, 1901, Baker Papers.
[30] *Ibid.*   [31] *Ibid.*   [32] *Ibid.*
[33] *McClure's*, XIX (Oct., 1902), 589.
[34] Baker to McClure, April 23, 1902, Baker Papers; Tarbell to Baker, May 6, 1901, *ibid.*; Jaccaci to McClure, July 8, 1902, Phillips Papers.
[35] Tarbell, *All in the Day's Work*, 202-30; McClure, *Autobiography*, 237-40.

Tarbell writes, "much talk in the office about it, and there came to the top finally the idea of using the story of a typical trust to illustrate how and why the clan grew. How about the greatest of them all—the Standard Oil Company."[36] Indeed, Miss Tarbell harbored a victim's knowledge of that trust. "Whisky and monopolies are fearful evils —and growing in their devilish power over the country," her mother had written after being bankrupted by Standard.[37]

Standard Oil was not only the first great trust, "the Mother of Trusts," but it was also principally the work of one man, John D. Rockefeller. This "Napoleon among businessmen" so dominated the company that the whole story could be reduced to the simplicity of a biographical treatment.[38]

It must be emphasized that neither McClure nor the staff was prepared to launch any journalistic indictment of trusts when Miss Tarbell began her research in the fall of 1901. An attempt was made to acquire some contributions favorable to the trusts. John Finley wrote Jeremiah Jenks, by then a sponsor of the Anti-Trust League, asking him to interview the famous trust lawyer, James B. Dill, for a possible article. Jenks felt the session produced nothing of interest to the *McClure's* editors.[39] Even the book department exerted itself on behalf of the trusts.

When Phillips sent a memo down the hall asking about the possibility of preparing a "Trust Book," the response was that either President Arthur Hadley of Yale, who opposed the trusts until he became President, "when his attitude was better balanced," or William Graham Sumner, "a trust man" from the same institution, would do an excellent job of preparing the volume.[40] The book department

---

[36] Tarbell, *All in the Day's Work*, 202.
[37] Mrs. F. S. Tarbell, Aug. 6, 1893, Tarbell Papers.
[38] McClure, *Autobiography*, 238.
[39] Jenks to Finley, Nov. 6, 1902, Finley Papers.
[40] Unsigned to Phillips, Aug. 4, 1902, Phillips Papers.

thought Hadley would make a "very simple, possibly a classical," tome, while Sumner "would probably make the more entertaining" one.[41] Phillips and McClure finally persuaded Jenks to write *The Trust Problem*, an objective account that went through three printings and two editions in three years.[42]

It was mainly the accumulation of facts that transformed the attitude of McClure, Phillips, Baker, and Steffens to one of hostility towards industrial combinations. Miss Tarbell was the vengeful collector of these facts. Originally McClure and the staff were "very anxious" to have the whole subject opened up for discussion, and all believed the trust articles the "most serious thing the magazine has on hand," yet there was caution in selecting "an adequate scheme."[43] After three chapters of *Standard Oil* were sketched out, McClure hastily assigned Baker to investigate the beef trust, "although there is none."[44] On the beef trust, as on Standard Oil, McClure wanted unimpeachable evidence before the magazine printed a series. Conclusions, he hoped, would be left to the reader. "Get at the facts," he told Baker, "find out just what stock men and farmers get for cattle on their hoof, and then find out how much they annually produce, and just see just how much money is made by the beef trust."[45] As the data flooded in, McClure had no hesitation in printing it. By the summer of 1902 he had Steffens writing Attorney-General Philander Knox to see if the Justice Department had any information on the beef trust.[46] Within a few years the magazine was running Baker's articles on Armour and his trust. Since the laudatory article on the Armour Institute in 1894, the magazine had made a reversal of policy. Miss Tarbell's investigations were the main ingredient in this editorial evolution.

[41] *Ibid.*

[42] Jeremiah W. Jenks, *The Trust Problem* (New York, 1900, revised edition, 1901, 1903).

[43] Tarbell to Baker, May 6, 1901, Baker Papers.

[44] McClure to Baker, May 31, 1902, *ibid.*   [45] *Ibid.*

[46] Unsigned to McClure, June 27, 1902, Phillips Papers.

Although Miss Tarbell felt committed to write an objective history of Standard Oil when she commenced her work in September, 1901, she was quite conscious that her endeavors were modeled after "Josiah Flynt's investigations" and the Wall Street stories of Lefevre which attacked the "evils of stock broking in an excellent form."[47] She noted in retrospect, "we were neither apologists nor critics, only journalists intent on discovering what had gone into the making of this most perfect of all monopolies."[48]

Indeed, most of Miss Tarbell's sources were in the public domain in the form of newspaper articles or hearings: House of Representatives reports, the Hepburn Committee reports, Interstate Commerce Commission Reports, court cases, and state records. An important guide through this material was *Wealth Against Commonwealth*, which Miss Tarbell had read in Paris several years before on the recommendation of her parents. Henry D. Lloyd, its author, often offered her advice, suggesting such works as the Final Reports of the United States Industrial Commission, before which he had been a witness.[49]

Miss Tarbell read the *Wealth* intently, a marked copy of which remains among her papers, and penned numerous inquisitive letters to its author, particularly as she began her study. She was especially impressed with Chapter Seven, in which Lloyd told of Rockefeller's taking a widow's property for a fraction of its worth. Indeed, Miss Tarbell came to share Lloyd's animus against the corporation.[50]

[47] Tarbell to Baker, April 29, 1901, Baker Papers. Allan Nevins, who has superseded Miss Tarbell's work with his Rockefeller volumes, thinks her emotional and biased. (Allan Nevins, *John D. Rockefeller: The Heroic Age of American Enterprise* [2 vols., New York, 1941], 524ff.; Nevins to Phillip Benjamin, Dec. 15, 1953, Tarbell Papers.)

[48] Tarbell, *All in the Day's Work*, 206.

[49] Henry Lloyd to Tarbell, May 6, 1902, Phillips Papers.

[50] Miss Tarbell's early chapters owe a deep debt to Lloyd's pioneering work and active collaboration. She used his knowledge of important sources, his contacts with friendly witnesses, and his specialized library to her advantage. (Lloyd to Tarbell, May 3, 6, Sept. 26, 1902, April 11, 1903, *ibid.*) But Lloyd's extremism frightened her. "His book

There were other important informants, often old friends of her father still living in the oil regions. Such was Edwin C. Bell, a resident of Titusville, who had amassed a large collection of periodicals and public papers in preparation for a history of Oil Creek Valley.[51] Additional testimony from lawyers, independents, and even Standard representatives themselves gave Miss Tarbell a mass of documentary evidence.[52] To help her arrange this material, McClure hired John Siddall, then working as secretary of Tom Johnson's board of education.[53]

Miss Tarbell waded through "appalling heaps of documentary stuff," and by Christmas of 1901, with her first chapter about finished, saw her way "clearer in the story of the Standard Oil matter."[54] By May, 1902, she had finished her first three chapters, and, in consultation with John Phillips and Henry Lloyd, had begun to revise them.[55] "Your story," wrote Lloyd, "grows more interesting every month."[56]

While Miss Tarbell was polishing up her articles, with publication scheduled for the fall of 1902, Lincoln Steffens was traveling beyond the Ohio River, having been ousted

---

was of course an argument for socialism," she later said, explaining why she did not follow him more closely. (Tarbell to Nevins, Aug. 22, 1940, Tarbell Papers; see Tarbell, *All in the Day's Work*, 206.)

51 Edwin C. Bell to Tarbell, Dec. 15, 1910, Tarbell Papers.

52 See Tarbell, *All in the Day's Work*, 233, Lloyd to Tarbell, Sept. 26, 1902, Phillips Papers. Not surprisingly even Standard vice-president Henry H. Rogers, an ex-independent producer who had known her father, showed an interest in Miss Tarbell's series. In January, 1902, he sent word through Mark Twain that he would like to talk with her about her findings. He discussed court cases and, on one occasion, went over an article in advance. (McClure, *Autobiography*, 239; Albert Britt, *Turn of the Century* [Barre, Mass., 1966], 32ff.) But such a truce was impossible, and soon after her break with Rogers, Standard-paid publicists were broadcasting their refutations of the *McClure's* series. (Tarbell to Boyden, July 30, 1905, Tarbell Papers.)

53 Phillips to Tarbell, Dec. 12, 1901, Phillips Papers; Tarbell, *All in the Day's Work*, 210-11.

54 Jaccaci to Tarbell, Nov. 23, Dec. 9, 1901, Phillips Papers.

55 Tarbell to Phillips, May 26, 1902, *ibid.*

56 Lloyd to Tarbell, May 3, 1903, *ibid.*

from the New York office by McClure. His mission was vague—to find a story and stay out of trouble.[57] Steffens had gone west on the train with a short list of men to inter-view, compiled by the obliging Albert Boyden. Because of Finley's interest, it is possible that Frederick Howe and Tom Johnson were on it.[58] The final name was "brother Bill" C. Boyden of Chicago.

When interviewed, William Boyden lengthened Steffens' list by suggesting Walter Fisher, his partner; Weyerhauser, a wealthy timber investor in St. Paul, deeply involved in politics; and Joseph W. Folk, circuit attorney for the St. Louis area. After interviewing all of these men, Steffens finally found in Folk's public prosecution of political crim-inality in St. Louis a familiar type of human drama that would go well in *McClure's*. It was a typical story of municipal boodlers being caught. Steffens matter-of-factly commissioned a St. Louis reporter to write up Folk's sen-sational exposures; then he returned to New York to find that Miss Tarbell's articles were coming together in an extraordinary fashion. Perhaps hoping for a series similar to Miss Tarbell's, he immediately took in hand the beef trust question which Baker was refusing to work with. But he had no time to stray, for on June 27, 1902, the "Folk St. Louis Man Story" came in and created a considerable stir in the office.[59] Even the quiet Jaccaci felt that "it can be made into a great McClure article."[60]

McClure excitedly called the diminutive reporter in and gave exacting instructions on how to rewrite the story, changing the title to "Tweed Days in St. Louis." Into the finished article went some of the ideas that Steffens had al-

[57] See Peter Lyons, *Success Story*, 195ff.

[58] Both Tarbell and Siddall were a chorus of praise about certain "admirable aspects of the city government of Cleveland." (McClure, *Autobiography*, 241.)

[59] Boyden to McClure, June 27, 1902, Phillips Papers.

[60] Jaccaci to McClure, July 8, 1902, *ibid*.

ready frequently expressed.[61] In fact, St. Louis could easily have been a case study conducted for one of Wilhelm Wundt's seminars on morals.

As Steffens rewrote the Folk article, rumors were circulating widely in the New York press to the effect that President Roosevelt was going to take action against the trusts. The Northern Securities case was being processed, and antitrust legislation appeared in the offing. "From all indications," the New York office wrote McClure, "it is going to be one, if not *the* great subject in the forthcoming Congress."[62] William Allen White saw the President during the first week of July, and a few days later Steffens attempted to get him into an interview again to discuss the trusts.[63] Roosevelt finally revealed an antitrust program patterned after the recommendations of the Chicago Convention on Trusts in 1899.[64]

This further whetted McClure's appetite. Could the Steffens article on St. Louis be expanded into a series? A series on municipal lawlessness to go with Miss Tarbell's series on corporate lawlessness would be excellent. Jaccaci helped these prospects. While reading the *New York Sun*, he found an article on "Graft in Minneapolis" and gave McClure the clipping. McClure immediately sent Steffens to investigate Minneapolis, assigning "the title and the thesis of the article . . . before I left."[65] Roughed out by November, the article was a "corker," said McClure, as he gave Steffens the usual inordinate attention in rewriting.[66] The "Shame of Minneapolis," as McClure named the piece, was scheduled for the January number. That way it would have the maxi-

---

[61] Steffens had published "Two Bosses" and "Politics" in *Ainslee's* in 1901. See Steffens to William F. Neely, July 14, 1901, Steffens Papers.

[62] Jaccaci to McClure, July 8, 1902, Phillips Papers.

[63] *McClure's*, XIX (Sept., 1902), 387; Jaccaci to McClure, July 8, 1902, Phillips Papers.

[64] See John Morton Blum, *The Republican Roosevelt*, Atheneum edition (New York, 1965), 57; U.S. Congress, *Bills and Debates Relating to Trusts, 1888-1918* (3 vols., Washington, D.C., 1903, 1914), 486ff.

[65] Steffens, *Autobiography*, 374.

[66] McClure to Steffens, Nov. 7, 1902, Steffens Papers.

mum effect upon the Minneapolis mayoralty election in the spring.[67] "I think," anticipated McClure with rare understatement, "it will probably arouse more attention than any article we have published for a long time. . . ."[68] A second series was thus inaugurated.

While Steffens was preparing his *Shame of the Cities* in the summer of 1902, he paused to write a short sketch on John Mitchell, directing a strike of the United Mine Workers in the coal fields of Pennsylvania. He wrote an article that "will do no matter what happens in the strike," which lauded Mitchell but accused the union of behaving like a "trust."[69]

By the winter of 1902 the strike was still on, and with the importation of strike breakers, violence erupted. It was to McClure another sign of civic lawlessness. McClure decided to try for a "hummer" of an article on the role of the 17,000 men who refused to strike with Mitchell, to be run as a companion article with Steffens' piece on Minneapolis.[70] What he envisioned, McClure explained to his staff, was an article like the "report of a sermon" he read in the *Sun*.[71]

There was only one experienced writer on the staff remaining who could prepare "a series of big industrial

[67] McClure to Steffens, Nov. 10, 1902, *ibid.*   [68] *Ibid.*

[69] *McClure's*, XIX (Aug., 1902), 257; Steffens to Phillips, June 24, 1902, Phillips Papers.

[70] McClure to Steffens, Nov. 10, 1902, Steffens Papers.

[71] *Ibid.* Although McClure was interested in industrial lawlessness, his views must have been colored by a strike which his firm suffered in September, 1896. He temporarily cut the wages of his press feeders from $12 to $10 a week, and when they went on strike, hired non-union labor. This resulted in all sixty of the firm's skilled hands leaving. The company won the strike, refused to re-engage any of the strikers, but was delayed in getting the October issue to the newsstands. (*Galesburg Evening Mail*, Sept. 26, 1896; Curtis P. Brady, "The High Cost of Impatience," 35-36.) This was the first strike the New York printing pressmen had ever lost, but the shop was subsequently re-unionized, although the 54-hour week prevailed. See S. S. McClure Co., *Manual Containing Rules Governing Compositors in the Composing Room of the S. S. McClure Co.* (N.Y., 1904).

articles that will touch in a vital way the principles, and give graphically the essential situations in this tremendous drama."[72] But Baker resisted all attempts to lure him away from his fiction. Relatively ignorant of the excitement in the New York office, Baker finally came east in the late summer of 1902, feeling, "the best thing in the August number was 'How the Fairies Came to Ireland.' "[73] His purpose was to gather additional material for a novel he was writing on labor conditions. McClure finally cajoled him into reporting on the biggest strike since the Pullman troubles eight years previously.

Baker went to Wilkes-Barre in October, 1902, to follow up Steffens' interview with John Mitchell. Henry Lloyd, Clarence Darrow, John R. Commons, and Louis Brandeis were already there, watching as the country prepared for a long winter without coal. While President Roosevelt labored behind the scenes, using the offices of Morgan and Wall Street, Baker looked at the human lot of the scab and the fink. His article, "The Right to Work," was a series of case histories of individual plights. Grounded in reality, it was dramatically superior to the stories of Miss Thanet. McClure, for the third time, was wildly enthusiastic over the possibilities of a timely, dramatic series. From New York he rushed down to Scranton to supervise the rewriting, and in November the piece was finished.[74]

[72] Tarbell to Baker, May 6, 1901, Baker Papers.

[73] Baker to Phillips, Aug. 23, 1902, Phillips Papers.

[74] See Baker, *American Chronicle*, 165-68. John Mitchell gave his side of the coal strike in *McClure's* of December, 1902. McClure's feelings at this juncture were clear to himself: "The struggle for the possession of absolute power which you find in your work among capitalists & Steffens finds among politicians & Baker finds among labor unions, is the age-long struggle & human freedom has been won by continual & tremendous effort. I hope that Baker will get the fundamental concept in his head. The central idea of his work is human freedom. Freedom for the laborer & for mankind involves the labor union & *the non-union laborers*. No body of men can be safely allowed absolute power. Yet employers would have absolute power if there were no unions & unions on the other hand would have absolute power if there were no non-union laborers. Therefore the

McClure took Baker's article, Miss Tarbell's third chapter on Standard Oil—the other two appeared in November and December—and Steffens' study of Minneapolis, and published them in January, 1903. It was, wrote McClure in an editorial, "a coincidence that the January *McClure's* is such an arraignment of American character."[75] In his autobiography McClure repeated the theme that the muckraking conception "came from no formulated plan to attack existing institutions, but was the result of merely taking up in the magazine some of the problems that were beginning to interest the people a little before the newspapers and the other magazines took them up."[76] And yet the three articles carried a common message, "The American Contempt of Law," and proved that capitalists, workingmen, politicians, and citizens were all engaged in this national pastime. Neither the judges nor the lawyers, McClure editorialized, nor the clergy, nor the colleges were free from the tint of lawlessness. The public had to pay, and "in the end the sum total of all the debt will be our liberty."[77] Thus muckraking was defiantly inaugurated in the exciting decennial volume which McClure wanted.

The emergence of muckraking was certainly no accident. The suppositions of Flynt, Finley, and the Boydens were documented by Steffens, the contentions of Maurice Low and Lefevre by Tarbell and Siddall. It was no new game to lift the rocks in twentieth-century America and watch the bugs scramble for cover, but what was new was the expertise and authority of the writing, the threats of Wall Street centralization that became daily more portentous, and the challenge accepted by Theodore Roosevelt in the

---

Open Shop is the central idea. The magazine believes in Unions, trusts, large aggregations of laborers & of capital, but the tyranny & power of large aggregations must be checked by the free laborer & the free merchant." (McClure to Tarbell, June 22, 1904?, Tarbell Papers.)

[75] *McClure's*, XX (Jan., 1903), 336.

[76] McClure, *Autobiography*, 246.

[77] *McClure's*, XX (Jan., 1903), 336.

White House. As Robert Wiebe has since shown us, the country was quickly fragmenting into militant economic interest groups bent upon class warfare. This fragmentation had been sensed by Garland, Crane, Lefevre, Flynt, and others. But by documenting this perilous national situation, by giving it reality, drama, and human interest, the January *McClure's* was ensured a success.

But muckraking was not a total commercial success, for an investigation shows that *McClure's* circulation underwent no spectacular growth. By 1908 even Miss Tarbell's *History of Standard Oil* was selling at the rate of only eighty-seven copies per year.[78] During the same period *The Shame of the Cities* sold only one copy more.[79] Yet in only six months of that year 980 copies of *He Knew Lincoln* were purchased.[80] There was to be much competition and little profit in alerting the nation to its new needs.

[78] Royalty Statement, Sept. 15, Jan. 6, 1908, Tarbell Papers.
[79] Royalty Statement, April-Dec., 1908, Steffens Papers.
[80] Royalty Statement, Sept. 15, 1908, Tarbell Papers.

Chapter VIII. The Second
Decade: The Problem
of Lawlessness

AFTER January, 1903, *McClure's* perceptibly changed, although not as much as generally maintained. The magazine invented little; rather it accentuated principles which had characterized it since 1893. At *McClure's* it was difficult to maintain that there was a decisive split between the old mugwump generation and the new progressives.[1] Rather *McClure's* was like a sprout worming its way about in the earth, finally breaking through to find the sun. By an alchemy as old as the Great Revival, *McClure's* had always closely identified the activities of the saloon and the dance hall with professional thievery and machine politics. But with Theodore Roosevelt's assumption of the Presidency, hailed nationwide by the reform press, the magazine's progressive principles became more obvious.

A careful reading of McClure's editorial in the January, 1903, issue gives the germ idea from which the magazine's contributions to muckraking ensued. The title, "The American Contempt of Law," wrote McClure, "could well have served for the current chapter of Miss Tarbell's History of Standard Oil. And it would have fitted perfectly Mr. Baker's 'The Right to Work.' All together, these articles come pretty near showing how universal is this dangerous trait of ours."[2] The law, the law, all were "breaking the law, or letting it be broken."[3] Who was to uphold it? Neither the lawyers, nor the judges, nor the churches, nor the colleges could do so. "There is no one left; none but all of us."[4] Illegal rebates, he continued,

[1] See Richard Hofstadter, *Age of Reform: From Bryan to F. D. R.*, Vintage edition (New York, 1955), 167.
[2] *McClure's*, xx (Jan., 1903), 336.
[3] *Ibid.*   [4] *Ibid.*

148

traction franchises which sold for a bribe, as well as law-less and violent strikes were worse in America than else-where. Railroads in particular and corporations in general, the city machines and the unions, exhibited the fatal native flaw of lawlessness. A toleration of vice and a contempt for order meant that vice was on the throne and the disintegra-tion of society had begun. Newton Bateman could not have spoken more apocalyptically.

A defense of order and propriety that would have been a credit to those more staid fixtures, *Century* and *Scrib-ner's*, pervaded *McClure's* after 1903. Most of *McClure's* muckraking articles can be classified as dealing with the breakdown of order, the birth of lawlessness, and the end of propriety. As Henry Adams might have seen it, in 1903 McClure was trying to defend in the twentieth century a unity of values based on moral absolutes, a naive assump-tion that moral and political laws had a clear meaning, and that answers could quantitatively be proved black or white by counting strikes or murders or other such external results. Henry May, in his *The End of American Innocence,* finds this is a characteristic of most American literature at the turn of the century. The situation was to change re-markably within a season, but at any rate the McClure journalists dished up heavy heapings of moral law and by it challenged society as the abolitionists had the slavocracy.

To point ahead, it must be said that initially, except where traditional moral judgments were dealt with, any appeal to a higher law, natural and unwritten, such as suggested by the Brandeis brief and the rise of sociological jurisprudence, was rather limited. But a generation with its Adamses, Spenglers, Einsteins, Spencers, Stoddards, Mc-Kinters, and Turners showed an unusual tendency to wrestle with metaphysical speculations about the order of the world. It was slowly—and this is the subject of later chapters—that the muckrakers came to terms with natural law and the axiomatic superstructure upon which institu-tions were built.

But more important than moral law in the early *Mc-Clure's* muckraking were man's conscious rules for governing himself. These rules were deemed valid by assuming that democracy itself was a moral condition, a metaphysical value. Laws, constitutions, and charters were the cohesive forces of society whose inviolability *McClure's* insisted upon. This defense of law was made more frantic by the country's condition. The McClure writers, it seems, confused the natural fragmentation of society resulting from social and economic forces—such as immigration, concentration of wealth, specialization of labor, technological development, and the rise of the cities—with the deterioration of the old order familiar to them. The first principle of *McClure's* muckraking, espoused even before the articles of Flynt and Lefevre, was that the conscience of the nation must be aroused to enforce existing laws, not to draft new ones.[5] Man's inability to live in conformity with these articulated rules was described *ad infinitum* by McClure as "lawlessness."

When the muckraking movement began, McClure proved more capable than ever of pressing his campaign against "lawlessness" through the magazine. None of the illnesses or absences of earlier years plagued him. After 1906 the magazine became a more accurate reflection of his mind and interests, for in that year many of the men who had acted as both a restraint and a catalyst for McClure's enthusiasm left the magazine. Probably the only person capable of awing McClure was President Roosevelt. Thus not infrequently Roosevelt's philosophy of government and society spilled into the magazine's pages under the name of one of the editors or staff journalists. Most of the staff knew the President well enough to write him informally for his views. McClure, at least partially in response to Roosevelt's attack on muckrakers in 1906, it would appear, made a substantial change in editorial policy. Not only did the magazine strive to portray more positive aspects of society,

[5] *Ibid.*, II (April, 1894), 475.

but it showed a limited evolution from its posture that reform consisted in getting various laws obeyed to the position that certain new laws and new organizational structures were necessary to preserve the old ideals. Indeed, this was the direction of the whole progressive movement. And so in time, for example, the magazine advocated the city manager and the city commission form of municipal government as a means of preserving the democracy inherited from the New England town meeting. And, still later, the very nature of social and economic laws had to be questioned.

Throughout the years of muckraking McClure held steadfastly to the axiom that a quantitative judgment could be made on the effectiveness of government.[6] "Governments," McClure paraphrased Locke, "are established and maintained chiefly for the purpose of protecting life and property."[7] The number of lives lost and the amount of property destroyed were unquestioned indexes to the ineffectiveness of government and the "lawlessness" of society. This theory, from the contract theorists of the seventeenth century, puts in perspective most of the muckraking publications of *McClure's* between 1903 and 1911, when McClure retired.

McClure's only important contribution to muckraking was "The Increase of Lawlessness in the United States," published in 1904. His article was filled with statistics gleaned from the *Chicago Tribune* which proved that crime had been significantly increasing since 1881 until the ratio of murders to the population in the United States was twenty times that of any European country.[8] In a speech before the Twentieth Century Club during the spring of 1904, the doughty editor developed his theme. There were

[6] See McClure to Phillips, 1903?, Baker Papers; McClure to Phillips, Nov. 21, 1903, McClure Papers.

[7] *McClure's*, xxiv (Dec., 1904), 163.

[8] *Ibid.*, 163-69; McClure to Baker, May 27, 1903, Baker Papers; Phillips to McClure, Feb. 17, 1904, McClure Papers.

more lynchings than legal executions in the United States which resulted in "more murders in the United States during the time of the Boer War than the entire number lost by Great Britain in that war by bullets and disease."[9] "You have," he pointed out to his sedate audience, "one man in the United States out of each two hundred and fifty who is a murderer."[10] It was statistically safer to commit murder than to embezzle bank funds. Only in the medieval atmosphere of Imperial Russia was a man's life confronted with such dire probabilities as in the United States. McClure was quick to place responsibility on three classes who kept the government from functioning as it should: the saloon keeper, the franchise buyer, and the corrupt politician. "These men destroy the law."[11] While McClure spent years intensely collecting and collating, at great expense, statistics on murder and criminality in nations, states, and cities, it was the broader question of lawlessness that was attacked by the magazine. This discussion has been developed at length because this is the matrix from which most of *McClure's* important articles sprang, including those of Tarbell, Baker, and Steffens.

The History of Standard Oil, wrote liberal New York lawyer George W. Alger in a review, was "an obvious desire to be exact in statement and to give all the facts, so that the reader may judge for himself whether the conclusions are justified."[12] Lawless rebates, coercion, bribery, and fraud were the gravamens of Miss Tarbell's detailed two-volume indictment, not size, efficiency, or even the demise of laissez-faire economics. "I was willing," she insisted later, "that they should combine and grow as big and rich as they could, but only by legitimate means."[13]

When Miss Tarbell finished with Standard Oil, Burton J. Hendrick's history of "Great American Fortunes and Their Making" replaced it. In a much less critical vein than

---

[9] McClure, Speech to Twentieth Century Club, Jan. 30, 1904, *ibid.*
[10] *Ibid.*   [11] *McClure's*, xxiv (Dec., 1904), 169.
[12] *Ibid.*, 223.   [13] Tarbell. *All in the Day's Work*, 230.

Tarbell or Gustavus Myers, Hendrick recounted the familiar successes of the Astors, Thomas Fortune Ryan, and Elkins, and then he turned his attention to other concentrations of wealth in "The Story of Life Insurance." In New York, Charles Evans Hughes had revealed shortcomings on the part of these supposedly conservative bulwarks of society who often behaved as "savings banks" or "lotteries."[14] Hendrick followed the New York exposures of fraudulence in detail. He explained the Tontine system— a gambling system whereby the insured bought a policy with an indefinite face value, depending for that upon the number of policy holders who survived him. The system had little relation to actuary tables, and it burdened and penalized persons who lived long—because by then company funds would have been exhausted by extensive advertising, large commissions and executive costs, and matured policies.[15] In 1910 *McClure's* last series on the malefactors of great wealth appeared as "The Masters of Capital," by George K. Turner and John Moody. John Moody, who authored *The Truth about Trusts* while editing *Moody's Magazine* and *Moody's Manual,* was a cousin of George Foster Peabody, who helped found the House of Morgan in America. A follower of John Stuart Mill's individualism and Henry George's humanism, Moody approached McClure about writing a series to counter-balance Tom Lawson's *Frenzied Finance* in *Everybody's.*[16] Though Moody and Turner worked in a "scientific manner," they admitted the "inevitability" of the concentration of wealth which in the final analysis could be controlled only by the state.[17]

Like Miss Tarbell, they criticized only the lawlessness of the economic system. The greed and lust of the great businessman was no more than that of lesser ones, they asserted

14 *McClure's,* xxvii (May, 1904), 37.
15 *Ibid.,* xxvii (Aug., 1906), 401.
16 John Moody, *The Long Road Home,* 161.
17 *McClure's,* xxxv (Oct., 1910), 617; xxxvi (Feb., 1910), 482.

in an article on Morgan. "What could be more vicious than the waste of the savings of the race in the duplication of machinery which it does not need to do its work?"[18] *McClure's* had finally advanced to the New Nationalist position without ever forsaking the original principles by which it had criticized the trusts. They should grow only by "legitimate means." While Miss Tarbell was deriding corporate machiavellianism, Baker exposed that of labor.

The lawlessness of labor was the central theme of Baker's *The Industrial Unrest*. The important question, McClure explained, was why non-union men "stick to their jobs in spite of the most horrible forms of boycott, not simply social, but business boycott, even suffering abuse and sometimes death."[19] Again McClure was particularly interested in the plight of the non-union miners of Colorado.

One of Baker's articles dealt with "The Reign of Lawlessness" in Colorado where a "State of insurrection and rebellion" followed the organization of the Western Federation of Miners in that state.[20] After Baker left *McClure's* Christopher P. Connolly continued the theme of miner violence in the west with his "The Story of Montana." A lawyer for twenty years and a county prosecuting attorney for one term, Connolly supplied the gruesome details of his state's "reign of lawlessness and its overthrow" by vigilantes who hanged from forty to fifty men.[21] Before Connolly's revelations were finished in 1907, another shocking series was begun. Harry Orchard, who, as a paid assassin for the International Workers of the World, supposedly killed eighteen men, published his autobiography in *McClure's* —after he first turned state's witness against Moyer, Haywood, and Pettibone, charged with the assassination of ex-Governor Frank Steunenberg of Colorado.[22]

When Baker finished *The Industrial Unrest*, McClure

---

[18] *Ibid.*, xxxvi (Nov., 1910), 17.
[19] *Philadelphia North American*, Aug. 15, 1905.
[20] *McClure's*, xxiii (May, 1904), 43.
[21] *Ibid.*, xxvii (Aug., 1906), 346.   [22] *Ibid.*, xxix (July, 1907), 294.

hoped to develop other studies of lawlessness. He particularly wanted a complete study of European crime. Finally he reneged, suggesting that "railroad accidents are also very interesting and something in the same proportion."[23] Soon Baker was writing "The Railroads on Trial," showing that the disregard for the law and life caused the deaths of nearly 20,000 people yearly in railway accidents. Subsequently the magazine asked "Can American Railroads Afford Safety in Railroad Travel?" and demonstrated that Europe had seventy-five percent fewer accidents than the United States because of advanced safety equipment and strictly enforced governmental regulations.[24] In 1909 the magazine attacked the steel trust for producing cheap rails in "The Problem of the Broken Rail." It was shown that low production costs resulted in increased accident hazards.[25] A year later the magazine delivered its *coup de grace* against the negligence of railroads in "The Cruelties of Our Courts." After a half dozen years of muckraking and progressive legislation, the railroads still refused to provide workers' compensation coverage or assume liabilities for injured or dead workmen, and often the rail magnates perverted the judicial process to maintain these prerogatives. Bismarckian Germany was a generation in advance of the United States in its protection of life and limb.[26]

While all of these articles fitted the *McClure's* pattern, still another subject, lynching, "was taken up by us simply as a study in lawlessness—the total overthrow of all restraints and forms of government. . . ."[27] "What is Lynching?" was a short series by Baker on mob justice, North and South, that served to introduce him to the controversial race question.[28] His conclusion was startling: A high incidence

23 McClure to Baker, May 27, 1903, Baker Papers.
24 *McClure's*, XXIX (Aug., 1909), 421.
25 *Ibid.*, 428.   26 *Ibid.*, XXXV (June, 1910), 151.
27 *Philadelphia North American*, Aug. 15, 1905.
28 *McClure's*, XXIV (Jan., 1905), 299; XXIV (Feb., 1905), 422.

of homicides almost universally accompanied a high lynching rate. Roosevelt was immensely impressed with the series
and sent Baker a list of the few crimes committed in the
District of Columbia, designed to show that his administration did not abet lawlessness. But the President's article
did not appear, probably because the staff agreed with
Steffens that "there are no murders down in the District of
Columbia, they are too busy stealing to stop for such a thing
as murder."[29]

McClure's abounded with articles on other aspects of
crime: the justice of the courts, the psychology of crime,
secret criminal societies, and famous trials of felons. In
"Some Follies in Our Criminal Procedures," a lawyer
analyzed the probability of a defendant's getting justice
in an American court where juries were often swayed by
considerations other than the evidence presented.[30] Not
surprisingly, the magazine held up as an example the
efficiency of English courts, with fewer judges and less delay
in litigation.[31] Later *McClure's* pioneered the advocacy
of probation as a part of the "New Gospel in Criminology,"
which would help eradicate crime and lessen prison costs
at the same time.[32] One of *McClure's* most knowledgeable writers in the field of criminology was Hugo Munsterberg, chairman of his department and head of the psychological laboratory at Harvard. Like Steffens and G. Stanley Hall, Munsterberg had studied under Wilhelm Wundt
at Leipzig. As early as 1893 he had published his views on
criminology in *McClure's*, but with the advent of muckraking he was called upon for more regular contributions.[33]
Munsterberg was responsible for several articles that viewed
the criminal as a diseased person, sharing responsibility for
his guilt with his environment. His behavioristic bent became
obvious in his studies of the third degree, hypnotism and

[29] Boyden to Baker, Jan. 10, 1905, Baker Papers.
[30] *McClure's*, XXXIV (April, 1910), 653.
[31] *Ibid.*, XXXIII (Sept., 1909), 552.
[32] *Ibid.*, XXXI (July, 1908), 358.   [33] *Ibid.*, I (Oct., 1893), 399.

crime, and the prevention of crime. He voiced a plea for penal reform reminiscent of Charles Sumner and Horace Mann in Massachusetts before the Civil War.[34]

A less sympathetic approach was that of George K. Turner, who wrote and collaborated on articles that exposed the organized criminality of the Black Hand in the politics of Tammany Hall.[35] In turn Theodore A. Bingham, an ex-police commissioner from New York, explained how Tammany infiltrated and made use of the police services in "The Organized Criminals of New York."[36] Meanwhile the activities of Western crusaders against organized lawlessness—such as Ben B. Lindsey of the Denver juvenile court and William J. Burnes who investigated the timber frauds in Oregon—were chronicled by the magazine.[37] But more sensational yet were the articles on famous trials: the I. W. W. leaders in Colorado; Ferrer, a revolutionary in Spain; and the Camorra trial of a Mafia chieftain in Italy, written up by Arthur Train.[38] Baker's articles on labor and lynching naturally led the magazine to undertake investigations on the other aspects of criminality in a statistical way methodologically more convincing than that of Josiah Flynt. Steffens' *Shame of the Cities* served as the same sort of catalyst.

From St. Louis to New York Lincoln Steffens described the struggle between the law defenders and those men who McClure said "destroy the law."[39] In *The Struggle for Self-Government,* his sequel which muckraked the states, Steffens continued to develop the theme of a lone fighter involved in a personalized fight against criminality. *The Up-builders,* likewise, is filled with vivid portrayals of men at-

[34] *Ibid.,* XXIX (Oct., 1907), 614; XXX (Jan., 1908), 317; XXX (April, 1908), 750.

[35] *Ibid.,* XXXIII (May, 1908), 41; XXXIII (June, 1908), 117.

[36] *Ibid.,* XXXIV (Nov., 1909), 62.

[37] *Ibid.,* XXVII (Oct., 1906), 563; XXXIV (Nov., 1909), 62.

[38] *Ibid.,* XXXIV (Jan., 1910), 327; see *The Independent Republican,* June 6, 1939.

[39] *McClure's,* XXIV (Dec., 1904), 169.

tempting single-mindedly to defend the legal order against a host of villains. This technique was also fondly, but less speciously, cultivated by Samuel Hopkins Adams and William Allen White. Adams' work included an analysis of the breakdown of the legal process in the Appalachian region. "The State of Kentucky vs. Caleb Powers" dealt with the insurrection that developed over the murder of Senator William E. Goebel in a contested governorship, and "Dan Cunningham: A Huntsman of the Law" depicted a U.S. Marshal's fight against the mountain clan system with its moonshining ways.[40] White, in turn, in his "Folk," wrote *McClure's* third article on the Missouri reformer in two years, and emphasized the fact that the young district attorney had won twenty of his forty cases against the St. Louis machine.

It can be seen that the writings of Steffens, Baker, and Miss Tarbell only stimulated further inquiries into the state of lawlessness current in the various fields of capital, labor, and politics, with the resulting loss of life and property through crime and accidents. But *McClure's* campaign against such destruction due to governmental inefficiency spread quickly into other areas such as public health and fire prevention.

McClure's was probably never as influential in the field of preventive medicine as *Collier's*. But Samuel Hopkins Adams, whose famous series on medical quackery appeared in *Collier's*, first wrote on the inadequacy of medical treatment for McClure. With articles on tuberculosis, typhoid, hookworm, and modern surgery, Adams blamed the unnecessary loss of human life on misgovernment.[41] Tenements and slums rather than the lack of medical technology were responsible for the scourge of the contagious diseases. Unguarded sewers and polluted water supplies existed because of irresponsible local government. In typical

[40] *Ibid.*, xxii (Feb., 1904), 465; xxiii (June, 1904), 215.
[41] *Ibid.*, xxv (June, 1905), 145; xxxiii (Oct., 1909), 617; xxiv (March, 1905), 482.

McClure's fashion Adams' articles made much of the better examples afforded by Europe in disease control—where cities were cleaner, airier, and more sanitary. This son of a minister and a graduate of Hamilton College also wrote on the New Orleans conquest of yellow fever through a campaign against the mosquito, "Rochester's Pure Milk Campaign," and the activities of various public health boards.[42] *McClure's* dealt with other facets of the health problem with articles on food faddism, pellagra in the South, and poisonous commodities. Undoubtedly, Upton Sinclair's *The Jungle* was more important than *McClure's* in securing the passage of pure food and drug legislation. But on occasion the magazine championed such projects vigorously. With editorial support Walter Fisher used the pages of *McClure's* to propagandize for a National Health Board in his "A Department of Dollars vs. a Department of Health."[43]

Public and private agencies engaged in health campaigns proved to be good copy. The Public Health Service had its successes publicized in "Our Duel with the Rats" in 1910.[44] In much the same manner as Miss Tarbell had written of the Pasteur Institute earlier, Burton J. Hendrick explained the Rockefeller Institute's early researches into spinal meningitis.[45] He also wrote other articles on municipal health problems, but this hardly exhausted *McClure's* concern with health.[46]

To be expected, one of McClure's most aggressive programs was directed against the consumption of alcohol. George K. Turner wrote much on the evils of that drink. Other problems were studied by George Kennan, who usually wrote on Russian life but devoted some time to the question of suicides, and Georgine Milmine, who exposed the supposed cures of the Christian Scientists.[47] All of this

[42] *Ibid.*, XXIX (June, 1907), 142.   [43] *Ibid.*, XXXV (July, 1910), 329.
[44] *Ibid.*, XXXV (May, 1910), 88.   [45] *Ibid.*, XXXII (April, 1909), 594.
[46] *Ibid.*, XXXV (Aug., 1910), 373.
[47] See *Ibid.*, XXXIII (Sept., 1909), 528; XXXI (June, 1908), 218; XXVIII (Jan., 1907), 227; XXXI (Aug., 1908), 427.

material, less graphic than Sinclair's *Jungle*, less masterful than Adams' series on patent medicines, *The Great American Fraud*, obviously was concerned with risks to life in an area far broader than that covered by the Pure Food and Drugs Act.

Much of McClure's concern for health grew out of his friendship with the vegetarian, James H. Kellogg, of Battle Creek, Michigan. Both John Phillips and McClure frequented Kellogg's "sanatorium" in Battle Creek and tried his "biologic living," as did many of the progressives, such as Irving Fisher and Ben B. Lindsey.[48] Kellogg was the son of ardent abolitionists who grew out of the Millerite faith and who opposed the use of tobacco, alcohol, spices, tea, coffee, and meats. Reflections of this health magnate's theories often appeared in *McClure's*. McClure paid his bills at the resort by giving Kellogg advertising, and on several occasions attempted to get publishable articles written on the program of the food faddist. Surprisingly, it was the *American Magazine* which first openly endorsed "biologic living."[49]

McClure's was no less concerned with the loss of property which resulted from misgovernment. McClure and his staff were particularly interested in the twin problems of conflagration and conservation. American municipalities, the magazine pointed out in "Fire—An American Extravagance," ignored the recommendations of such groups as the International Society of State and Building Commissioners in regard to fire prevention.[50] Arthur F. McFarlane especially indicted New York City, which permitted the building of skyscrapers when its fire department was unequipped

[48] Horace B. Powell, *The Original Has This Signature—W. K. Kellogg* (Englewood Cliffs, New Jersey, 1956), 14, 20, 80, 83; see Gerald Carson, *Cornflake Crusade* (New York, 1957), 18.

[49] Powell, *The Original Has This Signature*, 57. *McClure's*, at considerable expense, refused to accept advertisements that were "medical in fact or in appearance," used the word "cure," or promoted cigarettes. (Curtis P. Brady, "The High Cost of Impatience," 136, 142.)

[50] *McClure's*, XXXII (Nov., 1908), 99.

to fight fires in multi-storied buildings.[51] Factory and tenement tinder boxes were also exposed. "The Newark Factory Fire," published in 1911, graphically pictured the unsafe laboring conditions of one hundred New Jersey factories. Frequently fires resulted in extensive loss of life because no provision was made for evacuating the workers and because, on one occasion, doors to the fire escape were kept locked by the management.[52] The situation was worse in the slum dumb-bell tenements, crowded, with no fire escapes and little fire prevention care.[53] Unsurprisingly, American losses from fire were from five to fifteen times as great *per capita* as those of Europe.[54]

McClure's staff was also concerned with the conservation problem, although hardly as much as such magazines as *Collier's*, which first publicized the Ballinger-Pinchot controversy. McClure was content to follow in the wake, and never did he pursue this question systematically or aggressively. In "A Continent Despoiled," which appeared after Roosevelt left office, one writer lamented the national wealth lost through careless destruction of forests, mineral resources, and animal life.[55] Later George K. Turner wrote what amounted to *McClure's* only indictment of Ballinger. In "Billions of Treasure" he accused Ballinger of acting contrary to the public interest in the disposal of Alaskan property to the Guggenheim trust.[56] Articles on Gifford Pinchot and the "National Water Power Trust" completed *McClure's* concern with conservation.[57]

This summation should show that on one level much of *McClure's* muckraking was remarkably simple, a plea for

[51] *Ibid.*, xxxvii (Sept., 1911), 467.   [52] *Ibid.*, xxxvi (April, 1911), 663.
[53] *Ibid.*, xxxvii (Oct., 1911), 690.
[54] *Ibid.*, xxxvii (Sept., 1911), 467. Conflagration was generally a progressive concern. (Irwin Yellowitz, *Labor and the Progressive Movement in New York State* [Ithaca, New York, 1965], 127; Joseph G. Rayback, *History of American Labor* [New York, 1959], 264.)
[55] *McClure's*, xxxii (April, 1909), 639.
[56] *Ibid.*, xxxiv (Jan., 1910), 339.
[57] *Ibid.*, xxxi (July, 1908), 319; xxxiii (May, 1909), 35.

the enforcement of laws against lawlessness of corporations, labor unions, criminality, corrupt politicians, and especially municipalities which were derelict in their public duty to protect health and property. In every instance, like a Bryce or a de Tocqueville, McClure used the practices of Europe as a yardstick by which the effectiveness of American government might be judged. While not the whole reform message of *McClure's*, this defense of order ensured the magazine's appeal to the middle class, always concerned with the legal protection of life and property.

Before completing this analysis of the contents of *McClure's* in the muckraking era, it must be reasserted that muckraking did not change many aspects of the magazine. *McClure's* maintained its interest in popular science, exploration, and aerial navigation. The exploits of the Wright brothers, for example, were nationally publicized by George K. Turner's "The Men Who Learned to Fly."[58]

Nor did *McClure's* with the advent of muckraking cease to publish considerable material on the Civil War, that great illustration of lawless rebellion. During its second decade many of *McClure's* manuscripts came through the offices of Frederick Bancroft, and Miss Tarbell, working on Standard Oil, willingly surrendered much of her responsibility in this area to him. Perhaps their most significant collaborative venture was the securing of Carl Schurz's memoirs.[59] Since Bancroft had worked with the old inde-

[58] *Ibid.*, XXX (Feb., 1908), 442. Cleveland Moffett, Baker, and Henry Reuterdahl, American editor of *Jane—Fighting Ships*, also wrote on scientific developments. (*Ibid.*, XXI [June, 1903], 172; XXX [Dec., 1907], 163.) Reuterdahl precipitated a three-year controversy with Washington when he criticized the structure of American ships in "The Needs of Our Navy." United States ships, he found, had their heavy armor below the water line, had guns so positioned that they could not fire in high seas, and had their magazines in vulnerable, unprotected locations. (*Ibid.*, XXX [Jan., 1908], 251.) The Navy Department, Burton J. Hendrick added, was guilty of the "greatest waste of national funds in the history of the United States." (*Ibid.*, XXXII [Feb., 1909], 397; see *ibid.*, XXXII [Nov., 1908], 106; XXXVI [March, 1911], 523.) The taunt that European navies were building better ships was a familiar refrain.

[59] See Tarbell to Bancroft, Aug. 28, 1899, Bancroft Papers.

pendent reformer in the campaign of 1884, the two had developed a close friendship. It took twenty-seven installments for Schurz to get from the insurrection in Germany, where he drew a lasting portrait of Karl Marx, to his election as Senator from Missouri.[60] While the series was in progress, Schurz died in 1906.

In addition to his memoirs, Schurz published a review of the race problem for *McClure's* which no one else could have written and no other magazine would have published. This article, which preceded four attempted rebuttals by Thomas Nelson Page and Baker's progressive analysis of lynching and *Following the Color Line*, was a discussion of the aims of Reconstruction in the light of contemporary Negro disfranchisement and demogogic appeals by Vardaman and Tillman. Joshing the South for its fluttered feelings over Booker T. Washington's invitation to dine at the White House, Schurz strenuously argued that modern attempts to reassert peonage over the Negro were doomed.[61] Booker T. Washington immediately responded to this brilliant article: "I spent a portion of Christmas Day in reading your article in McClure's Magazine, and must say to you what I have just said to Mr. Baldwin in a letter, that it is the strongest and most statesmanlike word that has been said on the subject of the South and the Negro for a long number of years, and I want to thank you most earnestly for the article. I earnestly hope that it will have a large circulation in the South. McClure's Magazine is read a good deal by Southern white people, and I hope the results will be far-reaching."[62] Undoubtedly Schurz's great reform mind influenced Baker's approach to the race problem.[63]

In its earlier years, the magazine continued to cultivate even minor aspects of the Civil War. Together Bancroft

[60] *McClure's*, xxv (Oct., 1905), 671.
[61] *Ibid.*, xxii (Jan., 1904), 259.
[62] Booker T. Washington to Schurz, Dec. 28, 1903, Booker T. Washington Papers, Manuscript Division, Library of Congress.
[63] Baker to Boyden, Jan. 12, 1905, Baker Papers.

and Miss Tarbell served as a sort of Civil War brain trust for the magazine, ready to help any of their colleagues.[64]

On the other hand, with the genesis of muckraking, *McClure's* fiction underwent as much change as the politically oriented articles. One would like to say that the muckraking movement spelled an end to Victorian modesty, opened new areas for factual commentary, and ended the guise of fiction which factual articles had to carry. But such was not totally the case. Even *The Thirteenth District* and *The Jungle* paraded as fiction. Perhaps Henry May's setting of the pivotal year for the end of American innocence at a later date is justified.

But since muckraking preempted the fields of Lefevre and Flynt, *McClure's* fiction did change. In a sense it resumed its burden to entertain. The political fiction became a less serious way of commentary. For example, James M. Palmer published numerous stories on "Colonel Lumpkin." Lumpkin often gave long monologues on how to take over a city or a business, or he instructed a Mr. Boodle on the art of using the "pigeonhole vote," the party vote. Or else he revealed delightful accounts of rapid transit scandals of "Finances of the Shark System."[65] Undoubtedly Colonel Lumpkin was based to a great extent on Washington G. Plunkitt, the Tammany chieftain who held sway at a shoe-

[64] See Tarbell to Richard W. Gilder, March 7, 1908, Century Papers; Tarbell to William Dutcher, Jan. 8, 1909, A. W. Anthony Papers, New York Public Library; Tarbell to Markham, Jan. 3, 1900, Markham Papers, Wagner College. Bancroft served as the magazine's agent on his travels through the South searching for material. Miss Tarbell instructed him, "we shall be glad if you will let us know of anything that occurs to you as being suitable for McClure's, and anything that you may write we shall be glad to see." (Tarbell to Bancroft, Feb. 20, 1902, Bancroft Papers.) Bancroft obtained many manuscripts, but was not very successful in having his own writing published. (Bancroft to Finley, May 27, 1900, Finley Papers; *McClure's*, xxxv [Sept., 1910], 545; Tarbell to Bancroft, Nov. 9, 1901, Bancroft Papers; Phillips to Bancroft, Jan. 29, 1901, *ibid.*; Tarbell to Bancroft, Jan. 11, 1912, *ibid.*; George K. Turner to Bancroft, Aug. 7, 1908, *ibid.*)

[65] See *McClure's*, xxi (Aug., 1903), 372; xxiv (March, 1905), 522; xxv (May, 1905), 66; xxv (Aug., 1905), 406.

shine stand in Greenwich Village, educating listeners on the distinction between honest and dishonest graft. With only slightly more pathos Harvey O'Higgins, who served an apprenticeship with Steffens on the *Commercial Advertiser,* wrote in dialect of Irish ward politics. His "Tammany's Tithes" appeared in 1906 and was about the police-machine combine.[66] The suffragettes were the subjects of other humorous accounts.[67]

Although earlier writers such as O. Henry, Rex Beach, and Jack London continued to appear occasionally, slowly the field of short story writing was taken over by such writers as Theodore Dreiser, James Hopper, Mrs. Woodrow Wilson, Kathleen Norris, and Willa Cather. Octavia Roberts, a confidante of Brand Whitlock, was occasionally published, as was Alfred Damon Runyon, who wrote "The Defense of Strikesville" in 1907, a character sketch of a professional soldier who helped to put down strikes.[68] After 1905 an increasing amount of *McClure's* fiction came from the pens of its own staff. Miss Roseboro', Miss Cather, Steffens under the pseudonym of Adrian Kirk, James Hopper, and George K. Turner all supplied material. The poetry of Miss Roseboro' along with that of Witter Bynner often appeared, as did that of McClure's protégée, Miss Florence Wilkinson. Miss Wilkinson published more poetry in *McClure's* than any other poet.

Miss Wilkinson is worthy of further comment because there was deep suspicion that lines like the following were written for McClure: "I took you into my lonely arms,/ You were the soul of me;/ There was no speech between us twain,/ There needed not to be."[69] While this suspicion contributed to the catastrophe that was to follow, it must not be forgotten that on occasion her poetry throbbed with moving romanticism. An example is "The Tortured Millions":

[66] *Ibid.,* xxvii (Oct., 1906), 621. [67] *Ibid.,* xxxiii (Oct., 1909), 676.
[68] *Ibid.,* xxxiv (Apil, 1910), 629; xxviii (Feb., 1907), 379.
[69] *Ibid.,* xxiii (June, 1904), 166.

They are dying that I may live, the tortured millions,
By the Ohio River, the Euphrates, the Rhone.
They wring from the rocks my gold, the tortured millions;
Sleepless all day they mix my daily bread;
With heavy feet they are tramping out my vintage;
They go to a hungry grave that I might be fed.[70]

In conclusion, muckraking brought to *McClure's* a deepening concern for law, a concern that relegated literature
to a secondary status but permitted Civil War themes to
be continually developed. The magazine's reform program
was built upon the design of the old Galesburg reformers
who wanted the heavenly city, with temperance, racial
justice, feminine rights, and Sabbath observance. Lawlessness had no place in such a universe. But these noble aims
were threatened by numerous ills when progressive journalism had scarcely come into its own.

In the first place, several members of the staff felt an indictment of lawlessness might appeal to the middle class
but the magazine needed to balance its rather negative
attitude with something more positive. Baker was one of
the first members of the staff to show such a concern. Although writing of the industrial unrest, lynching, and the
railroads with great skill, he saw both sides of these great
questions. He admitted his doubts to McClure, who responded in 1903: "I think you are right, that we should in
some way offset the critical campaign of the magazine by
some articles that would show the real and conquering
American in his true character and aspect. It is, of course,
a little difficult to formulate such articles. . . ."[71] The President's growing impatience with muckraking only further
encouraged McClure to emphasize what he called the up-
building nature of the American people. Hendrick's series
on "Great American Fortunes" and Steffens' on "The Upbuilders" seem efforts in this direction. By 1910, in what

70 *Ibid.,* 167.
71 McClure to Baker, Feb. 6, 1903, Baker Papers.

could be considered either as a joke or an attempt at objectivity, the magazine published the memoirs of Senator Thomas Platt. This was the same Platt who threatened to sue the magazine over William Allen White's portrait of him a half decade before.[72] And so the second decade at *McClure's* witnessed an increasing dialectical strain between concern for "upbuilding" and for "lawlessness." It was becoming necessary for the staff to make crystal clear what its metaphysical notions were.

But there were many other problems that came with muckraking. Financial difficulties with mounting costs and competition were a major concern, and personality differences were no less significant. When the *McClure's* staff split up in 1906, the most articulate of the middle class monthlies suffered an irreparable blow to its prestige and well-being. This contributed in no small degree to the final disaster that befell McClure in 1911 when he lost control of his magazine.

Before undertaking an analysis of the varieties of reform thought found at *McClure's*, we should see what occasioned this great disruption, for it sheds some light upon the problems which confronted a reform journal, and it exhibits the contrary nature of the men who made *McClure's*. And, moreover, it helps to explain some of the motives and pitfalls of muckraking.

[72] *McClure's*, xxxv (Aug., 1910), 427; xxxv (July, 1910), 317; xxxv (Jan., 1910), 115.

Chapter IX. The Great Schism
and Afterwards

THE MYSTERY of why a popular magazine, so closely identified in the public mind with muckraking successes, should suddenly lose most of its staff, as *McClure's* did in the spring of 1906, was not totally explained by the participants in their autobiographies. William Allen White, who helped found the *American Magazine*, insisted that the rift came "over what seemed to us who followed John over to the American Magazine, a question of common honesty. Sam could not see it. That kind of insight was not his gift."[1]

Ray Stannard Baker credits Roosevelt's criticism of muckraking with being an irritant leading to the schism, but the "real break rested upon deeper and more personal reasons with which I had long been familiar. It had been growing more and more difficult, on the part of members of the staff, to work with S. S. McClure."[2] Steffens, rather dissatisfied because his material was heavily rewritten, "was in and out of New York, didn't have part in all the plans, and so don't know all that was said and done."[3] Providing more detail, Miss Tarbell credits McClure with attempting to use the *McClure's* group "to reconstruct the economic life of the country," by founding a new company providing for a *McClure's Universal Journal* allied with a bank, an insurance company, a textbook publishing firm and eventually a "McClure's Ideal Settlement in which people could have cheap homes on their own terms."[4] This was, she wrote, speculative and monopolistic, "as alike as two peas to certain organizations the magazine had been battling."[5]

There is very little additional information available in the contemporary newspapers, which almost universally saw

1 White, *Autobiography*, 397.
2 Baker, *American Chronicle*, 211.
3 Steffens, *Autobiography*, 536.
4 Tarbell, *All in the Day's Work*, 256-57.
5 *Ibid.*, 256.

the schism as precipitated by the President's man-with-a-muck-rake speech on April 14. The *New York Morning Telegraph* thought the strike in the "literary foundry" came because McClure was halting muckraking, and the event, if not instructive, added "greatly to the merriment of life."[6] The *Chicago Journal*, crediting Roosevelt with turning the tide, thought muckraking passé, a game "almost as popular as bridge, whist, or golf," while the *Inter-Ocean*, at one time so close to the syndicate but now conservative, felt that "McClure has parted with his muckrakers, a concession which, however, comes a trifle late to influence those readers who have parted with S. S. McClure."[7] A bad parodist at the *Long Island Sea Sickel Times* voiced the sentiments of many when he wrote:

". . . What makes you look so white, white?" said
                  Lawson-on-Parade.
"I'm dreading what I've got to hear," J. Lincoln
                  Steffens said.
". . . What makes Miss Tarbell look so faint?" said
                  Lawson-on-Parade.
"A touch of sun, a touch of sun," S. Hopkins
                  Adams said.
". . . What's all that noise that shakes the ground?"
                  said Lawson-on-Parade.
"It's Teddy Roosevelt's muck rake speech," a pale reformer
                  said.
They're exposing the exposers, there is trouble in the air.[8]

Other newspapers, such as the *St. Paul Pioneer Press*, the *Milwaukee Sentinel*, and the *New York World*, were full of invective at "Makecure's" discomfiture, as the *World* lampooned.[9] A few newspapers refused to make a public

---

[6] *New York Morning Telegraph*, May 5, 1906.

[7] *Chicago Journal*, May 5, 1906; *Chicago Inter-Ocean*, May 7, 1906.

[8] *Sea Sickel Times*, April 26, 1906.

[9] *St. Paul Pioneer Press*, May 6, 1906; *Milwaukee Sentinel*, May 7, 1906; *New York World*, May 13, 1906.

statement on *McClure's* household troubles.[10] Almost alone, Bennett's *New York Herald* adopted a friendly and accurate position. It printed a letter from McClure in May denying that there were any editorial differences within the staff or that Roosevelt's speech had anything to do with the magazine's policies.[11] Later the *Herald* explained that McClure had been planning a new magazine for over a year and this was a contributing factor in the disruption of the most renowned editorial staff in the country.[12]

Perhaps the most important ingredient in the *McClure's* split was McClure's proposed new magazine and allied projects which threatened the income of Miss Tarbell and John Phillips, large stockholders in the existing firm. McClure's growing impatience, after several years of delay, to "invent" another popular magazine, to start a cheap book reprint business, and generally to move society in a utopian direction coalesced in his great scheme of 1905. And indeed McClure's biographer agrees that the editor's futuristic, if not erratic, plans were the crux of the matter.[13] But there were other contributing factors, not the least of which was that McClure's staff believed him guilty of gross improprieties with several women, including the poet Florence Wilkinson. A manuscript by Miss Wilkinson entitled "The Shame of S. S. McClure, Illustrated by Letters and Original Documents," arrived at the office with the recommendation that it be published with other important revelations. The situation put the magazine and its program in dire jeopardy. Whether guilty or innocent of all the accusations, McClure had an intransigent staff by the summer of 1904. "He's a Mormon," Miss Tarbell wrote Phillips, "an uncivilized, immoral, untutored natural man with enough canniness to keep himself out of jails and asylums. He is

10 See *Denver Post*, May 5, 1906; *Topeka Capital*, May 6, 1906.
11 *New York Herald*, May 5, 1906?, clipping in McClure Papers.
12 *Ibid.*, May 11, 1906.
13 See Lyon, *Success Story*, 280ff, which also has a full account of McClure's amorous adventures.

not to be trusted. . . ."[14] This was a remarkable change of opinion, since she had worked so closely with McClure on the Standard series the year before. While McClure courageously resisted all efforts to reform him, the incident over his affair immediately created dissent and maliciousness within his otherwise cooperative staff.

The consensus of the editorial group, Phillips included, was that McClure's childish behavior was due to an inordinate emotional strain caused by overwork and, perhaps, guilt. The staff, fearing a scandal, asserted itself under Miss Tarbell's leadership. "That man," said Boyden a few months later, "was never so bad off as he is now," and Miss Tarbell, after talking with McClure, promptly wrote Phillips that she doubted if the sick man were "going to be hard to deal with in the business, except now and then."[15] She was wrong. The battle lines were quickly drawn. Even Hattie McClure, convinced of her husband's innocence, in her brief visits to the office thought the staff was beginning to over-assert itself. There was a "good deal of habitual lack of understanding on the part of these young men who have learned to work without McClure to contend against."[16]

McClure's constant absences and restless visionary scheming fanned rather than doused this lingering hostility. For over a decade he had sought to enter the book reprint business, and for almost as long he had wanted a companion magazine to go with *McClure's*. Shortly after the failure of the *Harper's* project he wrote Miss Tarbell, who "was dissatisfied with me in regard to stock in the S. S. M. Co.," that he looked "forward with eagerness to the time when you & I & Boyden & Baker will start our new magazine (Nov. 1903)."[17] A year later he told Miss Tarbell, rest-

14 Tarbell to Phillips (June, 1904?), McClure Papers; see items marked "L'Affaire" in Tarbell Papers.

15 Tarbell to Phillips, June?, 1905, copy in Tarbell Papers, New York Public Library.

16 Hattie McClure to Peggy Bisland, Sept. 14, 1904, McClure Papers.

17 McClure to Tarbell, Dec. 30, (1901?), Tarbell Papers.

ing before finishing the Standard Oil series, that "when you get strong we will side by side found McClure's Review."[18] Twenty months later in Europe, McClure was still thinking in terms of "the other magazine," hoping to "take from the two magazines together enough stuff to make one magazine for this side of the ocean and charge a shilling for it."[19]

Likewise, McClure had never completely forgotten his relationship with Heinemann in 1890 and the prospects of founding a reprint business. Methuen, of course, had taken up the project at the death of Wolcott Balestier in 1891. In the ensuing dozen years an English reprint series, *Dent's*, selling at a reasonable price, made some headway in the country. But, on the other hand, a set of large, beautiful books by Macmillan failed to sell.[20] The reprint business, like publishing as a whole, was becoming extremely competitive and highly risky. But McClure had mastered fortune before; why not again? With his book department barely three years old, McClure negotiated a contract with Professor George Edward Woodbury, who had spent twelve years building a strong graduate department of English at Columbia, to edit a *World's Classic Series* of cheap reprints for *McClure's*. The success of this venture hinged on its "exceeding cheapness."[21] It was to do to the book business what *McClure's* had done to magazine publishing. Professor Woodbury took a leave of absence and soon resigned his academic position with this uncertain work before him.

At this juncture, when all seemed to be going well, a surprising announcement appeared in the *Athenaeum,* an English periodical, to the effect that a cheap Methuen library was in preparation under the editorship of Sidney Lee, the Shakespearean scholar. Lee's reputation was con-

---

[18] McClure to Tarbell, March 18, 1902, *ibid.*
[19] McClure to Phillips, Nov. 21, 1903, McClure Papers.
[20] Phillips to Hattie McClure, June 29, 1904, *ibid.*
[21] Unidentified to probably Robert McClure, Jan. 30, 1904, McClure Papers.

siderable and solidly built upon his editorship of the sixty-three-volume *Dictionary of National Biography*, to which he himself contributed over eight hundred articles. After the index to that series was finished in 1903, Lee joined Methuen, prepared to edit the "most complete and perfect edition of Shakespeare that has ever been published."[22] Later he supervised an edition, published at Harvard, of over twenty volumes on the same subject. His work, popularized by a lecture tour in America in 1903, was well known and his association with Methuen was foreboding. When McClure saw the announcement, he immediately arranged an interview with Lee, sensing that competition between him and Methuen would be absolutely disastrous, particularly since the volumes of the latter were to cost about four shillings each, or 50 cents in America.[23]

Methuen knew his man and played his hand well. He informed McClure's London office that two American publishers, one later identified as Henry Holt, were eagerly vying to handle his books, and both had approached him prior to the public announcement of the project. Although late, McClure might have either the finished plates or the unseen pages simply by paying a royalty on the former.[24]

Methuen, with a half dozen volumes of classics at the printers, in the name of professional secrecy hesitated to quote a price for the plates until Phillips and McClure looked with favor on the project. It was only fair to other publishers to do so, he said. A lame proposal that both Lee and Woodbury work together met a quick and certain rebuff.[25] "Is it not possible," McClure asked his staff, "that we might withdraw from the Woodbury understanding?"[26] He feared his product might be too highly priced and that Holt, with Methuen's aid, might steal a quick march on him.

---

22 Unidentified to probably Robert McClure, Jan. 27, 1904, *ibid.*
23 *Ibid.*   24 *Ibid.*
25 Unidentified to probably Robert McClure, Feb. 3, 1904, *ibid.*
26 Unidentified to probably Robert McClure, Jan. 30, 1904, *ibid.*

By June, 1904, McClure, with little agony, had decided to drop Woodbury.[27] John Phillips still dissented, "You understand, of course, that Sidney Lee's name would not be so beneficial in America as Prof. Woodbury's. . . ."[28] In fact, he was unenthusiastic about the whole business of reprinting. Phillips' principal objection was economic. The Methuen series would be cheaper only if one took twenty or thirty titles, but the McClure-Phillips book company was "not in a position to sell it," having "a set of books now, secured from D. Appleton & Company" that with good fortune would make a profit.[29] The book company had no capital to finance the Methuen venture, and the "magazine is making less and less on account of the great increase in the costs."[30] Indeed, the magazine's profits had "been knocked down to almost nothing."[31] In fact the magazine lost $8,000 in 1904, and the future of magazine publishing in general was uncertain.

Both John Phillips and Miss Tarbell strongly argued against using the magazine's credit to finance a doubtful and expensive enterprise. Their considerable financial interest in, and years of selfless labor for the magazine, as well as their slight chance to profit by McClure's highly speculative venture convinced them of the absolute "need to work on our present problem calmly, sensibly, and persistently."[32] With anxiety both appealed to Hattie McClure to assert herself because they felt "deeply that the office and business cannot endure permanently the strain which has been felt. . . ."[33]

It seems evident that both Phillips and Miss Tarbell were legitimately more than a little concerned with their investments, one having large family responsibilities, the other responsible for herself. Phillips owned 146 shares of stock

[27] N. W. Gillespie to Robert McClure, June 28, 1904, *ibid.*
[28] Phillips to Hattie McClure, June 29, 1904, *ibid.*
[29] *Ibid.*   [30] *Ibid.*
[31] Phillips to McClure, July 7, 1904, *ibid.*
[32] *Ibid.*
[33] Tarbell to Hattie McClure, July 12, 1904, *ibid.*

in the S. S. McClure Company, and together with Miss Tarbell's 15, they accounted for sixteen percent of the control of the company. The shares, originally worth $100 each, were valued at $1,000, since *McClure's* had a value of about one million dollars. In addition, Phillips owned 110 shares in the book company, worth $100 each, while Miss Tarbell owned 50, and D. A. McKinlay, an executive, owned 100. The total value of this stock was $187,000.[34] Save for lesser amounts of stock owned by Robert McClure and other relatives, August Jaccaci, and Arthur Conan Doyle, who owned 50 shares of the magazine, the control, some 600 odd shares, was in the hands of Sam McClure, now hell-bent upon risking it to grab a greater place in the New York publishing sun. Could anything deter him?

Stalled until the fall of 1905, McClure suddenly returned from Europe vigorously determined anew to pursue his projects to the end. In November he drew up a prospectus for founding a new journal, *The Universal Magazine, McClure's Journal,* or *McClure's Universal Journal* to cost exactly one-half as much as *McClure's,* five cents per copy or fifty cents per year. McClure envisioned a journal "at least as large as the *Nation,* or probably as the *Saturday Evening Post,* or *Success.*"[35] In fact the magazine was to look a great deal like *Public Opinion* which his brother, Robert, shortly bought. It would contain 40 large pages of small type commentary, as much material as the *Century* had in 160 pages. Twenty-four pages of advertisements would cover most of the costs of publication. Howard Pyle, the artist, was contracted at $18,000 a year as art manager. He produced an expensive dummy filled with his original drawings.

This new magazine was to be a family magazine, said McClure, with something for the children and the women

34 Phillips and Tarbell to McClure, April 12, 1906, *ibid.*; McClure to Mrs. Horace Van Deventer, Sept. 21, 1909, *ibid.*

35 McClure to Robert Mather, April 14, 1906, *ibid.*; see Curtis P. Brady, "The High Cost of Impatience," 182ff.

of the household—as if *McClure's* had not been that for years. The first great series of articles envisioned was to come from Samuel Hopkins Adams, whose patent medicine series for *Collier's* had made such a success. Adams was to study the alcohol question in all countries along with the closing of the saloons on Sunday, themes that were soon accentuated in *McClure's*. The new magazine was to use fiction accumulated by the syndicate and *McClure's*: "I have thereby acquired a larger collection of capital short stories than we would need to supply both McClure's and this new magazine with for two or three years. . . ."[36] Having worked for *McClure's*, why would not this plan work for the new journal?

McClure liberally calculated a probable circulation of one million, an anticipated circulation among almost five percent of the country's households, and an income of almost two million dollars. That was quadruple the income of the new *Collier's Weekly*. McClure optimistically estimated that he would earn from eight to ten times as much from advertising as from circulation. The initial costs of the magazine, however, would be minimized by using the *McClure's* staff, the company presses at the new plant on Long Island, and accumulated literary material. "I believe that this has in it the germ of the greatest periodical ever published in America," he added.[37] It may have had. But practically the entire staff felt it would be the greatest bust possible.

McClure also had plans to establish several subsidiary enterprises. He probably saw them as only vague, hopeful possibilities: a Universal Library to publish reprints of classics, a People's Life Insurance Company, a People's Bank, and a People's University, evidently a Chautauquan

[36] McClure, "Proposition for Founding of a Magazine," Nov. 27, 1905, Tarbell Papers.

[37] *Ibid.*; Miss Tarbell was rather shocked when McClure revealed his "little secret," that he had raised $255,000 in the course of a few days to finance this venture. (McClure to Tarbell, Nov. 27, 1905, Tarbell Papers; Phillips to Tarbell, "Saturday," 1905, *ibid.*)

type scheme for which Frank N. Doubleday had just found it successful to publish.

As a part of this last, democratic program, it seems that McClure, reflecting on the utopian community which the abolitionists had created in Galesburg, dreamed of a model village like that of Pullman in Illinois or Gregg in South Carolina. Several years earlier James L. Ford, with good-natured humor, had portrayed a "McClure's Model Village for Literary Workers" for the *New York Journal*. Samuel "Syndicate" McClure, as the *New York Town Topics* dubbed him, had named the town "Syndicate." Boats arrived at Syndicate and unloaded memoirs or photographs from Palestine, and then reloaded with material produced by specialized workers doing biographies, fiction, or articles under the watchful eye of a foreman. Young men discovered by William Dean Howells awaited their assignments patiently. Having read the magazine for some time, Ford expressed surprise that child labor was not used in the model village.[38] At any rate McClure's intense interest in settlement houses makes it probable that Miss Tarbell's account of a McClure benevolent foundation to establish settlements and ideal housing projects sprang from some valid interpretation of his utterances.[39] Years later he helped establish some of the Houses of Childhood to promulgate the Montessori method of teaching.

McClure sincerely wanted the new magazine; the rest of his schemes depended upon its success. He meant to stake his fortune on it. To this end he intended to found a company with $12,750,000 stock: $12,000,000 common stock and $750,000 preferred. Four hundred common would go as a bonus for each hundred preferred bought. The preferred stock was rather like a bond. Not one share of the

[38] Quoted in *Galesburg Evening Mail*, Oct. 12, Dec. 12, 1896.

[39] See Lyon, *Success Story*, 601 for opposite view, McClure mentions the "four subsidiary enterprises" but omits all reference to a model village in his instructions to Robert Mather concerning the proposed company. (McClure to Robert Mather, Jan. 22, 1906, Tarbell Papers.)

common stock was to be sold; it was to be given away to writers and others for services. While McClure was determined to support the whole financial structure with *Mc-Clure's* stock, in the new corporation, "I and my associates . . . will retain only common stock. I have no doubt that the common stock will pay a dividend of eight per cent within five years."[40] About this Miss Tarbell and Phillips had horrifying doubts. Their stock could become worthless.

With McClure determined to found a competing magazine, in name little different from the existing one, and to begin the long desired reprint house over their wishes and best interest, jeopardizing their livelihood, Tarbell and Phillips had little choice but revolt. The scheme, Steffens wrote his father, "was not only fool, it was not quite right, as we saw it. It was a speculative scheme, and . . . he took counsel from financiers who have been exploiting (which means robbing) [with] railroads, and it looked as if he were willing to do the very things the rest of us had been 'exposing'."[41] Of course Steffens' reference was to the Bancrofts and Robert Mather, who had connections with International Harvester, Westinghouse, and several dozen railroads. McClure, it would appear, needed remarkably little counsel, nor heeded it when given.

In desperation Miss Tarbell wrote her brother, who was counsel for Pure Oil. She was obviously motivated by possible loss of revenue from her holdings in *McClure's*. The fair thing to do, morally, her brother William decided, was to force McClure to organize the new proposition "as he should . . . with the S. S. McC Co. Ltd. owning the interest he is intending for himself."[42] Should McClure "use the name or refer in any way to the name of the existing com-

[40] McClure, "Proposition for Founding of a Magazine," Nov. 27, 1905, Tarbell Papers; for additional details see "Memo for Universal Magazine," 1905, Tarbell Papers, and Tarbell to McClure, April, 1906, *ibid.*

[41] Lincoln Steffens, *The Letters of Lincoln Steffens*, eds. Ella Winter and Granville Hicks (2 vols., New York, 1936), I, 173.

[42] W. W. Tarbell to Tarbell, Jan. 16, 1906, Tarbell Papers.

pany to its detriment," he added, she might get either an injunction or a court-appointed receiver to protect her minority rights. Otherwise, she was "up against it." With a note of glee, William Tarbell, who had many misgivings about the whole muckraking movement, suggested that since *McClure's* had published "numberless sermons" on business ethics, why not expose the whole business scheme?

While these were reasons enough to cause a break-up, there were other circumstances that militated against peace in the Lexington Building. The new magazine, proclaimed McClure's prospectus, would have little problem attracting advertising from corporations since it stood ready and "eager to do them absolute justice."[43] It had always been McClure's position that lawless behavior emanated from all levels of society, but, perhaps, he thought a time for "up-building," at least temporarily, was approaching. The month before McClure drafted his magazine prospectus, Roosevelt had written him, "as I said to you and Steffens to-day, I think Steffens ought to put more sky in his land-scape. . . . It is an unfortunate thing to encourage people to believe that all crimes are connected with business, and that the crime of graft is the only crime. I wish very much that you could have articles showing up the hideous iniq-uity of which mobs are guilty, the wrongs of violence by the poor as well as the wrongs of corruption by the rich. . . . Put sky in the landscape, and show, not incidentally but of set purpose, that you stand as much against anarchic vio-lence and crimes of brutality as against corruption and crimes of greed. . . ."[44] McClure undoubtedly pondered the President's request soberly.

McClure, too, had long had qualms over Steffens' sardonic pen; "his articles are far & away the most terrible stuff we can handle."[45] McClure's passion for facts was not a pas-

[43] McClure, "Proposition for Founding of a Magazine," Nov. 27, 1905, *ibid.*
[44] Theodore Roosevelt to McClure, Oct. 4, 1905, Baker Papers.
[45] McClure to Phillips, Oct. 15, 1904, McClure Papers.

sion for heavily negative conclusions, the emotive titles of his articles notwithstanding. As a result he always forced Steffens to do detailed research and heavy rewriting. For example, in dispensing instructions from Berlin in late 1903, McClure assigned Steffens first to do "The Boodling in St. Louis, and 2nd., The Royal Baking Powder struggle for supremacy as set forth" in legal and congressional investigations. The court records, he told the diminutive reporter who disliked such instructions, were to be carefully examined so as to be sure that alum powder was secretly added to baking powder. But once the case was made, "then ask, 'Did Mr. Ziegler really believe all this' and say that you are compelled to believe that he did not, else he himself would not have manufactured alum baking powder. Then after making that point clear you can end with the testimonials in favor of alum baking powder and it can be stated that it is only reasonable to suppose that Mr. Ziegler took the view of the harmlessness of alum baking powder or he would not have himself made it for profit."[46] McClure usually dictated conclusions in such a manner. In this case, and often, his staff suspected him of patronizing business.

As the office squabble grew more heated, McClure's instructions, often practically justified in order to prevent suits, irritated most members of the staff. Undoubtedly he heeded Roosevelt's advice concerning his letter, "Do show this to Baker; it applies . . . to his future articles also."[47] Roosevelt himself communicated his cautiousness to Baker several days prior to the man-with-a-muck-rake speech: "I feel that the man who in a yellow newspaper or in a yellow magazine (I do not think it worth while to say publicly what I will say to you privately, that Hearst's papers and magazines are those I have in mind at the moment, as well as, say the New York Herald and similar publications, daily and monthly) makes a ferocious attack on good men or even

[46] McClure to Phillips, Nov. 21, 1903, *ibid.*
[47] Theodore Roosevelt to McClure, Oct. 4, 1905, Baker Papers.

180

attacks on bad men with exaggeration or for things they have not done, is a potent enemy of those of us who are really striving in good faith to expose bad men and drive them from power."[48]

On the same day, April 9, 1906, two months after Miss Tarbell had heard from her brother, McClure reported to his stockholders that he believed "a study of municipal and other questions abroad would be a very good thing to do."[49] Lawlessness abroad was an overdue investigation. "I believe," he continued, "that during the present insensate wave of reaction against the magazine exposures it will be well to take up now these other constructive sides, as there will soon be a wave of reaction against reaction and we can then go on with our work." How soon would this work go on? Shortly, McClure probably thought. "I believe to go on now with the heavy exposure articles would not convert those who disagree with us, and those who agree with us don't need conversion." McClure seemed to his staff to be putting a damper on muckraking. As already seen from the contents of the magazine, this was certainly not his intent. But all of this was immaterial, for Phillips and Tarbell had already determined to leave for other reasons.

Miss Tarbell, conscious of participating in a historic drama, kept a diary of the emotionally exhausting last days.[50] On March 21 McClure suddenly arrived from one of his trips. John Phillips was cabled to meet Hattie McClure for a conference, to see if peace could be arranged between friends over the many points in dispute, the new magazine, the reprint business, etc. Since McClure had no intention of surrendering his project, Phillips immediately declared that he was severing relations after twenty-five years of close comradeship. In distress McClure interceded

---

[48] Theodore Roosevelt to Baker, April 9, 1906, Baker Papers.

[49] McClure to McClure Company Stockholders, April 9, 1906, Tarbell Papers. The whole paragraph is from this source.

[50] Tarbell, Diary, March 22, 1906, *ibid.* The next three paragraphs are from this source.

with Miss Tarbell in the office to support him. She "refused to argue—told him it was just as before in my mind," that she must wait until John Phillips had talked with everyone about the possibilities of starting a new magazine before making her final decision. After a long discussion with her, McClure seemed to admit that his fabulous schemes, "point by point," were inadequate. Was any scheme worth his friends, he must have thought? Miss Tarbell felt, "he seems to acknowledge these crazynesses now." When McClure wished to talk about the value of the stock, Miss Tarbell "refused to discuss" it. Finally she told him, "I see no reason he should not go ahead."

Finally, McClure was hesitatingly persuaded to face John Phillips, the good friend who had been his partisan supporter in so many old controversies, at Knox, with Doubleday, with Jaccaci. McClure suggested that Phillips needed a long rest. They had fought before, but after vacations the controversies had ended. Would Phillips take a three-year vacation on full salary? Then he could decide whether or not to stay. But Phillips refused, said he was going, said he could not stand it. The time-worn friend offered to sell his stock, and McClure agreed "to buy." When McClure asked if anyone else were going, Miss Tarbell admitted she was if Phillips went, "I can't stay without him or some one like him. . . ." Then McClure emotionally offered to take all of her work for three years. Was anyone else going? "I said Boyden was the only one who had told me so directly," Miss Tarbell responded.

By afternoon McClure's emotional poise was utterly shaken, and, deserted, he swung from affection to vengeance. After lunch, continues Miss Tarbell, "I am in P's office when S. S. enters." McClure said, "John I can't buy your stock; the staff is leaving and it isn't worth $1,000. (Price agreed on in money)." Phillips made a determined reply: McClure owed him that for his long service. "The only fair & manly thing for S. S. to do now," he insisted, was "to buy him out." But McClure insisted that Phillips should buy the company, and when Phillips agreed, McClure finally left in gloomy silence.

Miss Tarbell followed McClure to his office, and he was weeping. "It's all right," he said when she gave him her hand, "I am at peace for the first time in days. My wife is praying for me. I telephoned her before I went in there to pray for me. I am satisfied." McClure, who no doubt loved Miss Tarbell deeply, "referred to his love for me" and admitted it "had lured him in *affaire* Wilkinson. . . ." Miss Tarbell begged him to go home, "I only talk once—to tell him that it has ceased to be a question of S. S. & JSP. To save his manhood he must get out of this situation." McClure kissed her and left weeping, and Miss Tarbell sat "down & sobbed hysterically" but remained "more convinced than ever that we are right."

A week later McClure returned to the now disorderly office for another emotional scene with John Phillips on how the assets should be dissolved, and again he agreed to "sell out (so he says now at least)."[51] "We'll never have as good a business opportunity," Boyden wrote Baker, "Miss Tarbell, Steffens, Bradys and I each want to put in $50,000—I hope we can keep nearly all the stock in the group. . . . It's a relief to know that the magazine is to be preserved—that's bigger and more important than any of us."[52]

Still McClure was of a divided mind on whether to buy or sell. He wrote his good friend Robert Mather, upon whose legal advice he now relied, that his "continual wavering was caused by my utter inability to face the separation," and yet his mind, "has always come to this point of preferring to sell out" because whatever "excellence a man may achieve his contemporaries quickly equal, and I am not well fixed to advance forward so as to secure that position of leadership that I have had in the past."[53]

51 Boyden to Baker, March 27, 1906, Baker Papers.
52 *Ibid.*
53 McClure to Robert Mather, April 14, 1906, McClure Papers.

Nevertheless, McClure decided to retain the company by forming a new corporation, with a capital stock of $1,000,000 in common and $200,000 in preferred stock to take over the business of the S. S. McClure Company.[54] The preferred was to pay for the new building contracted on Long Island which was quickly becoming a major liability. The stock owned by the insurgents could be sold to the new concern, the McClure Publishing Company. And indeed, the final terms of settlement were governed by the staff's desire to buy the proffered *American Illustrated Magazine*. The new corporation was to pay Phillips and the dissenters $3,000 a month for four months, $5,000 a month for thirty-five months, and allow them the right to start a new magazine. In return the parting journalists could not start a syndicate for three years. Also they were to finish various articles already contracted. Miss Tarbell was working on some Lincoln articles. The insurgents were to continue getting their regular salary for six months.[55] The terms were more liberal than McClure's unsound finances justified.

Steffens and Baker, both of whom were absent during most of the crisis, rejected lucrative positions, Baker $10,000 with *Collier's* and Steffens $20,000 with Hearst, to join Phillips, Tarbell, John Siddall, Albert Boyden, Harry McClure, and Ed Phillips in "buying an old magazine which we propose to make the greatest thing of the kind that was ever made in the world—sincere, but good natured; honest, but humourous; aggressive, but not unkind."[56] While the lure of starting a new magazine may have contributed, it was mutual respect that bound the group to leave together. "I feel," wrote Baker, "that I should remain with my associates, who are not only my friends, but who have contributed largely to whatever success I have obtained."[57]

Leslie's Monthly Magazine, after uncatalogued vicis-

[54] McClure to McClure Company Stockholders, April 9, 1906, *ibid.*
[55] McClure, "Suggestions for a Settlement" (May, 1906?), *ibid.*
[56] Steffens, *Letters*, I, 173.
[57] Baker to Father, May 31, 1906, Baker Papers.

situdes, had come under Ellery Sedgwick's control and become the *American Illustrated Magazine*. Over this property the insurgent journalists hoisted their banner. The price was $360,000.[58] The magazine, never a muckraking organ, had a solid diet of contributors, including Stephen Crane and Stuart Edward White, when the Phillips Publishing Company assumed responsibility and changed the name to the *American Magazine*.[59] The sale was negotiated in May, 1906, and Ellery Sedgwick, after six years in the editor's chair, transferred to *McClure's*, where he stayed for a season during that magazine's transition.

To buy the magazine Phillips' company undertook to sell 400 shares of 6½ percent preferred stock at $1,000 a share, with one share of common stock, worthless until the preferred was redeemed, going as bonus. The 2,400 shares of common stock were nominally worth $250, but really represented the ability of the journalists to make the magazine pay.

Phillips hoped to turn the money realized from the sale of his *McClure's* stock into the magazine, but when that settlement was not realized immediately, he quickly refunded the debt for paper owed by the magazine to Warren of Boston. Then he talked the major bond holder, Ayers of Philadelphia, into accepting stock for his lien, and hustled among the monied reformers for more capital.[60]

Among the insurgents $50,000 was realized almost immediately with Baker putting in enough to get one-sixth of the total stock value of the company.[61] "I have put into it practically all I have, outside of my home," Baker wrote his father in Wisconsin. "I stand to lose everything or make a good deal of money."[62] But that was hardly enough money. "Knock down everybody for dough! That's the cry . . . ,"

[58] Siddall to Baker, May 29, 1906, *ibid.*
[59] See Mott, *A History of American Magazines*, IV, 510-16.
[60] Siddall to Baker, office memo, n.d., Baker Papers.
[61] Siddall to Baker, May 29, 1906; Baker to Father, Oct. 3, 1906; Phillips to Baker, Oct. 1, 1906, *ibid.*
[62] Baker to Father, June 30, 1906, *ibid.*

wrote Siddall, destined in time to become editor of the enterprise.[63] In Chicago Baker raised another $50,000, principally from reformers William Kent and Charles R. Crane.[64] In Kansas, with William Allen White helping, Walter Roscoe Stubbs bought some stock.[65] Steffens also worked the west. He saw Everett Colby, who pledged $5,000, toyed with soliciting from Scripps, and got $2,500 from Stuyvesant Fish, the son of Grant's Secretary of State. Miss Tarbell worked among reformers in Cleveland, Pittsburgh, and Philadelphia. At the latter city she interviewed the wealthy Wanamakers, already owners of a daily paper.[66] By July over $100,000, by August $250,000, and by October over $300,000 had been raised to finance what seemed to be a sensational venture.[67]

Before the legendary James B. Dill, a close friend of Steffens by now, had finished drawing up the formal papers incorporating the firm, the magazine was "devilish hard up for stuff . . . ," and getting "kind of nervous over the November number."[68] But William Allen White and Finley Peter Dunne filled the breach and soon Baker's fiction, written under the pseudonym of David Grayson, was gracing the magazine along with his exposés of church, labor, and racial problems. For the *American* Miss Tarbell wrote her great series on the tariff as well as some revisitations to the practices of John D. Rockefeller. Steffens, who remained for only two years, worked principally with San Francisco municipal politics.

"We hear more from our friends the enemy," wrote McClure to his wife, "Ed. Phillips and Steffens think that soon

[63] Siddall to Baker, n.d., *ibid.*

[64] Baker to Father, Oct. 3, 1906, *ibid.*; Phillips to Steffens, April 1, 1907, Steffens Papers.

[65] White, *Autobiography*, 387.

[66] Siddall to Baker, n.d.; Siddall to Baker, May 29, 1906, Baker Papers.

[67] Siddall to Baker, June 14, 1906; Phillips to Baker, Aug. 30, 1906; Baker to Father, Oct. 3, 1906. *ibid.*

[68] Siddall to Baker, n.d., *ibid.*; Boyden to Baker, July 24, 1906, *ibid.*

my failure will appear. . . ."[69] In fact Steffens was telling his father, "as for Mr. McClure, he has lost his staff, but he is organizing a new one, and he will succeed with it."[70] *Mc-Clure's* survived well. For a few days Witter Bynner took Boyden's place as managing editor, then McClure thought of promoting his old Knox classmate Charles Churchill to the position, but finally he installed Will Irwin, a young San Francisco reporter from the *New York Sun*.[71]

Irwin's stay with McClure was a short one, and Bynner soon left too. But Willa Cather and George K. Turner, aided by Henry Kitchell Webster, Percival Gibbon, C. P. Connolly, and Burton J. Hendrick soon took the magazine's helm. Miss Cather, long a friend of Viola Roseboro', who happily remained, had just authored one book of verse and *Troll-Garden*, when she replaced Miss Tarbell. Born in Virginia, reared in Nebraska, Miss Cather's interests lay in literature rather than in reform. She did general editing, working on Georgine Milmine's critical and detailed essay, "Mary Baker G. Eddy."[72] George K. Turner inherited the task of writing about political corruption, alcoholism, and prostitution. While John Phillips was trying to get Baker to write an article on Chicago, the "most American and Democratic city," in an effort to boost the *American's* Midwestern circulation, Turner, an ex-news-

[69] McClure to Hattie McClure, July 25, 1906, McClure Papers.
[70] Steffens, *Letters*, I, 174.
[71] *New York Times*, May 11, 1906; Siddall to Baker, n.d., Baker Papers; Siddall to Baker, June 8, 1906, *ibid.*
[72] Miss Cather worked hard writing and worried little about politics. Feminine suffrage she equated with "tea-party legislation." (Willa Cather to Elizabeth Sargent, Sept. 28, 1914, Cather Papers.) Possibly out of awe of McClure she exerted little influence upon the editorial policy of the magazine. Curtis Brady wrote that she was considered "by all in the office . . . a 'yes man' and a bad influence." (Curtis P. Brady, "The High Cost of Impatience," 235.) But of her relationship to McClure, Edith Lewis wrote, "she never flattered him, never compromised her own judgment in order to please him." (Edith Lewis, *Willa Cather Living* [N.Y., 1953], 70-71.)

paper man, hammered home the typical *McClure's* exposé of that city's lawlessness.[73]

As already mentioned, in the wake of Tom Lawson's *Frenzied Finance* for *Everybody's*, John Moody, the single-tax editor of Moody's *Statistical Manual*, strengthened *Mc-Clure's* with his long series on "The Masters of Capital."[74] And Burton J. Hendrick, after several articles on the insurance companies, wrote the popular "Great American Fortunes" in 1907 and 1908.

But despite a brilliant response to catastrophe, *Mc-Clure's* came upon hard days. In order to satisfy John Phillips' claims, McClure had to put his stock in the hands of a board of trustees to whom he was responsible.[75] A publishing plant begun on Long Island at an estimated cost of $105,000 eventually required an outlay of over a third of a million dollars. Likewise, the McClure book company, with Phillips competing heavily for authors, ran deeply into debt. These problems, in addition to purchasing the stock of Phillips, Tarbell, and McKinlay, placed the firm in a precarious position. Moreover, the depression of 1907 tumbled advertising revenues to a fraction of their former height. Thus *McClure's* declared no dividends for 1906, nor subsequently.

In order to meet these tremendous obligations, amounting to about $800,000, McClure took in as a partner Harold Roberts, a New York financier with interests in several tobacco firms.[76] Roberts bought the insurgents' stock and paid $130,000 for that of the Bradys as well. But in 1907 McClure separated from Roberts, who he thought was trying to undermine him. New arrangements were made to carry the debt with the West Virginia Pulp Wood and Paper Company at an annual interest of 16 percent. Still

[73] See Phillips to Baker, May 8, 1908, *ibid.*
[74] John Moody, *The Long Road Home*, 161.
[75] McClure to Hattie McClure, Sept. 15, 1906, McClure Papers.
[76] For an excellent discussion of finances see McClure to Mrs. Horace Van Deventer, Sept. 21, 1909, *ibid.*

McClure retained control of a firm that was a half million dollars in debt and had little income.

Neither the sale of the book company and the printing plant nor the leasing of the building on Long Island helped. The fate of *McClure's* was established long before McClure lost control of the company in the fall of 1911.[77] But McClure's loss of his magazine came only after years of heroic journalism in which his voice had served as the tocsin for progressivism. The end of muckraking at *McClure's* came as a result of the subtle mixture of journalistic competition and personal ambition. The conspiratorial hand of capitalism was nowhere to be seen.[78] But then there were enough cardinal sins already laid at that door. The *American*, until purchased by outside interests, also in 1911, gropingly sought to emulate the role of the parent magazine.

It is time to analyze the nature of *McClure's* role in the progressive movement and to grapple with the question of why reform journalism proved so powerful a stimulant to the forces of change.

[77] *Ibid.*

[78] For a dozen years *McClure's* carried more advertising than any magazine in the United States. This eventually amounted to over 224 pages per issue and an advertising income in excess of $700,000 per year. After 1907 *McClure's* position was successfully contested by *Everybody's*, and by 1911 *McClure's* and *Everybody's* carried practically the same lineage of advertisements. Incidentally, only two companies ever cancelled advertising in response to *McClure's* editorial policy, the business manager attested. Burton J. Hendrick's "The Story of Life Insurance," which started in May, 1906, cost the advertising of Mutual and Equitable. To their credit neither Royal Baking Powder nor Armour stopped advertising when muckraked. (Financial Report, n.d., Tarbell Papers; Curtis P. Brady, "The High Cost of Impatience," 165, 184-91, 256.) *McClure's* advertising pages remained remarkably stable. For the month of November, usually a premium month, the magazine carried the following pages of advertising: 104 (1895), 100 (1896), 146 (1898), 174 (1899), 154 (1900), 146 (1901), 178 (1903), 184 (1905), 162 (1906), 164 (1907), 130 (1909), 166 (1910), 154 (1911).

Chapter X. Government by
Magazine

WHEN A question has arisen about the nature of muckraking, some have responded in this spirit: Muckraking "consisted in adhering strictly to the literal truth, but in so arranging and proportioning statements of fact as to show most disadvantageously some person, corporation, or other organization of which the public was predisposed to believe the worst."[1] The writings of the journalists themselves may be quoted to substantiate this. Steffens thought, "Mr. McClure was interested in facts, startling facts, not in philosophical generalizations." Baker agreed, "that it was not the evils of politics and business, or the threat to our democratic system, that impressed him most, but the excitement and interest and sensation of uncovering a world of unrecognized evils—shocking people! Many of Sam McClure's ideas were the ancient and more or less banal stand-bys of editors who sought large circulations."[2] Such disparaging remarks can be supplied almost indefinitely from other sources. To Hamlin Garland, who wrote voluminously for the magazine in its early years, "Sam McClure represented the conquering side of the editors' guild. . . . Striving for wider 'circulation' and knowing that for every added hundred thousand readers, advertising rates could be advanced, the business man consulted the wishes of the average reader—or the reader below the average."[3] Even Richard Hofstadter has adopted this image of McClure as a businessman for whom muckraking "was the most successful of the circulation-building devices. . . ."[4] These judgments for the most part originated with the pens of men like Ellery

[1] *Cambridge History of American Literature* (3 vols., New York, 1917-21), III, 317.
[2] Steffens, *Autobiography*, 393; Baker, *American Chronicle*, 96.
[3] Hamlin Garland, *Roadside Meetings* (New York, 1930), 341.
[4] Hofstadter, *Age of Reform*, 192.

Sedgwick, Theodore Roosevelt, and jealous newspaper editors, and have not been demonstrated.[5]

As already seen, after 1903 *McClure's* circulation grew but slowly, and after 1907 the magazine gradually fell behind its competitors. While some journals such as *Everybody's* reaped benefits from their exposures, *McClure's* did not. In 1905 McClure made his last profit on the magazine. Lincolniana paid far more handsomely than muckraking. Advertising, circulation, and profits were of interest to McClure, as they are to any publisher, and he calculated well the effect of articles upon circulation. But muckraking cannot be solely explained, at *McClure's* or elsewhere, as Luther Mott and others have done, as only a circulation-builder.[6] McClure and his staff were very conscious of participating in a political and economic movement intent upon reshaping many of the country's institutions. Their close ties first with Roosevelt, then with La Follette and Wilson, evidence this. The criticism of progressive journalists, based on the assumption that they were economic men, publishing with an eye on income and circulation and unable to attack the economic and political power structure without a vote of confidence from the "average reader," has only limited value. Criticism of a capitalistic society can, and did, emanate from a capitalistic press.

McClure's principal intent was to publish a credible, exciting journal. In imitation of the new historians or the new naturalists, London, Dreiser, and Hopper, he and his journalists evinced an unusual preoccupation with facts and possessed a desire to let events and documents speak for themselves. Baker, long before he remembered McClure in his autobiography, explained it well. He wrote Oswald Garrison Villard, then editor of the *Nation*, "I remember once in the old days at McClure's of getting a red-hot letter from a man out west about one of my articles on the Beef Trust, in which he trounced me soundly for my fail-

[5] See *American Magazine*, LXII (May, 1906), 112.
[6] Mott, *American Journalism*, 573ff.

ures, after describing the villainies of these men in Chicago, to 'skin them alive,' as he expressed it."[7] Baker responded to the old man, he continued, "if I got mad, you wouldn't." "I always had a feeling," he added, "that if I let off steam in my articles the reader himself would feel quite relieved and never want to do anything."

The men who trained in the McClure "foundry" considered well the lesson and power of the restrained statement. Like a conductor, McClure could play pianissimo as well as fortissimo. He was a hard taskmaster when his own thesis was not played in major key. McClure felt his mind—and perhaps Munsey's—was uniquely attuned to the nation's average taste. And so McClure and Phillips published carefully; they were in the tradition of responsible journalism. McClure often responded, as he did to one of Steffens' early articles, "I wish to go over the Pittsburgh article very carefully before it is published. . . . I think that the article to begin with should be free from bias, just the same as a news article or newspaper. . . ."[8] While concerned with circulation and possible suits, McClure also demanded good, accurate, persuasive writing. This was explained to Willa Cather after she joined the staff. George K. Turner was the case in point although Steffens was a far worse offender: "If Turner has any defect in writing it is a defect that almost all writers lean towards; that is a certain distaste towards documentation."[9] McClure felt, "when a writer himself knows the facts he does not realize how important it is to put the reader into possession of the same convincing proofs."[10]

McClure demanded articles with realism as convincing as that infused by Miss Roseboro' into the magazine's fiction. With regard to one article on the Lexow Committee, McClure pointed out, "things that will bear out the color of

[7] Baker to Oswald Garrison Villard, March 15, 1922, Baker Papers. Rest of paragraph from same source.
[8] McClure to Phillips, March 20, 1903, McClure Papers.
[9] McClure to Cather, March 16, 1909, *ibid.*
[10] *Ibid.*

our statements, will be very valuable. This article will be violently attacked and unless is is documentarily backed up it will lose a good part of its influence."[11] McClure was willing to test his theories in the market place of ideas, hoping he could bring home considerable public support. Perhaps it was the old debating society motif transposed to a new environment. It pleased McClure to note of Mrs. Milmine's series that "a number of people talk about our Christian Science articles, and the note invariably was the presentation of Mrs. Eddy's own writings and the presentation of documents."[12]

Consequently, McClure's remarks to his staff were full of editorial reproofs. Rather than use words like "stealing" and "lying," he suggested to Baker, "I think that better than such an assertion as this is to give an illustration of the sort of falsehood they issue."[13] It was hardly enough to say that a particular politician was "sly," "cunning," or "cowardly," as Steffens was wont. The incidents had to be allowed to speak for themselves.[14] And so the adjectives were deleted. While sensational adjectives like "shame" or "lawlessness" often graced a story's title, they are relatively rare in the text.

Save for Miss Tarbell, a trained and restrained historian, the *McClure's* staff often chafed under these restrictions. Steffens, subdued by numerous rewritings, thought that "for the most part our ideas & feelings should, I hold, go with the facts into narrative articles."[15] Baker, too, felt that "after seeing men & things and thinking about them for many years, a writer develops a desire to put down some of his conclusions, something that will be more than a report."[16] When Baker was trying to get at the essence of one of his series (and all of them, race, labor, and religion, were

[11] *Ibid.* [12] *Ibid.*

[13] McClure to Baker, Dec. 6, 1905, Baker Papers.

[14] Phillips to Steffens, June 29, 1907, Steffens Papers; McClure to Phillips, March 20, 1903, McClure Papers.

[15] Steffens to Baker, March 3, 1904, Baker Papers.

[16] Baker to Father, Nov. 24, 1906? *ibid.*

highly emotional topics), Steffens delighted in mocking McClure to him, "look out for editorializing. That's easy and it doesn't count without the facts."[17] Baker did not agree. "A fact is not true," he wrote, "only a *man* can be true, and a man can be true (unified) whether he writes stories or comic-operas. . . ."[18] Baker probed the metaphysics of his profession when he saw that basically a fact was only a falsification: "I have just finished an article . . . & these reflections occur to me: That it is . . . an approximation, at most an impression."[19] Even Miss Cather somewhat "objected" to being a happy gatherer of facts.[20] The legwork, the interviewing, and the research were hard, but McClure and Phillips demanded them.

In addition to being well documented, a second characteristic of the McClure article, perhaps contradictorily, was its shocking nature. McClure succinctly expressed this policy, "it has been customary from the beginning of humanity to carefully break bad news to people so as not to shock them, and in the same way you can minimise [*sic*] the effect of good news by letting it leak out gradually. . . ."[21] The point in question was of no great issue. Steffens simply insisted on crediting the title of his second series, *The Enemies of the Republic*, to Joseph Folk. Possibly in a whisper, McClure told his brother: "The United States is full of people who are honorable, upright men, and in order to carry out their ends, even rightful ends, bribe officials of the Government. We want to shock public opinion into the belief and knowledge that this is a terrible crime, and this phrase will do for this subject what the word 'shame' did for the other. Also it is most important to keep to ourselves all these plans and schemes that we have in hand, important for the sake of the effect we expect it to

[17] Steffens to Baker, March 3, 1904, *ibid.*
[18] Baker, Notebook "L," 27-28, *ibid.*
[19] Baker, Notebook "XI," 109-11, *ibid.*
[20] McClure to Cather, March 16, 1909, McClure Papers.
[21] McClure to Robert McClure, June 12, 1903, copy in Steffens Papers.

have on public opinion. I should have regarded it as a disaster to the whole scheme to have looked upon this phrase as coming from Mr. Folk."[22] McClure's twist of Machiavelli's edict to the prince as to when to release good and bad news has been a commonplace in the publishing profession, but the shock was no value in itself. It was employed to mobilize opinion to correct a glaring lawless act. So often McClure came back to the theme that "above all things I want this idea and scheme kept secret, for the effect of our campaign will be infinitely greater if everything comes out as a complete surprise."[23] All the same, an investigation of publications contemporary with *McClure's* makes it seem likely that the shock value of the "yellow press" and the muckraking journals has been overrated by historians and journalists alike.

A third tendency of the McClure group was to personify conflict. Phillips' advice to Baker during his labor investigations serves as one illustration of this: "I take it you will make your articles compact with incident and fact. Your strong point is in making things alive, human, with stories of individuals. . . ."[24] This, of course, was vintage *McClure's*, to insist that "an article must have great human interest, a great news interest; the human interest, of course, includes a great many varieties, it may be personal, it may be what man is doing or achieving."[25]

There were still other standards that *McClure's* articles had to meet. "The story is the thing," McClure always said; "when Mr. Steffens, Mr. Baker, Miss Tarbell write, they must never be conscious of anything else while writing other than telling an absorbing story: the story is the

[22] *Ibid.*   [23] *Ibid.*

[24] Phillips to Baker, June 18, 1903, Baker Papers.

[25] Phillips to Baker, June 15, 1900, *ibid.* This theme was assumed by the fledgling *American Magazine* in its first announcement, "whatever will best interpret the human panorama we shall use. There is no literary form and no real human material that does not belong in a great magazine." (*American Magazine*, LXII [Oct., 1906], 575.)

thing."[26] The McClure articles imitated the short story with quickly initiated action and a climax. But the most weighty criterion with McClure was that the story be readable, that it be as interesting and exciting on its second or third reading as on its first. But more, like all great Victorian literature, the article needed a moral, but the "ethical element" was present "unconsciously."[27] Not always—perhaps never—was it wholly unconscious after 1903.

These principles go far towards explaining the wide success of the *McClure's* muckraking articles. These portraits in words, often worked over by everyone on the staff until polished, did not lack an editorial content. One sees the extent of McClure's editorializing in 1904 when he lectured his staff on advertising. "The advertisements," elucidated McClure, and he could have been speaking of the whole magazine, "should convey to the reader of it as truthful an impression as possible of what the goods to be sold are."[28] Yet he felt, "it is necessary for an advertisement to really be the expression of the magazine."[29] There was no solution other than that "the writing of the advertisements of McClure's Magazine must be done practically with the same minds that edit McClure's Magazine."[30] By analogy the factual articles were to be true, yet carry an editorial burden. Incidentally, McClure's favorite advertisement was a testimonial.

The editorial burden of the magazine was weighty. "The editorial policy of the magazine," McClure instructed Phillips, "belongs to you and me. This is just as true of the editorial policy of articles as it would be of editorials."[31] For many years *McClure's* had no editorial section, and later little distinction can be made between the editorials and the articles. The magazine's editorial position was

[26] *Philadelphia North American*, Aug. 15, 1905.
[27] *Ibid.*, Aug. 14, 1905.
[28] McClure, Staff speech, fall, 1904, McClure Papers.
[29] *Ibid.* [30] *Ibid.*
[31] McClure to Phillips, March 20, 1903, *ibid.*

often arbitrary: Secretary of State Bayard had made no major blunders under Cleveland; unless Senator Spooner of Wisconsin was elected by bribery "we must clear him"; and "Steffens has a notion that the business man is a coward, and that the business man is to blame for political corruption, and he makes every fact bend to this notion. Now, he must disabuse himself of any predilections in the matter. . . ."[32] Although McClure dominated the editorial policy of the magazine, the individual writer's feelings and style came through as a strong undercurrent.

McClure's magazine was a "gentleman," visiting in a home, and despite Miss Roseboro', its characteristics of speech were only those permitted "in ordinary conversation in the family gathering," for a gentleman would not enter a household "with oaths on his lips, or with words that violate the universal canon of good breeding."[33] McClure could never understand why some felt his journal full of "fault finding and complaining," because he intended to depict a "picture of civilization dealing mostly" with the triumphant.[34] He meant to transcend the negative. "With one or two exceptions," he thought, "all of our stories have been stories of achievement—as of how Folk achieved in St. Louis—and the result has been enormous encouragement for right minded people in other cities."[35]

How did these various ingredients of skill and intention blend to make *McClure's* the phenomenal muckraking organ that it was? Among contemporaries perhaps it was Will Irwin who most competently assessed the impact of *McClure's* upon the country. It is of more than peripheral interest to mention that Irwin not only served as a *McClure's* editor, but during World War I he directed foreign

---

[32] Rogers to Tarbell, May 1, 1900, Phillips Papers; McClure to Phillips, Oct. 15, 1904, McClure Papers; McClure to Phillips, March 20, 1903, *ibid.*
[33] McClure to Arthur Hoffman, Sept. 3, 1927, *ibid.*
[34] *Ibid.*
[35] *Philadelphia North American*, Aug. 15, 1905; see McClure to Baker, Feb. 6, 1903, Baker Papers.

propaganda for the United States. Both he and Walter Lippmann, who learned his art from Steffens, came out of the war students of persuasive tactics. In a lengthy series for *Collier's* as early as 1911, and later in *Propaganda and the News* (1936), Irwin attributed the power of the muckrakers in general, and *McClure's* in particular, to the fact that local news for the first time was truly nationalized. Irwin maintains that muckraking was not especially flamboyant or sensational, and although "McClure drew magazine journalism into politics" in a new and vital way, this does not explain its power.[36] McClure, he says, exposed not only city gangs, political bosses, and rich practitioners of lawlessness, but "exposed our lack of a national journalism."[37] This theory seems valid.

Steffens' *Shame of the Cities* is a case in point. Criminal activities in each locality were an open book, and journalists who knew the truth often refused to tell it for fear of reprisals through loss of advertising. Often the local newspapers printed regular accounts of bordellos and boodling, read alike by a complacent public and an unmoved government. What Steffens showed in his articles, and this he acknowledged in his *Autobiography*, was already common knowledge. It was in showing the universality of the system of lawlessness, that "influential business usually stood behind the boss, who served its ends as well as his own," that he obtained his reputation.[38] In terms of Walter Lippmann, who studied the problem firsthand, the *Shame of the Cities* gave to the public at large a simple formula for understanding a government; it gave them images, symbols, by which not only the power and position of their own traction monopolies could be understood, but which acted as a guide of American misgovernment from hamlet to metropolis. But Steffens did more than portray the "system" and show its universal manifestation in seventeen

---

[36] Will Irwin, *Propaganda and the News* (New York, 1936), 69.
[37] *Ibid.* [38] *Ibid.*, 70.

cities and, in major key, in eleven states.[39] He and *Mc-Clure's* nationalized local episodes of corruption, fitted them into the general pattern, and went far towards creating what William Allen White called "Government by Magazine."[40]

"No newspaper," McClure told a reporter for the *North American*, "is national in influence; few newspapers influence a population of more than 10,000,000 people."[41] England, smaller, might have national papers, but America was five days wide, so "in influencing public opinion the magazine is a division or branch of the press which is absolutely essential. . . ."[42] The magazines not only nationalized local news events in a way that the press services and dailies could not, but they retained a freedom from partisan politics and financial pressures. This, McClure explained, was why a "boodling Alderman may not feel particularly injured by the charges of a partisan newspaper," and yet could be ruined by having "his picture printed in the magazine and seen by people all over the country."[43]

Such a press, McClure felt, was the "real tribune of the people," and in the final analysis the fourth estate was an "infinitely greater guard to the people than any government officials."[44] In what way did nationalizing news perform a public service?

In terms of interest groups, in the vocabulary of Arthur F. Bentley or Elmer Eric Schattschneider, who write of the atoms of society into which men cluster on the basis of occupation, religion, or race, *McClure's* role becomes more understandable. Although the newspaper press might be a captive of its local environment, a national magazine could appeal directly for support to a segment of society larger than the particular problem at hand. *McClure's*, by virtue

[39] Steffens, *Autobiography*, 343.
[40] White to Phillips, May 25, 1908, White Papers.
[41] *Philadelphia North American*, Aug. 14, 1905.
[42] *Ibid.*   [43] *Ibid.*   [44] *Ibid.*

of its large circulation, could appeal a particular local conflict between small groups to a larger national public, and eventually make it an issue between political parties. "*Mc-Clure's* is representative of many people's interests," its editor said; "if I were still more representative it might have a million circulation in place of half of that. . . ."[45] It was in this escalation of political conflicts, in this intent to be a vital participant in the political process and an agent in decision-making, that one finds the real goal of *McClure's* muckraking. The techniques were as old as Garrison or Birney, or even Thomas Paine.

The muckrakers did not see themselves appealing to a larger interest group than any of their opponents; they felt they appealed to the "only force that rules nations"—public opinion.[46] Publicly they said they were "out to illuminate and inform public opinion and to cure these evils" by applying the direct "force of the minds of the people themselves. . . ."[47] The extent to which this was believed will be seen later. The sentiment, of course, reflects Platonic, or German, idealism.

Conscious of the power of his writing for such a periodical as *McClure's*, Baker felt that "if I had a large means I should not endow universities or build churches."[48] Rather, "I should start able young students of economics & sociology to work finding out the truth about our modern conditions: . . . and in publishing that truth broadcast among our citizens" because "it is the density of misapprehension, the ignorance that . . . causes most of our troubles."[49] Baker's own particular role in muckraking, to which he turned in his thinking quite often, centered on "more publicity, more information, more preaching in the wil-

[45] *Ibid.*; see Joel A. Tarr, "William Kent to Lincoln Steffens: Origins of Progressive Reform in Chicago," *Mid-American*, xlvii (Jan., 1965), 51ff, as an example of how national publicity affected local struggles.
[46] *Philadelphia North American*, Aug. 14, 1905.
[47] *Ibid.*
[48] Baker to Father, Jan. 7, 1906, Baker Papers.
[49] *Ibid.*

derness. If once the people can be got to know the facts & to think about them, we need not fear for the future."[50]

This was the same goal of Steffens' exposures, but he gave them a subtle twist: "to sound for the civic pride of an apparently shameless citizenship."[51] Researched data was hardly the quest of this psychologically oriented and trained reporter. Rather the mores, unconscious and accepted, which tolerated city gangs, had to be verbalized, brought to the surface, and exposed, so that the unconscious act could be squared with the conscious moral principle. As will be seen later, Steffens' role was even more complex than this.

Rousseauesque, Steffens dedicated his writings "to the accused—to all the citizens of the United States," who reasoned that it was not bad to give a bribe, but to take one.[52] Steffens wanted to show that the "wail of the typical American citizen" was an irrational contradiction in that it "deplores our politics and lauds our business"—while both used similar methods.[53] Thus the "corruption that shocks us in public affairs we practice ourselves in our private concerns" because the "condemned methods of our despised politics are the master methods of our braggart business."[54] The public was part and parcel of both systems. And so the people were guilty, and only the exposure and dissolution of their walls of rationalizations could cure their ills.

But muckraking was more than Steffens' therapy, or Baker's sermon, or McClure's attempt to participate in government. Muckraking was more than the nationalization, personal and emotional, of local scandal. At its best it consisted in an almost prophetic appeal to the national consensus, the vigorous application of sophisticated moral,

[50] *Ibid.*
[51] Steffens, *Shame of the Cities* (New York, 1904), 3.
[52] *Ibid.*, 26.   [53] *Ibid.*, 5.
[54] *Ibid.*, 10. Both Steffens and Phillips studied under Jean Martin Charcot at the Sorbonne, whose analysis of the unconscious so influenced Freud.

social, and economic laws, and a sense of urgency that transcended class and party. The issue, be it with the tariff, the corporation, or the machine, was joined with no less intensity than an earlier generation had closed with slavery.

The line of demarcation between fact and opinion, between informing and deceiving public opinion, was hardly the problem for the *McClure's* muckrakers that it should have been. Allan Nevins may speak of Miss Tarbell's history as being a bit biased, and Samuel Hays may see the *Shame of the Cities* as inadequate, but the journalists themselves had few such misgivings.[55] Laden with copiously researched documentary evidence, they spoke with an almost absolute sense of confidence in their rightness. It was, perhaps, an age of confidence. Before looking at some of the areas to which the muckrakers addressed themselves, we should perhaps investigate the extent to which they were propagandists.

One of *McClure's* most revealing articles on propaganda was written by Baker. As a part of the "Railroads on Trial," he developed a "very strong and interesting" article on "How Railroads Make Public Opinion."[56] The railroad executives, with the techniques of modern business, had defeated the original Townsend-Esch bill of President Roosevelt, and, allied with the National Association of Manufacturers, planned the same fate for the Hepburn rate fixing bill in the offing in 1905.[57] To this end the businessmen, together with the Morgan interest, organized and hired a publicity organization to carry out the "most sweeping campaign for reaching and changing public opinion ever undertaken in the country."[58] Operating extensively

[55] Samuel P. Hays, "The Politics of Reform in Municipal Government in the Progressive Era," *Pacific Northwest Quarterly*, LV (Oct., 1964), 157-69.

[56] McClure to Baker, Dec. 6, 1905, McClure Papers; *McClure's*, XXVI (March, 1906), 535.

[57] Blum, *The Republican Roosevelt*, 82. Robert H. Wiebe, *Businessmen and Reform: A Study of the Progressive Movement* (Cambridge, 1962), 51-55.

[58] *McClure's*, XXVI (March, 1906), 535.

through newly established regional offices, the railroad agents inundated county editors with pro-railroad material and pressured to get it published. In Nebraska during the first week of July, 1905, immediately following the Congressional hearings on railroad legislation, there were 212 columns of news inimical to the railway interests and only 2 favorable. But within eleven weeks there were 202 favorable and 4 unfavorable columns.[59] The vast lobbying activities of the interest were so well organized that even public forums such as conventions and governmental investigations produced favorable propaganda. Supplementary to its pamphlets—and there were tracts for various professions, including teachers, workers, farmers, lawyers, and editors —the organization aggressively undertook to influence legislators directly by petitions and letters.

How much did such a program differ from muckraking? Baker was careful to point out why such propaganda was wrong. Although the organization had a right to carry on its various activities, it had no right to operate in secret, to organize county editors clandestinely, employing free passes and control of advertising, or to hide its motives. This sinister behavior was accentuated by the use of unlimited funds to represent a "private interest which wishes to defeat the public will."[60] By contrast muckraking was open and represented the interests of the general public.

Baker's assumption was simple: There was a definable public interest, and the "people are unorganized, they have no money to hire agents" to defend their interest as did the railroads or the shippers.[61] Baker did not believe that a struggle between diverse social and economic groups seeking control of the political arena naturally resulted in the public's interest being cared for. Rather, he believed in the Platonic idea of the general good, against which, somehow, the special railroad interests militated. And certainly

[59] *Ibid.*, 538.
[60] *Ibid.* This "public will" coincided with the interests of the shippers of commodities.
[61] *Ibid.*

in his view the propagandists of the railroads did little to help the general welfare by keeping silent about free passes, rebates, monopolies, accident rates, or accumulation of great wealth. The railroads not only constructed a false view of the world but obstructed public progress. While many world views might be valid, only one presumably could represent the greater interests of society.

The role of the muckraker in such a situation was evident, "if we can let in light and air, if the people understand . . . they will at least proceed forward."[62] Baker's idea of a valid world view was one where the underdog's position was fully portrayed, and his interests were integrated with those of society: "What then, is my job as a journalist? My job is to see as straight as it lies in me to do. . . . Nor must I forget in doing it that love after all is the goal. . . . I must see the mill owners as honestly as I see the strikers, I must see the strike-leaders though they are anarchists, with the same patience that I see the absentee capitalist in Boston. . . . What makes people love? One way is to make them share a little of the other fellow's pain & woes."[63]

The muckrakers, seeking a balanced picture of the world, often picked second-seeded interests of local conflicts to bring into national focus. They championed the shippers against the transporters, the small traction companies against the large, and independent oil companies against the monopolies. And to an extent this interpretation holds true of the power struggle between the bosses and the reformers, where the muckrakers supported the latter in their endeavor to remove the informal power structure of boss rule, so that public contracts and benefits could be opened to new interests. By the process of muckraking the struggle between the underdog and his local oppressor was transformed into a conflict between the "people" and the "interests."

In order better to essay the style of the *McClure's* journal-

[62] *Ibid.*, 549.
[63] Baker to M. F. Woodlock, July 2, 1912, Baker Papers.

ism, it might be fruitful to review two tales of Pittsburgh, both told by staff members at different times. For ten years before coming to *McClure's*, Willa Cather, fresh from Nebraska, had been a resident of that city. Pittsburgh, by 1900, with its great steel and glass factories, supported by a quarter million population, rested at the confluence of the Allegheny and Monongahela Rivers much the same as when Hamlin Garland wrote of it for *McClure's* in 1894. As a reporter on the *Pittsburgh Daily Leader* and a city employee, Miss Cather knew much about the machine politics of William Flinn and Christopher Magee. Magee's power was built on the immigrants, who numbered one-third of the city's population. Steffens, for his own reasons, called Pittsburgh a "Scotch-Irish-American city."[64] Magee, for his efforts, owned two city papers, the Consolidated Street Car Company with 8,000 miles of track, a bank, and practically the entire city. Miss Cather, whose newspaper opposed the machine and eventually helped expose its pilfering, was an admirer of Magee, even though knowing of his rascality.

Miss Cather has left a picture of the boss which Steffens could not have painted and which serves to put the muckrakers' montage into perspective. Shortly after the election of McKinley she called upon Magee for a job. Miss Cather found his office filled with the usual types—of which she was one—"poor women who wanted work for their husbands on the car line; men who had been fired for drunkenness and wanted to 'try again'; men who wanted to sweep the streets and seedy looking newspaper men in last summer's tan shoes and red neckties whose appearance told plainly why they were there."[65]

The center of all this activity was Magee, "a little ugly man, carelessly, almost shabbily dressed with an intensely nervous manner."[66] Miss Cather was amazed that Magee

[64] Steffens, *Autobiography*, 400.
[65] Cather to Will Owen Jones, Jan. 15, 1896, Cather (Brown) Papers, Yale University.
[66] *Ibid.*

"had a kind word for everyone" of his callers, "and it wasn't unctuous patronizing kindness, just the simple sort that a man whose heart was good might let drop to his less fortunate fellows as he hurried through the thousand gigantic plans of his busy life."[67] The little man with the kind manner left her deeply impressed: "I'd work for the fellow just to study him, this queer fellow who controls the politics of Pennsylvania, 'owns Pittsburgh,' edits two papers, rides in a carriage, lives in a palace, wears dirty collars, and shoes run down at the heel and talks to street car conductors' wives like they were his friends. . . ."[68] After having given letters to various petitioners, Magee did "the big generous thing" for Miss Cather, and offered to take her writing and get her a job on one of his papers.[69] "Nothing may come of it," Miss Cather wrote, but she insisted that, "my admiration for . . . Magee will be just the same."[70]

This genial view of the boss, supported by recent historical research, explains why he was in power. He was a man of the minorities of Pittsburgh. He tolerated their foibles and old world mores—and they tolerated his peccadilloes. While the Westinghouses, the Carnegies, and the Heinzes may not have liked Magee, they dealt with him. When Steffens arrived in 1903 for a muckraking article to follow his second on St. Louis, what did he find? "It looked like hell, literally," he wrote.[71] "Arriving of an evening, I walked out aimlessly into the smoky gloom of its deep-dug streets and somehow got across a bridge up on a hill that overlooked the city, with its fiery furnaces and the two rivers which pinched it in. The blast ovens opened up periodically and threw their volcanic light upon the cloud of mist and smoke about the town and gilded the silver rivers, which were high and threatening floods."[72] Such was Steffens' reproduction of what Garland saw a decade earlier.

---

[67] *Ibid.*   [68] *Ibid.*
[69] *Ibid.*   [70] *Ibid.*
[71] Steffens, *Autobiography*, 401.   [72] *Ibid.*

With the aid of a local reporter, Steffens began to construct his picture of Pittsburgh's politics. He accumulated a great deal of data, but "I didn't print much of it. It was too detailed and dull; the public won't read figures."[73] He researched and wrote his article in less than three months; he was anxious to get on to Philadelphia. Steffens' article contrasts sharply with Miss Cather's letter.

A "giant," Miss Cather called Magee. Steffens in his muckraking article in *McClure's* made him responsible for a city described as "Hell with the Lid Off."[74] Misgovernment by a "deliberate, intelligent organization . . . was conceived by one mind," and that was Magee, Steffens wrote. Magee was charged with criminally plundering the town financially.[75] Where Miss Cather saw a man kind to drunks, Steffens portrayed a brutal boss who used the "bartenders, saloon-keepers, liquor dealers, and others allied to the vices, who were subject to police regulation and dependent in a business way upon the maladministration of law."[76] Magee's lawlessness had routed the reformers like Oliver McClintock. Miss Cather's boss who "talked to street car conductors' wives like they were his friends," Steffens saw as president of a thirty-million-dollar traction company, with a perpetual franchise, paying practically nil in taxes.[77] Miss Cather's bank president was Steffens' politician who controlled businessmen and banks through "control of public funds and the choice of depositories."[78]

Miss Cather is a weak foil for Steffens, but the point remains that his facts were correct, that they were aimed at enhancing the position of the Pittsburgh reformers, that the reformers in Pittsburgh faced the same "system" as other communities, and that the people had to follow the reformers if government was to be saved from the interests.

A recent analysis of Pittsburgh politics has questioned Steffens' conclusions. Although employing the ideology of

[73] *Ibid.*, 405.
[74] Steffens, *Shame*, 147-89.
[75] *Ibid.*, 150.
[76] *Ibid.*, 155.
[77] *Ibid.*, 175-76.
[78] *Ibid.*, 157.

popular democracy, Samuel Hays writes, Steffens was really attempting to engineer a coup d'état of the bankers, corporation directors, and upper echelon of professionals. While Hays' study probingly questions the supposed middle class origins of progressivism assumed by Hofstadter and Mowry, his identification of Steffens' muckraking with a municipal elite of 745 upper class citizens is open to challenge. Steffens, like the other *McClure's* muckrakers, often, perhaps too often, indicted Hays' business elite for municipal corruption. Indeed, Magee himself was a successful businessman, listed in the Social Register, and presumably a member of the elite.[79]

The muckraker stood before a society which he tended to view as an organistic whole; he envisioned lawlessness as a ubiquitous condition. His role was to preach. Perhaps Baker best explained what the *McClure's* writers were attempting with their highly personal articles: "The journalist is a true servant of democracy. The best journalist of today occupies the exact place of the prophets of old: he cries out the truth & calls for reform. . . . The news is the way God speaks to men."[80]

The success of this patient, yes, prophetic, journalism that cost almost $2,000 per article was such that *McClure's* got "more newspaper notice . . . than any four of the other magazines."[81] This gave the magazine its tremendous national influence from the rural homes of the West to the White House. Joseph Folk credited Steffens' articles on St. Louis with turning the "mass of public opinion in Missouri at a critical time in his favor."[82] But while Steffens'

[79] Hays, "The Politics of Reform in Municipal Government in the Progressive Era," *Pacific Northwest Quarterly*, 161ff; *Dictionary of American Biography*, XII, 197. See also Whitney R. Cross, "The Muckrakers Revisited: Purposeful Objectivity in Progressive Journalism," Neiman Reports, VI (July, 1952), 10-15; *Readings in Municipal Government*, ed. Chester C. Maxey (New York, 1924), 190ff.

[80] Baker, Notebook, "I," 21-23, Baker Papers.

[81] *McClure's*, XXIV (Nov., 1904), 112; Baker to Father, March 27, 1904, Baker Papers.

[82] *Philadelphia North American*, Aug. 14, 1905.

Chicago piece "strengthened the League" in that city and helped William Kent's career, "The Pittsburg article had no effect in Pittsburg, nor that on Philadelphia any results in Philadelphia."[83] The lot of the prophet was not an easy one.

After Ellery Sedgwick wrote that the muckraker used "exaggerations, perversions, distortion, truths, half-truths, lies . . . ," William Allen White was inclined to respond, "Gentlemen in the pillory of public sentiment blame their discomfiture upon the newspapers and magazines."[84] This was wrong:

> They merely voice sentiment.
> Often they make clamor,
> > but public sentiment grows.
> It is as evanescent as the wind,
> > and as resistless as the waves.[85]

When men like Sedgwick responded, government by magazine had proved itself at *McClure's*. It could make a thunderous din; it could defy the President; it could elevate or destroy. It was the vanguard of the new revolution and a force to be reckoned with. But what was the nature and cause of lawlessness against which the muckrakers crusaded? How could the erring state and economic system be called back to the ways of order and progress? In sum, what the illness and what the cure whereof these angry young journalists prophesied? To see if muckraking had substance beneath its sermonizing, it is necessary to go into the metaphysical thicket and seek to identify some basic presuppositions.

[83] William Boyden to Steffens, Aug. 25, 1903, Steffens Papers; Steffens, *Shame*, 23.
[84] *American Magazine*, LXII (May, 1906), 111; William Allen White, *The Old Order Changeth* (New York, 1912), 133.
[85] *Ibid.*

Chapter XI. The State of
the State

IN TIME the muckrakers constructed a coherent analysis of why government had failed in its basic functions. In fact there is a chronological sequence between *McClure's* pre-muckraking concern with intemperance and prostitution, its identification of these problems with misgovernment after 1903, and, finally, its advocacy of such reforms as the city manager and the city commission which supposedly alleviated these conditions. If the muckrakers viewed themselves as prophets, they also saw themselves as young scientists accumulating data on lawlessness and searching for the laws of misanthropy.

Governmental institutions were perhaps the muckrakers' earliest concerns. This was explicit in Steffens' articles on municipalities and inherent in Miss Tarbell's writings on Standard Oil. A political theory evolved despite the obstacles of fragmentary, hasty writing and the necessity of retailoring old traditional assumptions and values to the new sciences, sociology and biology. At every step there were the ubiquitous pressures from segments of the public which elaborated upon Roosevelt's challenge, "shall every 'exposer' be our prophet?"[1]

The existence of a political theory forged by the *McClure's* group has generally eluded modern commentators, one of whom sees no "definite doctrinal preconceptions of set pattern of reform" in these progressives. The insistence that *McClure's* "sought no change in the actual form of government other than making it more responsive to the will of the electorate" is supported substantially by John Chamberlain's *Farewell to Reform* and Walter Lippmann's *Preface to Politics*.[2] More specifically, a biographer of Lincoln

[1] *American Magazine*, LXII (May, 1906), 111; see Louis Filler, *Crusaders for American Liberalism*, 222.

[2] Quotations from David Chalmers, "The Social and Political Ideas

Steffens has found that caustic journalist's "cure for corruption," as developed in a lengthy study of Boston, a "vague, circuitous, and repetitious document which skirted the causes of political depravity."[3] Steffens was in the no-man's land before turning to socialism when he sponsored "Boston 1912," but the same impatient criticism has been lodged against the entire movement of reform journalism.

In a convincing, if general, way Louis Filler attempts to refute the charges that the muckrakers were negative and ignorant of Bunyan's heavenly city (or that they were ignorant of Howe's American city). "The aim to find constructive remedies for corruption was inherent in the muckraking articles," he writes, "particularly in those which most bravely and conscientiously sought to analyze entire situations as a prelude to prescribing for them."[4] And although a scattering of other historians have agreed that "every muckraker restlessly considered alternatives to the conditions he was describing," or that "each of the journalists developed his own reform theories," little attention has been paid to the political philosophy which evolved at *McClure's*.[5]

The principal cause of governmental corruption, of the breakdown of orderly legal processes, was, the *McClure's* staff believed, the rise in the United States of a shadow government, a fragment of which existed at every electoral level from the precinct to the highest office in the land. This extra-legal apparatus, ruled by a hierarchy of bosses, was called the "superficial government" by William Allen White, the "real" government by S. S. McClure, and the

---

of the Muckrakers," doctoral dissertation, University of Rochester, 1955, 193. In revised form this dissertation has been published as *The Social and Political Ideas of the Muckrakers* (New York, 1964); these documents will be cited independently.

[3] Irving G. Cheslaw, "An Intellectual Biography of Lincoln Steffens," doctoral dissertation, Columbia University, 1952, 159.

[4] Filler, *Crusaders for American Liberalism*, 222.

[5] *Ibid.*, 223; Chalmers, *The Social and Political Ideas of the Muckrakers* (New York, 1964), 109.

"invisible" government by Steffens.[6] The strength of the shadow government exceeded by far that of the legal constitutional government. The sum result of machine government was a corruption of the decision-making processes and a perversion of legal, rational order. McClure diagnosed the general ills caused by the machine before a meeting of the Twentieth Century Club in 1904: "Under a weak form of government you have tyranny; under an inefficient form of government you have tyranny; under a corrupt form of government you have tyranny. This is the condition that the political machine has brought about in the United States, and this is general."[7]

Varying somewhat were the explanations of how the anti-government came to be organized. To McClure, for whom Tammany Hall was an especial *bête noire*, the popular explanation of bossism was sufficient. He felt from the beginning of muckraking that the boss arose with the "incoming of alien and frequently inferior breeds" which resulted in making "our country the asylum of the weak and destitute."[8] These "inmates of the asylums," the Ulsterman felt, had seized the "power of government" through their padrones and bosses.[9] The foreign mores which tolerated saloons and prostitution were the same forces which created bosses like Magee in Pittsburgh. One must not confuse such statements with the ideas of the American Protective Association, Stoddard, General Kearney, or Homer Lea. Like those other immigrants, Godkin, Bok, and Schurz, McClure wanted the alien assimilated into the New World culture. McClure's views seem identical with the President's: "We are a new race, composed of many Old-World stocks."[10] With

[6] See White, *Old Order Changeth*, 12; *McClure's*, xxxvi (Nov., 1910), 118; Steffens, *Autobiography*, 393.

[7] "Discussion at the Twentieth Century Club, Brooklyn, Between S. S. McClure and Hon. Timothy L. Woodruff," January 30, 1904, McClure Papers.

[8] McClure, Speech before the Canadian Club, Nov. 26, 1910, *ibid.*

[9] *Ibid.*

[10] Theodore Roosevelt to Finley Peter Dunne, Dec. 3, 1904, Dunne Papers, Manuscript Division, Library of Congress.

his background McClure's respect for European cultures and the efficiency of European governments was profound. But he felt that the immigration process was selecting the least likely candidates for American democracy, the poor and weak who became the tools of bosses.

Steffens, sired by Canadian immigrants, went to great lengths, however, to reject the contention that aliens formed the pedestal of machine government. "When I set out on my travels," he satirized McClure's position, "an honest New Yorker told me honestly that I would find that the Irish, the Catholic Irish, were at the bottom of it all everywhere."[11] But Steffens saw Pittsburgh full of Scotch Presbyterians, "and that was what my New York friend was. 'Ah, but they are all foreign populations,' I heard."[12] This was "one of the hypocritical lies that save us from the clear sight of ourselves."[13] Steffens also rejected other theories of misgovernment more ably propounded. Bryce's suggestion that corruption originated in the relative youth of the nation's institutions, the Republican insistence that it was part of the nature of the Democratic party, and the Southern contention that it was a phenomenon of the Northern cities were all held inadequate.[14]

Rather, from the beginning, Steffens believed that the boss was "not an accidental consequence of the wickedness of bad men, but the impersonal effect of natural causes," which might be identified without blaming anyone.[15] From his studies of the psychological and physiological evolution of man, Steffens felt that the boss was an institution, "an American institution," which reflected the business acquisitiveness, the selfishness, and the peculiar ambition of the American people. Again and again, from his earliest writings to the *Autobiography*, he returned to the theme that the boss was a "natural growth, not a legal device like a mayor" built upon the habits of a people.[16] He was an

11 Steffens, *Shame*, 4.   12 *Ibid.*, 5.   13 *Ibid.*
14 See Steffens, *Autobiography*, 374.   15 *Ibid.*, 407.
16 *Ibid.*, 409.

expression of American mores, not those of aliens. The *Shame of the Cities* embodied this sentiment: "The enduring strength of the typical American machine is that it is a natural growth—a sucker, but deep-rooted in the people."[17] In a word, the shadow government had developed as economic forces external to government had overshadowed and challenged civil authority with the acquiescence of the people.

William Allen White agreed with the gravamen of this charge against the American commercial spirit. Democracy became modified, he wrote in *The Old Order Changeth*, "when little by little the alliance was established between business and politics,—between capital and democracy,— the two governments were cemented into the customs and traditions of the people."[18] While Miss Tarbell, White, Steffens, and Baker were in agreement that materialistic institutions, so loved by Burke and so hated by Rousseau, had joined forces with the state to bind the country in subjection, McClure hesitated at first to accept a precept so closely identified with economic determinism.

"It is certain," a historian writes of McClure, "that he did not begin to understand the substance of Steffens' writings, which described the interrelationship between misgovernment and the 'better' members of the community."[19] This was hardly the case. By the time of Steffens' third article on municipalities there was no misunderstanding his predilections. His logic was simple. First, "the typical American citizen is the businessman." Secondly, "the typical businessman is a bad citizen." And finally, because of the unbridled profit motive, all Americans were responsible for bad government and for the existence of the machine which exploited it on all levels.[20] When Steffens wrote, "misgovernment of the American people is misgovernment by the

---

[17] Steffens, *Shame*, 198.
[18] White, *Old Order Changeth*, 13.
[19] Cheslaw, "An Intellectual Biography of Lincoln Steffens," 76-77.
[20] See Steffens, *Shame*, 5.

American people," McClure stiffened.[21] "I have been thinking seriously of the attitude Steffens always takes in regard to the people," he confided to John Phillips, "and I not only feel that he is wrong in his attitude, but that such an attitude is discouraging and calculated to lessen the value of the article."[22] While *McClure's* editors permitted Steffens to call the big businessman a "self-righteous fraud" because he bought political favors, they defended the small businessmen "who were despoiled and beaten by the large."[23] Even Steffens later equivocated, at times lauding businessmen reformers such as William Kent of Chicago.

These two theories—that the shadow government had its origins in the mores of an alien people and that it was based on the natural acquisitiveness of Americans—were both combined in the position which *McClure's* finally espoused. And eventually both Steffens and McClure adopted much of the other's position.

Three particular groups, McClure insisted, created the shadow government and pursued vocations which depended upon the breaking of the law and the undermining of governmental institutions. First and most important were "those who are engaged in occupations, like saloon-keeping and gambling houses and policy shops, etc., who like to have the laws broken that are made for the purpose of protecting the morals of the community."[24] A second class of men were those in the public service corporations who "make money by buying franchises for paving streets or by undertaking other contracts for cities."[25] These two

21 *Ibid.*, 4; This logic was first developed in Steffens' article, "Great Types of Modern Business: vi Politics," in *Ainslee's Magazine*, viii (Oct., 1901), 211ff. Here Steffens finds "politics is a businessman with a specialty" in supplying vice, privileges, immunities, and appointments.
22 McClure to Phillips, March 29, 1903, McClure Papers.
23 *Ibid.*; Steffens, *Shame*, 5.
24 McClure, Speech to the Twentieth Century Club, Jan. 30, 1904, McClure Papers. "The principal source of all police corruption was the saloon," Steffens wrote of New York in 1898 ("The Real Roosevelt," *Ainslee's Magazine*, ii [Dec., 1898], 483).
25 *Ibid.*

groups combined with a third, "the men who want public office," and the machine was born.[26] America, being "singular among nations" possessed these classes in almost every locality.[27] In his autobiography, Lincoln Steffens drew a graph of how these three influences interlocked to control municipal government.

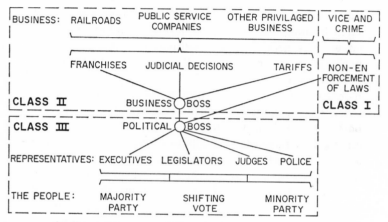

Steffens' Structure of Governmental Corruption[28]

Steffens agreed with McClure that the criminal, political, and financial classes created a market for illegal government favors. Using principally a controlled vote, the political boss doled privileges to the business community in the form of franchise grants, judicial decisions, etc. The professional criminals bought protection and repaid whenever possible by delivering a corrupt vote. *McClure's* attempted to expose this relationship between the official government and the machines, between the machines and business, between the criminal class and the voting public, and between the local

[26] *Ibid.*

[27] *Ibid.*; see Steffens' *Autobiography*, 407, where he wrongly accuses McClure of believing corruption "exceptional, local, and criminal."

[28] Steffens, Autobiography, 596. A variation of this appears in Steffens' "Great Types of Modern Business: VI Politics," *Ainslee's Magazine*, VIII (Oct., 1901), 218ff.

and the state machines. The endeavor was so inclusive, McClure insisted, that "when I was younger and more forceful and less rational and more worked up, I said we could have an article in McClure's Magazine based upon data that could be entitled, 'From the Whore House to the White House.' "[29]

Of the three lawless classes, *McClure's* was most concerned with the criminal. Hofstadter endeavored to explain why the muckrakers, usually concerned with bosses and trusts, veered to attacks on such "objects of reform as the liquor traffic and prostitution."[30] Relying completely upon the "thought and sensibility" of *McClure's*, Hofstadter concludes that the Progressives inherited the moral traditions of rural Protestantism, and they came from a "rural simplicity and village neighborliness" to the city, where they were "still freshly horrified by phenomena that we now resignedly consider indigenous to the urban existence."[31]

McClure's championship of a moral order, of course, had a direct linkage with the Great Revival via Galesburg. But it cannot be presupposed that Lincoln Steffens, who saw Europe as a student, if not a man of the world; nor Ida Tarbell, who lived among the toughs of Pennsylvania and the students of the Left Bank; nor S. S. McClure, whose curiosity drove him to many things, if not adultery; nor any of the young writers of *McClure's*, whose careers as police reporters had been a ticket to view hoodlumism for a decade, were the noble savages which many have maintained. *McClure's* opposition to organized criminality came from complex motives. Clearly from the Galesburg community came a traditional, Christian sense of "ought." But these values were quickly reinforced by a new social code based on the Social Gospel and social Darwinism. And probably, too, the pragmatic results of such anti-social be-

29 McClure, Speech before Race Betterment Conference, Jan. 10, 1914, McClure Papers.
30 Hofstadter, *Age of Reform*, 204.
31 *Ibid.*, 202, 205, 204.

havior influenced their decision. Clearly the liquor traffic and prostitution played an important part in debauching politics. But there was little Jeffersonian repugnance to cities in these men—if one excludes the pose of William Allen White.

As has been seen, *McClure's* from it earliest days had been an advocate of prohibition. Kate Field in the syndicate and Theodore Roosevelt in the magazine had indicted the liquor traffic long before the Spanish-American War. Later, throughout the *Shame of the Cities*, the saloon-keeper was portrayed as the base of a pyramid of corruption. Incorporating what seems to be an old saw, Steffens wrote of St. Louis in 1903: "Many of the legislators were saloon-keepers—it was in St. Louis that a practical joker nearly emptied the House of Delegates by tipping a boy to rush into a session and call out, 'Mister, your saloon is on fire,' —but even the saloon-keepers of a neighborhood had to pay to keep in their inconvenient locality a market which public interest would have moved."[32] In a review of this volume, William Allen White took occasion to agree that anti-government was created when saloon owners, gamblers, and prostitutes formed an alliance with the "thing we call capital."[33] If professional criminals "did not operate at the polls," they found themselves "facing the written law."[34] Indeed, White believed in 1904 that reform consisted in conforming "to the normal written governments of charters and constitutions."[35] He shed this notion in time.

The journalists evolved a theory as to how this criminal condition developed. Following the Civil War, American cities had begun to change, with the social center becoming the neighborhood saloons.[36] "The Pleasant Saloon-Keeper—Ruler of American Cities," an article appearing

[32] Steffens, *Shame*, 34.
[33] *McClure's*, XXIII (June, 1904), 221.
[34] White, *Old Order Changeth*, 11.
[35] *McClure's*, XXIII (June, 1904), 221.
[36] See White, *Old Order Changeth*, 11.

in *McClure's* in 1908, chronicled the manner in which this change came about.[37] Supposedly the saloon-keeper's strategic position allowed him to abuse the cupidity of men dependent upon drink. The ability to influence a few votes on election day, compounded by the absolute necessity of operating illegally in order to make a profit, as pointed out later in "The Experience and Observations of a New York Saloon-Keeper," made the dealer in alcohol a politically conscious denizen.[38] Financial straits drove the dealers to operating on Sunday, in illegal locations, and without licenses, *McClure's* maintained. Many were captives of the monopolistic policies of breweries. In order to obtain special favors, the saloon-keeper, like the gamblers, the opium peddlers, the prostitutes, and the crooks, had to arrange for political protection. The saloon-keeper either used inebriates to vote since his saloon was often a voting place or a party headquarters, perhaps forcing his own way into politics, or he bought his privileges. This was what Steffens called the "system," where every favor had its price, fluctuating only with the market. Even a saloon-keeper, he said, would soon learn that votes costing only a dollar could be sold for much more.

Convinced of this, William Allen White even developed a grudging admiration for his fellow Kansan, the hatchet-wielding Carry Nation. "Is it altogether impossible," he asked in Bok's *Saturday Evening Post*, "that this frantic, brawling, hysterical woman in the Kansas jail, brave, indomitable, consecrated to her God, may be a prophetess whose signs and wonders shall be read and known of men by the light of another day?"[39] White even apologized for Miss Nation's bizarre behavior with a paradox in 1901. Partly by her own example of lawlessness she had "aroused the law-abiding people of Kansas to the disgrace of law-

[37] *McClure's*, XXXI (Oct., 1908), 713.
[38] *Ibid.*, XXXII (Jan., 1909), 301.
[39] Quoted in Mott, *A History of American Magazines*, IV, 210.

breaking. . . ."[40] The logical problems of law were beginning to present themselves.

But the system existed everywhere, not only in Kansas. Steffens exposed a dozen cities. George Kennan found boodling in San Francisco's labor government, and George K. Turner contrasted vice-ridden Chicago with Galveston, Texas, under the reform commission government.[41] "Why," Turner asked in 1907, "have the primary basic guarantees of civilization broken down in Chicago?" The answer lay in a hundred-million-dollar-a-year liquor traffic, in a prostitution business worth twenty million a year, and in large gambling and drug rackets.[42] This effected a pronounced influence on government. The magazine found on the boards of aldermen in such cities a "percentage of saloon-keepers with foreign names which is astonishing."[43]

Understandably *McClure's* participated in a far-reaching campaign against alcohol. As a part of this program George K. Turner drafted a series on the saloon in 1909. He intended to arouse public opinion "to the dangers of this most evil political influence, which has degraded the government of American cities in a fashion utterly unparalleled among nations."[44] His principal villain was the saloonkeeper: "It has probably never happened before that men so ignorant and engaged in business so degrading have secured the complete mastery of the law-making and law-enforcing institutions."[45] Endeavoring to give the prohibition movement a more thorough investigation "than has ever been accomplished before," the magazine defended temperance as "perhaps the most vigorous and important ethical movement ever originated on this continent."[46] Again the question was being drawn—was it vio-

[40] Emporia *Gazette*, Feb. 11, 1901.

[41] *McClure's*, XXIX (Sept., 1907), 547; XXX (Nov., 1907), 60; XXVIII (April, 1907), 574.

[42] *Ibid.*, XXVIII (April, 1907), 575-76.

[43] *Ibid.*, XXXI (Oct., 1908), 713.   [44] *Ibid.*, XXXII (Dec., 1908), 195.
[45] *Ibid.*   [46] *Ibid.*

lations of statute law or moral law that made the state "lawless"? Clearly, it was both.

The alcohol problem was dealt with exhaustively in the magazine. Writers on this question included Dr. Henry S. Williams, who allegedly had studied the problem for twenty-five years in an asylum. He explained "how the poison works" upon the user and unborn generations.[47] Supposedly his experiments showed that every function "of the normal human body is injured by the use of alcohol—even the moderate use; and that the injury is both serious and permanent."[48] In a small way this shows how the new science was brought to the aid of the theology of the Great Revival. Dr. Williams attributed to the beverage not only mental illness but crime, pauperism, and broken homes. Later, a scientist and physician bolstered this view with additional "Evidence Against Alcohol."[49] *McClure's* also used testimonials as good and instructive copy. The inner life of moral deterioration brought about by drink was chronicled by two autobiographies, "The Story of an Alcoholic Slave" and "Confessions of a Moderate Drinker."[50] Anyone left with a thirst was told that Lincoln thought the drink a "cancer in society," and was invited to read Henry Parker Willis' "What Whisky Is."[51] What it was, with false labels, with added contents often poison, made Packingtown look like a Boy Scout barbecue.

Simultaneously with the prohibition campaign, the muckrakers attacked the practice of white slavery. In what must have been popular reading, Mrs. Fremont Older explained the role of this evil in San Francisco's labor government, and Turner, like E. J. Edwards, Flynt, Steffens, and Gustavus Myers, retold the story of Tammany's alliance with such criminality in 1909.[52] The dance halls of the large cities

47 *Ibid.*, XXIX (Oct., 1908), 705; XXXII (Dec., 1908), 154; XXXII (Feb., 1909), 419.
48 *Ibid.*, XXIX (Oct., 1908), 713.   49 *Ibid.*, XXXII (March, 1909), 556.
50 *Ibid.*, XXXIII (Aug., 1909), 427; XXXIV (Feb., 1910), 448.
51 *Ibid.*, XXIV (April, 1910), 687, 701.
52 *Ibid.*, XXXIII (July, 1909), 277; XXXIII (June, 1909), 117.

were the reputed places where young Jewish immigrant girls were recruited for the sordid business.[53] "These unfortunate women," said McClure, were "compelled" to rent their rooms from the local machine, which got "these houses at from twenty-five to forty dollars a month and rent them to these women at fifty dollars a week."[54] In addition, the prostitutes were forced to purchase their furnishings, clothing, jewelry, liquor, everything, "at exorbitant prices from certain people."[55] Edith Wyatt prepared a series on the conditions and salaries of working girls which most ably explored the economic causes of such sexual immorality.[56]

The *McClure's* exposures stimulated a national panic, and, finally, national action. Chicago and Illinois immediately passed laws against white slavery.[57] Soon President Roosevelt proclaimed adherence to the international white slave treaty, excluded prostitutes by the immigration act of 1908, and helped create a public sentiment favorable to the Mann Act of 1910.[58] Frederick Howe soon found himself on Ellis Island asking rather un-Victorian questions of young immigrant girls. Obviously popular opinion agreed that the disorderly house and the saloon were the base upon which the political machine was built, the factors which were "Tammanyizing" a civilization.[59]

A second segment of the shadow government, according to *McClure's*, organized the vice rackets and used them for its own purpose. The political machine thus became the alter ego of the political party. With free institutions, where

[53] *Ibid.*, XXIX (May, 1907), 67; XXXIV (Nov., 1909), 45.
[54] McClure, Speech at the Twentieth Century Club, Jan. 30, 1904, McClure Papers.
[55] *Ibid.*
[56] *McClure's*, XXV (July, 1910), 346; see *ibid.*, XXXVI (Dec., 1910), 201.
[57] For a discussion of this campaign see Henry May, *The End of American Innocence* (New York, 1959), 343ff; Harold U. Faulkner, *The Quest for Social Justice* (New York, 1931), 160; *McClure's*, XXXIV (Nov., 1909), 123.
[58] Faulkner, *The Quest for Social Justice*, 162.
[59] *McClure's*, XXXIV (Nov., 1909), 117, 126.

"every man was called fit to participate in the government," the migrants and immigrants flocked to urban centers to find themselves organized by a boss into a paternalistic machine.[60] Between 1890 and 1910 immigration averaged almost a million a year, and most of the coastal cities were composed of over one-half foreign born. But the uprooted included native rural Americans who migrated to the new metropolitan environment, evidently only to find corruption. This was the public which cast its votes in the wards.

Government faced insuperable problems. The structure of city government was modeled on that of the national government and had little usefulness in an urban environment. Fragmented, it had less power than the social and financial forces external to it. It was urban political parties which organized the forces outside of government and sought the reins of power. It was the machines, finally, which manipulated the parties. The political boss organized the "pigeon-hole" vote—those who voted the straight ticket—and "won elections by swinging the purchasable votes of the minority of worst citizens to the worst ticket. . . ."[61] From the ward to the state house, the boss was then prepared to do business in governmental favors.

The *McClure's* group had little patience with parties that allowed themselves to be undermined. People were herded into "parties according to some one or more relatively simple issues and thus get some few things decided."[62] Permanent grouping meant permanent stagnation and permanent boss control. Parties became alliances of feudal-like chieftains, but since machines were external to the parties and adaptable to any party situation, there was little faith that non-partisan elections were a panacea.[63] Both parties represented the same thing: the business of the ma-

[60] McClure, Speech to the Twentieth Century Club, Jan. 30, 1904, McClure Papers; *McClure's*, XXXIV (Nov., 1909), 117.

[61] Steffens, *Autobiography*, 394.

[62] Baker, Notebook "XI," June 22, 1916, 48-49, Baker Papers.

[63] White, *Old Order Changeth*, 18ff; Steffens, *Shame*, 232-33; Baker, Notebook "XI," June 22, 1916, 48-49, Baker Papers.

chine. Steffens concluded, after watching Kent, Crane, and Boyden function in Chicago, that perhaps the reformers should organize their own machines by utilizing a shifting or independent vote.

Outside of Tammany, perhaps the most publicized machine in the country was that of Missouri, a state which incidentally had pioneered legislation designed to protect the cities with home rule and general legislation provisions. Yet the written law which protected municipal citizens from the fiat of the state legislature did not defang the informal power structure of St. Louis. Indeed, the written law became a dead letter when attempts were made by Joseph Folk to oust the machine from St. Louis. The pattern was for the local boss to appeal to the state machine for aid against the reformers. The same was true in Ohio. There, Brand Whitlock in Toledo and Tom Johnson in Cleveland had to fight the state capital to keep control of their cities, because the local boss "had relations with the still more powerful groups of bosses that controlled the state conventions and state legislatures of his party."[64] The hierarchy was fluid, but always there was a "local boss," an intermediate "high-grade boss," and the "big boss" who controlled the state capital clique.[65]

Such an abstract scheme, evolved by the muckrakers, is too far removed from practical politics to be of more than a rule-of-thumb guide. But the political turmoil instigated by Joseph Folk in St. Louis proves it to be of aid in analyzing the political dynamics of that situation.[66] The young Vanderbilt-educated district attorney, originally put in power by the machine, aroused great local antipathy with his subsequent indictments of municipal officials and their corrupt allies in 1902. Unable to be re-elected to municipal office, Folk should, Steffens advised, "appeal over the heads of the people in St. Louis to the people of Missouri by run-

[64] White, *Old Order Changeth*, 19.   [65] *Ibid.*
[66] See *McClure's*, XXVI (Dec., 1905), 115; XX (March, 1903), 544; XIX (Oct., 1902), 597.

ning for governor."[67] In other words, the conflict should be escalated. Folk hesitated until the state machine proved its strength by having the Missouri Supreme Court release a dozen of the twenty men convicted of graft.[68] With *McClure's* support, Folk then twice ran successfully for governor. His program further endeared him to *McClure's* but alienated much of the state. A good fundamentalist, he passed blue laws, practically forcing the railroads to close down on Sundays, outlawed gambling, and stringently enforced temperance legislation.[69] When he could not have been reelected governor, wrote Steffens, Folk was "a possibility for president. . . ."[70] Such was the structure of machines. Although McClure led the campaign to make Folk president, the effort met with only limited response.

The hierarchy of bosses, as Missouri showed, paralleled the structure of government from the precinct to the state capital. Wherever there was an election to manipulate, they were present. But the counter-government did not cease here. The state legislatures at the turn of the century were relatively far more powerful than at present. They exercised greater arbitrary control over the rising metropolitan areas; they elected members of the U.S. Senate; and they enjoyed, for the time being, principal responsibility for controlling the worst features of capitalism, namely the trusts, labor unions, and working conditions, not yet under vigorous national control. "The central power in American government is the State Legislature," McClure accurately stated in 1905.[71] Because of their crucial importance, the machines wanted to control them. But despite their power the states were impotent before the great economic forces external to them. What chance, McClure asked, had forty or fifty odd little republics, "mostly corrupt," to control the strong national economic combines,

[67] Steffens, *Autobiography*, 396.
[68] *McClure's*, xxvi (Dec., 1905), 120.
[69] *Ibid.*, 127, 131.   [70] Steffens, *Autobiography*, 397.
[71] *The North American*, Aug. 14, 1905.

especially those mobilized by the trusts?[72] To succeed, the legal government had to be as powerful as any force it was supposed to control. In terms of either employees or capital investment, U.S. Steel or Standard Oil completely dwarfed the state legislatures. The inability of the states to enforce their thirty odd anti-trust laws, Miss Tarbell showed, was proof of their impotence.

Business which bought its political favors became the third villain of *McClure's* tragic troika. Businessmen interested in public franchises, tariff protection, and non-enforcement of laws regarding working conditions, rebates, concentration of wealth, and other limitations on laissez-faire made the state legislatures "the core of corruption in politics."[73] By 1905 McClure had come to share much of Steffens' view. To the capital "leads every line in every State; and the State Legislature makes the United States Senate, which is the most powerful national ruling body in the world."[74] Thus the U.S. Senate was "the shadow and mouthpiece of the great trust and railroad magnates of the United States."[75] Long before David Graham Phillips' *Treason of the Senate*, McClure counted the real rulers "not as numerous as the Senators, but they absolutely control them."[76] The chief business boss of the United States came from the "state for sale," Rhode Island.[77] Senator Nelson W. Aldrich had "no equal as a man of power at Washington. . . ."[78] This was the conclusion of Steffens in his article on Rhode Island in *Enemies of the Republic*. As a state boss Aldrich manipulated railroad franchises and "made himself fifteen million dollars in a few years. . . ."[79] In Washington he became the guardian of the protective tariff and the symbol of entrenched vested interests.

[72] *McClure's*, XXXVI (Nov., 1910), 118.
[73] *The North American*, Aug. 14, 1905.
[74] *Ibid.*   [75] *Ibid.*   [76] *Ibid.*
[77] See Steffens, *Autobiography*, 464ff.
[78] McClure, Speech at the Twentieth Century Club, Jan. 30, 1904. McClure Papers.
[79] *Ibid.*

McClure's, beginning with the corruption of an individual Midwestern city, traced the trail to Washington. There Steffens was to find the greatest of business bosses, Aldrich, allied with the greatest of political bosses, Mark Hanna. Roosevelt, intent upon using Hanna and Aldrich for his own ends, disputed such conclusions. Finally, when Steffens hinted that the President was a boss himself and began prying into the administration of the federal government, Roosevelt broke with the entire muckraking movement.[80] By so accusing the President, Steffens had distorted the concept of the shadow government into a meaningless generalization, a vague conspiracy which might include anyone hostile to *McClure's* ideology. The critical tools were ready. In time Taft was to be weighed and found wanting—when his policies were weighed against the feather of Progressive intentions.

It was obvious to the *McClure's* group that the legal government had failed because of its weakness in harnessing the extra-constitutional powers of the community. These new nationalists saw the United States Constitution as one of the principal allies of the shadow government. Like William Lloyd Garrison and Charles Sumner, they wanted no dreadful league with a document that enthroned a shadow oligarchy. William Allen White, Ray Stannard Baker, and probably McClure had read J. Allen Smith's *The Spirit of American Government*, a work which paved the way for Charles Beard's economic interpretation of the Constitution. "We have made of the Constitution," Baker wrote shortly after leaving McClure's, "a sort of fetish. . . ."[81] The authority of the written word had enshrined "the worship of ancestors," but "now we need *self-regulation*."[82] White questioned in *The Old Order Changeth* whether "this capture of the Constitution by our only aristocracy— that of capital—was not in truth merely a recapture of what

---

[80] See Cheslaw, "An Intellectual Biography of Lincoln Steffens," 112ff.

[81] Baker, Notebook "K," 1908, 145.   [82] *Ibid.*

227

was intended in the beginning by the fathers to belong to the minority."[83] He agreed with Baker and McClure that checks and balances "bound the nation to the rule of the privileged classes" as they had "protected slavery for fifty years" by delivering political control over to a minority of the population.[84] Sam McClure, as was his wont, went even further. He told a conference of leading Progressives that "I suppose there has never been a body of printed material so absurd and so far removed from actual facts and principles as the body of material which constitutes the various charters and constitutions under which the cities and states and this nation are governed."[85] The fact that the muckrakers, so concerned with boodling and lawlessness, should have challenged the very foundations of constitutional government needs further investigation.

First, in their thinking the muckrakers separated public law from the structure of government and moved only slowly towards attacking public law. The Constitution, they contended, came from an economic oligarchy which drafted an undemocratic and unworkable document. This error was compounded when state and city governments were modeled on the national. The political elite who had filled the Constitution with their own errors of thinking had done so because they drafted the document at one stroke. Had it not been for the American Revolution, a questionable good in itself, the United States would have "gradually developed our political system and freedom" imitating most nations who took "from three hundred to five hundred years to invent a government."[86] Indeed, as will be seen later, McClure was already making an appeal to a higher law of evolution and custom when he said after Wilson's election that the various constitutions were the

---

[83] White, *Old Order Changeth*, 22.   [84] *Ibid.*

[85] McClure, Speech at the Race Betterment Conference, Jan. 10, 1914. McClure Papers.

[86] McClure to F. C. Woodman, Feb. 7, 1910; McClure, Speech to the Canadian Club, Nov. 26, 1910, *ibid.*

"one single important body of documents in the United States that is not the result of observing the laws of men."[87]

Not only were the advantages of an evolutionary government and an unwritten constitution ignored in America, but, secondly, the very structure of government ignored the laws of administrative efficiency worked out by Frederick Taylor in his time and motion studies. McClure held that Montesquieu's "principles of the division of powers & democracy, or self-government cannot exist together."[88] And William Allen White agreed that "certainly these checks and balances are chafing us now in our struggle to express the widening moral intelligence of a democracy in terms of government."[89] The tripartite division of government, imitated on state and municipal levels, inhibited the orderly functioning of the state, hindered it from doing what it should. Government, McClure wrote years later, although his sympathies were the same in the muckraking period, was like a wagon going up hill: It needed no brakes in the form of "absurd theories . . . evolved by the deductive method of reasoning. . . ."[90] Admitting this radical assumption was to question the existence of "the Supreme Court and a government run upon the courts," as McClure pointed out to Chancellor Day at Syracuse.[91]

Long before Roosevelt advocated the direct election and recall of judges, William Allen White was writing that "the courts were not corrupt" in their practice of governing by injunction; "they were merely human."[92] The courts, "the

[87] McClure, Speech at the Race Betterment Conference, Jan. 10, 1914.

[88] McClure, "The Science of Political and Industrial Self-Organization," 1933, manuscript in the New York Public Library. This document, begun many years earlier, reflects many ideas which McClure expressed before the Progressive campaign of 1912; in fact it is filled with excerpts from his earlier work.

[89] White, *Old Order Changeth*, 22.

[90] McClure, "The Science of Political and Industrial Self-Organization," Ms in New York Public Library.

[91] McClure to Chancellor James R. Day, Dec. 29, 1910, McClure Papers.

[92] White, *Old Order Changeth*, 23.

last citadel of capital," implemented the "assumed right to declare legislation 'unconstitutional,' " and perpetuated "one of the most ruthless checks upon democracy permitted by any civilized people."[93] This became the stance of *McClure's*.[94] For example, Christopher P. Connolly's long series on the disorders of Montana recommended that the judicial power be curtailed. Connolly suggested, and Roosevelt eventually supported, the recall of judicial decisions in order to make the interpretation of the law conform to the public sense and justice.[95]

The nature of federalism itself did not go unquestioned as the *McClure's* staff analyzed misgovernment. Reminiscent of Governor Edmund Randolph at the Constitutional Convention, McClure felt that "a great number of independent sovereign states . . . make a very difficult government at best."[96] In Hamiltonian fashion he recommended, "I would reduce the status of the provinces to about that of city charters and make it a real nation, not an assemblage of more or less semi-sovereign states."[97] The nationalist posture of the *McClure's* muckrakers did not end here.

A third conclusion that they reached about the nature of American government was that popular democracy was desirable, not necessarily for its own ends, but to keep Wall Street and its allies from getting a corner on political power.[98] McClure believed in popular, honest government, but hesitated at accepting the doctrine of the "absolute equality of man, that is in his right to participate in government."[99] The immigrant, of course, was the principal

[93] *Ibid.*, 54, 57.
[94] *McClure's*, XXXIV (Nov., 1909), 117; XXXVI (Nov., 1910), 118.
[95] See Chalmers, *The Social and Political Ideas of the Muckrakers*, 31.
[96] McClure Speech to the Canadian Club, Nov. 26, 1910, McClure Papers. This was a widely held view among Republican businessmen, maintains Robert Wiebe in *Businessmen and Reform* (Cambridge, Mass. 1962), 50, 55, 202ff.
[97] *Ibid.*
[98] McClure, Speech to the Twentieth Century Club, Jan. 30, 1904, *ibid.*
[99] *Ibid.*

reason why American civilization "has not come up to the expectations of others."[100] And later Baker agreed with McClure to the extent that "the hope of America lies not so much in the reign of public opinion as in the *intelligence* of that reign," because "a blind public opinion is quite as likely to go wrong as to go right."[101] It was left for White in 1912 to paraphrase the classical fears of democracy, "government of the many by the many is not necessarily more desirable than the government of all by one" since at times the "tyranny of the mob was known . . . to be as cruel as the tyranny of a king."[102] Demagogues could use democracy, flatter it, and "make it mad with power."[103] Since wisdom and self-restraint were frail commodities, "there must be a check on the power of the masses. . . ."[104]

But as long as the public was well informed and well led, the muckrakers retained faith that the state would uphold the public welfare and morality; it would indeed impose the general will upon all the disintegrating facets of American life. They did not deign to "restore popular government as they imagined it to have existed in an earlier and purer age."[105] Their ultimate aim was not stopgap panaceas such as the primary, direct election of Senators, initiative, referendum, recall, the short ballot, or even the various modifications proposed for municipal government.[106] These were but means of achieving a national consensus regarding the greatest good for the greatest number. The legal government could not be made the equal of the shadow government solely by grafting new heads and tails onto it. Something more revolutionary had to be done if

---

100 McClure, Speech to the Canadian Club, Nov. 26, 1910, *ibid.*
101 Baker, Notebook "I," 1905-11, 17, Baker Papers.
102 White, *Old Order Changeth*, 65.
103 *Ibid.*, 64.   104 *Ibid.*, 65.
105 Hofstadter, *Age of Reform*, 257.
106 John Phillips advised Steffens that "nothing can be settled by a mechanical means such as the initiative and referendum. . . . Any device of that kind can be used by the wicked and the corrupt." (Phillips to Steffens, Dec. 10, 1907, Steffens Papers.)

the needs of the people in an evolving industrial society were to be met.

The muckrakers' shock at the extra-constitutional developments—such as political parties, the role of the Speaker of the House, the United States Senate's representing economic rather than political interests, and the rise of political machines built on patronage—are not shared today. But their analysis, also shared by Lord Bryce, that it was the mis-structuring of American government that permitted so much vice and mediocrity, has many modern supporters, including Harold Laski. The muckraking solution for such governmental ills was quick in coming. This, the topic of the next chapter, is significant enough to look at in detail.

Chapter XII. The Structuring
of Power—The Way Out

THE SHADOW government had resulted in a twofold malignancy. Naturally, misadministration was engendered; this was seen quite early. But, secondly, the process of law-making was impeded, and the state was hindered in coming to grips with the great new social forces. Only slowly, with the beginning of the Progressive movement, did the muckrakers finally conclude that obedience to a written code was not the sine qua non of reform. This change of the impetus of reform towards the restructuring of political power and the implementation of laws based on the great social and economic realities of the time is quite marked.

"Every new invention," McClure was moved to say in 1910, "demands new laws" governing social control and defining exploitation.[1] In a half dozen years the magazine had made a radically new interpretation of lawlessness. Just as the slavocracy had prevented new laws from being passed governing the control of inventions based on steam and steel, the shadow government obstructed needed legislation. As a result the United States remained "years and years" behind other countries "in the march of socializing new forces and ideas that have come into civilization."[2] This "legislative lag," as Baker defined it, resulted because law was the tortoise and society the hare in the pace of evolution.[3] McClure's staff agreed with his sentiment that "we are, broadly speaking, behind most of the other civilized nations in the various socialized laws dealing, for example, with the compensation of working men and so on and in methods of ameliorating the conditions of the poor and

[1] McClure, Speech to the Canadian Club, Nov. 26, 1910, McClure Papers.

[2] *Ibid.*; McClure, Speech at Race Betterment Conference, Jan. 10, 1914, *ibid.*

[3] See John Erwin Semonche, "Progressive Journalist: Ray Stannard Baker, 1870-1914," 100.

233

of the workers."[4] What was the way out when the "wealth and criminality" of the country arrayed themselves against the natural development of society as a whole and state functions in particular?[5]

The muckraker's solution lay in strengthening the formal government, in structurally unifying sovereignty, power, and responsibility. This was necessary, as Acton or Bagehot might have agreed, because "we cannot quarrel with a law of nature: water always flows downhill; government always seeks a strong hand."[6] The *McClure's* group undoubtedly concurred with the conclusions of John R. Commons in *A Sociological View of Sovereignty* that society was an organistic unity which preceded either the state, the family, or the individual in importance.[7] The principal responsibility of the state was to represent some consensus of the societal interests and to serve as a bulwark against centralized wealth.[8] The old arguments about the contract theory of the state, natural rights, and states rights had ceased to be meaningful in the light of the transformation of society with the concomitant growth of national powers of the first magnitude in the Wall Street-criminality combine. Perhaps, under these conditions, even democracy had become an unrealizable ideal.[9]

The process of society was Spencerian, from an "indefinite incoherent homogeneity to a definite coherent heterogeneity," and each epoch required revolutionary adjustment, particularly in government. In addition to Commons, the *McClure's* group was undoubtedly influenced by other nationalists in the Darwinian tradition such as Weyl,

[4] McClure, Speech at Race Betterment Conference, Jan. 10, 1914, McClure Papers.

[5] McClure, Speech at Twentieth Century Club, Jan. 30, 1904, *ibid.*

[6] *McClure's*, xxxvi (Nov., 1910), 118.

[7] John R. Commons, *A Sociological View of Sovereignty* (New York, 1965), 3.

[8] See Allan G. Crunchy, *Modern Economic Thought* (New York, 1947), 140; Joseph Dorfman, *The Economic Mind in American Civilization* (3 vols., New York, 1946-59), iii, 326.

[9] Steffens, *Shame*, 101, 181.

Croly, and John W. Burgess, the ex-Knox professor whose *Political Science and Comparative Constitutional Law* gave the concept of national sovereignty "its fullest and most systematic treatment in America."[10]

Hofstadter sees two schools of political thought among the Progressives: a Jeffersonian attempt to return power to the people and a Hamiltonian scheme to rest it in the hands of a great leader. The muckrakers fit neither category easily. They wanted popular support for uniting power and responsibility in the executive branch of government. The muckrakers' love of the short ballot, with most administrative posts being appointive, is well supported by McClure's belief that popular elections by nature were unfair since everyone's interests would not be represented in an individual elected by majority vote. "Partial representation" was the result when large numbers of voters cast their ballots for unsuccessful candidates.[11] The "direct election of the chief executive and other state officials has caused the degradation of the representative body, and weakened the official body," he wrote in later years.[12] It was by no means incompatible, then, for the muckrakers to favor structuring a powerful government in the image of the machine-capital combine and to use democracy to accomplish this feat.

As Samuel Hays has pointed out, all of this has the semblance of a very sophisticated type of class warfare, with the impotent plutocracy, not Hofstadter's white collar class, seeking to wrest governmental control from the lower strata which ruled through the extra-constitutional machine. He charges that the "reformers demanded electoral changes not because they believed in certain political principles but because they hoped that new techniques in

[10] Alan Pendleton Grimes, *American Political Thought* (New York, 1955, 1960), 285.
[11] McClure, "The Science of Political and Industrial Self-Organization," 1933, manuscript in New York Public Library.
[12] *Ibid.*

politics would enable them to overcome their opposition."[13] But semblance is not fact. The muckrakers were not class-conscious. On the whole they accepted an organistic view of society developed from social Darwinism. At any rate, no one, including Hays, has demonstrated how progressive reforms in the elective process could have aided, or did aid, the Marxian bourgeoisie's seizure of power. (It is difficult to identify the dominion of the boss with the rule of the proletariat, which is the logical conclusion of his argument.) Rather, the muckrakers were nationalists in the tradition of Hamilton, who wanted the state to be greater than any of its parts in order to make the needed social and political adjustments demanded by the industrial revolution.

The *McClure's* group, including those who went to the *American*, proposed to create a constitutional government which was stronger than the shadow government. The boss, the machine, and the corporation—all techniques of power manipulation—were deemed beneficial towards this end. This was only the imitation of eminently practical methods transformed to good ends. "The boss you like is a leader; the leader you dislike is a boss," philosophized the bard of Emporia.[14]

To the muckrakers the good boss was much like Carlyle's or Emerson's great man. It was he, presiding over the apparatus of the financial and political world, who was to chart the course towards the cause of light. Roosevelt, dubbed the "dictator," was one of the most consistent supporters of this theory.[15] The President opposed a device of "checks and balances so elaborate that no man shall have power enough to do anything very bad," and felt that the only way to get good public service was to "give somebody power to render it, facing the fact that power which will enable a man to do a job well will also necessarily

[13] Samuel P. Hays, *The Response to Industrialism* (Chicago, 1957), 155.
[14] *Emporia Gazette*, June 13, 1902.
[15] Steffens to Heney, April 18, 1908, Steffens Papers.

enable him to do it ill if he is the wrong kind of man."[16] It was a Progressive consensus that what was "needed is the concentration in the hands of one man, or of a very small body of men, of ample power to enable him or them to do the work that is necessary" with proper public safeguards.[17] It was an administrative logic which persuaded the *McClure's* group.

Lincoln Steffens admitted the necessity of the good boss only after finding "that the form of government did not matter; that constitutions and charters did not affect essentially the actual government," and that the "American theory of checks and balances" was archaic.[18] Undoubtedly, it was McClure who forced this conclusion upon Steffens and the entire staff. "You will either have strong men with power and responsibility in Government," McClure had contended, "or you will have strong men with power and without responsibility" because "real government" meant "strong men to govern."[19] Government was "just like running any railroad business or university."[20] McClure, a staff member later wrote, "was sure of that which he had learned by his experience on *McClure's Magazine* and by observation in all other business—that the dictatorship of one strong, wise man (like Sam McClure or Judge Gary) would abolish our political evils and give us a strong, wise administrator of cities. We had a pretty hot fight, and McClure won."[21]

The pattern of *McClure's* political exposures was to discover in every community a natural leadership, one man or group representing the shadow government and one

[16] Theodore Roosevelt, *Theodore Roosevelt: An Autobiography* (New York, 1913), 170-71.

[17] *Ibid.*, 171. Or as William Kent phrased it, "government by all of us thro the best of us" was desired (quoted in Joel A. Tarr, "William Kent to Lincoln Steffens: Origins of Progressive Reform in Chicago," *Mid-American*, XLVII [Jan., 1965], 57).

[18] Steffens, *Autobiography*, 409.

[19] McClure, Speech to YMCA, 57th New York Branch, April 10, 1911, McClure Papers.

[20] *Ibid.*   [21] Steffens, *Autobiography*, 375.

the moral order. This was a dialectical struggle between opposites where the good leader represented the forces coming to terms with technological evolution. In the *Shame of the Cities* the Hegelian dualism ran this way. In St. Louis the young righteous district attorney, Joseph Folk, opposed Edward Butler, the party boss. In Minneapolis, which "bore out Mr. McClure's certainty," a businessman, Hovey Clarke, who chanced to become foreman of a grand jury, confronted the corrupt Ames brothers, who as mayor and chief of police organized the racketeers.[22] In Pittsburgh bosses Magee and Flynn were challenged by the small Municipal League, while in Philadelphia the Republican successors of the Gas Gang, bosses Daniel Martin and Iz Durham, with their master Matthew Quay, fought dry goods capitalists John Wanamaker and his son. In Chicago William Kent, William Boyden, Walter Fisher, and Charles Crane through the Civic Federation and the Municipal Voters League guarded the public good against the successors of Charles Yerkes, and in New York Seth Low did the same with Croker and Tammany Hall.[23]

Nor did the theme of heroic combat enjoined between highly personified forces stop here. *The Struggle for Self-Government* and the *Upbuilders*, Steffens' later volumes, were constructed on this thesis. In what might be considered his first article on the cities, "The Shame of Minneapolis," Steffens wrote, "Whenever anything extraordinary is done in American municipal politics, whether for good or evil, you can trace it invariably to one man."[24] That man came from either the shadow government or the elite of "good people," "two forms of autocracy which has [sic] supplanted the democracy here as it has everywhere democracy has been tried."[25] The great man theory permeates the *Upbuilders*, where Steffens personified the good in Mark

<hr />

[22] *Ibid.*, 379.
[23] See Cheslaw, "An Intellectual Biography of Lincoln Steffens," 87-88.
[24] Steffens, *Shame*, 63.   [25] *Ibid.*

Fagan and Everett Colby of New Jersey, Ben Lindsey of Colorado, Rudolph Spreckels of California, and William U'Ren of Oregon. Six years after Minneapolis, Steffens still felt that "wherever the people have found a leader who was loyal to them; brave; and not too far ahead, there they have followed him, and there has been begun the solution of our common problem; the problem of the cities, states, and nations—the problem of civilized living in large communities."[26] In this leadership principle much of Progressive political theory was anchored.

The principal reason why the muckrakers married reform to progressive leadership was that they felt that the complexity of public administration was beyond the understanding of the average citizen and the exercise of rational authority beyond his ability. The natural leader was like a district attorney who showed the people, "a jury that can't be fixed," the alternatives and methods of political action— and yet stood "between the people and their raw undigested impulses."[27]

Nearly all of the Progressives were deeply influenced by the German use of the burgomasters, the professional municipal administrators who enjoyed an almost indefinite term of office. A month after the magazine's exposure of St. Louis, McClure wrote from the continent, "so far as I can find out many German cities, probably the majority of them, are about as well organized as our best business is in America."[28] Conscious of the efficient oil and oatmeal millers' monopolies, he could "not say that they are as well organized as, for example, the 'Standard Oil' or 'Canadian' concerns, but they remind me of those concerns in their accuracy, their experts, their carefulness and economy and so on, and the sense of honour in public matters is as keen as that of the most sensitive business man in busi-

[26] Steffens, *Upbuilders* (New York, 1909), vii.
[27] Steffens to Heney, June 1, 1908, Steffens Papers; *Emporia Gazette*, Jan. 2, 1902.
[28] McClure to Phillips, Dec. 9, 1903, McClure Papers.

ness relations in America."[29] Just as the Pennsylvania Railroad needed specialists to make engineering decisions, so did government need trained personnel to decide questions which the people could not solve "because they are incompetent to do so."[30]

As early as 1900 Baker had reported a deep interest "in what I called the 'bureaucracy' of Germany," and he, along with Phillips, Steffens, and Miss Tarbell, all familiar with German governmental practices, contrasted them favorably with those of America.[31] Many of *McClure's* articles extolled the superiority of the German system, and McClure himself longed to send Steffens abroad to write it up. Germany's low murder, disease, and fire rates pleased him immensely, but there were other reasons. "I had a most interesting talk with the Professor of the University of Leipsic," he wrote in 1903; "he told me that the City of Leipsic owned a certain tract of land which would have been very suitable for the building of working-men's homes, but they held the land until it became greater in value and then sold it at a larger price, too large for working men to buy, and he spoke of this as a bad thing for the people."[32] McClure was astonished: "if an American city did this it would be looked after as a model."[33] The socialization of natural monopolies and the care of the city's poor were administered "with an expert knowledge and a carefullness [sic] that is astonishing."[34] McClure was conversant with Frederick Howe's work on European cities and agreed with him that German cities "are true democracies."[35] Eventually, McClure and a whole generation of reformers were to

[29] *Ibid.*

[30] McClure, Speech at Race Betterment Conference, Jan. 10, 1914, *ibid.*

[31] Baker, *American Chronicle*, 103.

[32] McClure to Phillips, Dec. 9, 1903, McClure Papers.

[33] *Ibid.*   [34] *Ibid.*

[35] McClure, "The Science of Political and Industrial Self-Organization," 1933, manuscript in New York Public Library.

identify the city manager type of government with the burgomaster system.

The good boss was not only a specialist in political administration, a counterpart to Veblen's engineers who could make the economic order hum without the captains of industry; he was a leader, like Tom Johnson or Governor La Follette, who roused the citizens to action against privilege. "What we need," Baker wrote during Taft's presidency, "is a leader who will lay down fundamental principles, then tell us how we should meet immediate problems."[36] As revealed in the *Upbuilders*, the leader possessed this characteristic and more. He was part of the natural elite, one who stood for morality against the interests, who not only articulated political questions which the electorate decided, but like Walter Fisher in Chicago, actually manipulated behind the scenes in the precinct to get the public good effected. The role of the leader was much like the "Legislator" in Rousseau's *Social Contract;* he stood above faction, representing in himself the interests of the people. He was a lawgiver whose instinct rose above popular mandate.

"Is Democracy possible?" Steffens asked of St. Louis.[37] He soon concluded that not democracy but a leader could end government by injunction, general lawlessness, and unregulated laissez faire. In the final analysis the fight for a free count was not as important as the struggle against the shadow government after election. "What do you think of a civilization which makes it necessary to fight for the mere chance of fighting for the right?" he wrote Francis Heney, who was thinking of a political career; "it can't be a superficial disease can it?"[38] While both were desirable, democracy was not so important finally as good gov-

[36] Baker, Notebook "M," July 2, 1911, 6, 7, Baker Papers.
[37] Steffens, *Shame*, 101, 281.
[38] Steffens to Heney, Sept. 26, 1909, Steffens Papers.

ernment. And it was the "man nearest to the key to the situation," the strategic leader, who made for good service.[39]

Not surprisingly, these new Hamiltonians believed that a powerful executive made such Populist-oriented reforms as the initiative, referendum, and recall of little use. Despite the fact that *McClure's* ran Burton J. Hendrick's series on William S. U'Ren's experimentation in Oregon in 1910, Seattle's use of the recall, and the Des Moines system, which combined the initiative and the referendum with the city commission, the staff remained skeptical of such devices.[40] "Ask a business manager if a new way of discharging an employee is going to help build up an efficient organization," McClure told his Progressive friends, adding: "how can people determine laws of initiative and referendum?"[41] While McClure wanted to "throw away this bizarre stuff," Steffens was closer to the consensus, feeling, "I don't regard them as cures, but only as tools designed to make government represent the common interest of a community of human beings. . . ."[42] Nor did any think that the resulting "representative government will correct all evils"; only with a properly led attack against privilege could the nation "make such intelligent progress as they are making in England, France, and Germany toward the solution of the social and economic injustice which underlies most of our so-called political and moral evils."[43]

Who was the man in whom these lovers of the father image placed their eschatological hope for national redemption? Who was to attack the injustices? Certainly the ebulient Roosevelt, a veritable Thor, had the prerequisite character and energy. But he spurned the muckrakers when the

[39] Steffens, *Letters*, I, 190.

[40] See *McClure's*, xxx (May, 1910), 97; xxxvii (July, 1911), 235; xxxvii (Aug., 1911), 435; xxxvii (Sept., 1911), 505; xxxvii (Oct., 1911), 647.

[41] McClure, Speech at Race Betterment Conference, Jan. 10, 1914, McClure Papers.

[42] Steffens, *Letters*, I, 195; Baker, Notebook "K," 158, Baker Papers.

[43] Steffens, *Letters*, I, 195.

muckraking movement had hardly begun, only to seek their support with the creation of the Progressive Party. But in the Progressive campaign Baker insisted that Roosevelt "obscures everything, reduces the campaign to one of rabid discussion of personalities."[44] Miss Tarbell agreed, "I wabble terribly whenever I see him face to face. If I don't mistake, the day is going to come when The American Magazine will have to fight the Colonel."[45] A few years later, still firmly behind the Progressive program, Phillips was permanently soured on the old Rough Rider: "personally, I would not vote for Theodore Roosevelt for any position of trust."[46]

Robert La Follette was "a dictator dictating democracy" and a likely candidate for Legislator.[47] But neither he, nor Eugene Debs, for whom many of the reformers felt a deep affection, could leave his imprint upon the movement.

Even William Randolph Hearst, who attempted, "like a rich man, to give the people democracy, as others of his sort gave charity or an art museum," was worthy of consideration.[48] Steffens chose Hearst as a biographical subject for the fledgling *American Magazine* because he "was driving toward his unannounced purpose to establish some measure of democracy, with patient but ruthless—force."[49] After the *American* article appeared, the *San Francisco Examiner* growled, "Mr. Steffens' Hearst is not just the one we know."[50]

After 1912, Progressivism's noisiest hour, many of the muckrakers flocked to the banner of Woodrow Wilson, whom they had often met through Boyden while at Princeton.[51] As Arthur Link has shown, Wilson self-consciously adopted enough of the nationalist program to attract

44 Baker, Notebook "M," Aug. 31, 1912, 22, Baker Papers.
45 Tarbell to Baker, May 3, 1911, *ibid.*
46 Phillips to White, April 5, 1916, White Papers.
47 Steffens, *Autobiography*, 485.
48 *Ibid.*, 543; *American Magazine*, LXIII (Nov., 1906), 1.
49 Steffens, *Autobiography*, 543.
50 E. C. Walcott to Baker, Oct. 25, 1906, Baker Papers.
51 Baker, Notebook "M," Aug. 21, 1912, 22, *ibid.*

broad Progressive support. With unabashed idol worship, Baker remained a Wilson partisan and published a half-dozen volumes on the President. Even the aged Andrew Carnegie concluded his autobiography expecting a sort of messianic renewal under Wilson.

A decade later, almost without exception, the *McClure's* muckrakers looked admiringly at the regime of Benito Mussolini.[52] Their support of a fascist dictatorship in their mature years probably bespeaks the influence of German ideals rather than the pragmatic utilitarianism of John Stuart Mill and the classical liberals. How else could William Allen White have justified his statement that "it is the character of the man elected and not the method of his election that really counts"?[53]

Not only did the *McClure's* muckrakers want the leadership principle legitimatized, but the counterpart of the criminal machine had its place as the benevolent boss's instrument of public welfare. The strong man needed his supporters. "I do not object to a machine," McClure stated in a debate with a member of the New York Republican machine of Senator Platt.[54] "In all human history, in private and public life alike, the strong man . . . always rules, as he always will and until God makes all the same height, that will be true," and yet he needed his *posse comitatus*.[55] And White, who felt "our leaders are the clean-bred children of a natural selection unknown before in human history," argued that the best method of ousting the boodlers was by "establishing another machine."[56]

The reformer's machine, as Steffens pointed out in articles on the Chicago Municipal Voters League and La Follette's

---

[52] Tarbell to Roseboro', Feb. 21, 1934, Tarbell Papers; Steffens, *Autobiography*, 812; Tarbell, *All in the Day's Work*, 38off. See John P. Diggins, "Flirtation with Fascism," *American Historical Review*, LXXI (Jan., 1966), 492.

[53] Emporia *Gazette*, Nov. 11, 1904.

[54] McClure, Speech at Twentieth Century Club, Jan. 30, 1904. McClure Papers.

[55] *Ibid.*   [56] White, *Old Order Changeth*, 252, 39.

Wisconsin Republicans, either created its own independent vote or else worked within the framework of a given party. In Chicago, "like the politicians, too, they were non-partisans."[57] Often they played off one party against another, or, if neither would cooperate, they ran independents. They organized the wards, made lists of voters, dickered with the local leaders and corrupt politicians, and traded their way towards better men. In short, Chicago had in Walter Fisher, "a reform boss, and in the Nine of the Municipal Voters' League, with their associated editors and able finance and advisory committees, a reform ring."[58]

Much along the same lines, Governor La Follette was a "proud man begging for the blessing of justice upon the meek, whom he organized and inspired to take it—any way."[59] The reformers of Wisconsin harkened to the message of the little giant, and "he showed them what the job was, asked them if they would do their part in their district; and so he built up an organized following so responsive to him that it was called a machine."[60] According to Steffens, even La Follette's opponents agreed that it was a "powerful political machine which came to control the Republican Party in Wisconsin."[61] In a like manner wherever reform leaders arose, they built an organization which served the practical function of funneling power into the hands of the civic-minded members of the community. This was the machinery necessary for the power struggle with the special interests. As White said in 1904, "methods are clean enough in and of themselves, it is dirty men who make dirty politics."[62] The final prize was to forge and enforce the laws. Laws represented a resolution of the power struggle in which the public played only a peripheral part. This was the system that dominated the church, the legislature, and the corporation.

[57] Steffens, *Shame*, 245.   [58] *Ibid.*, 263.
[59] Steffens, *Autobiography*, 458.   [60] *Ibid.*, 459.
[61] *Ibid.*
[62] Emporia *Gazette*, Nov. 11, 1904.

On the whole, "it is a good system," being "the best system of government there is."[63]

At times the leaders represented the people, as in the case of Bryan or Roosevelt, but their organizations stood for the interests. "I was at the last two national conventions," Steffens stated in May, 1908, "and the special interest controlled both of them."[64] Both parties were in danger of being dominated by economic interests, and "that interest is not the interest of the people of this country."[65] In the final analysis, he wrote in Steffenese, it was the "dominating personalities" which made "these organizations stand for the people public [sic] against private interests."[66] A political machine, then, characterized by a program of common interest to the people was a beneficial, necessary, and natural development.

A third principle of muckraker theory was the conversion of business' corporate plan of management into a benevolent institution. Applied to city government, this structure was known as the commission form of municipal government. McClure took a fancy towards the commission while Steffens was muckraking the states. But Steffens refused to write the project up, as he later insisted, because "didn't I know that the form of government did not matter?"[67] Both Washington, D.C., and Memphis had experimented with the commission, and in Washington a carnival of corruption had resulted. Steffens felt that administrative control of the cities, whether in the hands of reformers or politicians, remained for the most part extra-constitutional. With his general animus towards business, he was suspicious of the corporate structure applied to government.

McClure soon persuaded George K. Turner, who surrendered much of his hostility towards business in the process, it seems, to report on the experimental government of

---

[63] *Ibid.*, Dec. 30, 1901.
[64] Steffens to W. B. Colver, May 29, 1908, Steffens Papers.
[65] *Ibid.*   [66] *Ibid.*
[67] Steffens, *Autobiography*, 450.

246

storm-devastated Galveston, Texas.[68] "When masses of individuals set out to co-operate together to produce some given result or carry on some given enterprise," McClure argued, "it has been found that there is only one successful method of organizing and that method is by the election of what corresponds in all cases, without any exception, to what a board of directors is to a corporation."[69] Consisting of five departmental specialists, one a titulary major, the commission differed from the old mayor-council government as a "Board of Business Men" or a "body of Bank Directors" differed from a "body of politicians playing to the galleries and catering to friends."[70]

In October, 1906, *McClure's* published Turner's "Galveston: A Business Corporation." The result was extensive nation-wide modification of state codes to permit municipal adoption of the commission. The article, the first national notice taken of the commission, had an estimated reprint circulation of some 12,000,000 copies in the United States.[71] Several newspapers printed the piece in full, and Seattle, Washington, alone circulated 20,000 copies.[72] Such prominent personalities as Charles Eliot of Harvard became proponents of the new system.

Turner's "revolution in local government" had occurred when a storm destroyed one-sixth of the lives and one-third of the property of Galveston. A local committee of fifteen, organized by the businessmen to get national funds for harbor improvements, assumed control of the town.[73] "Galveston was viewed as a great ruined business, not a city," and the commissioners, owning most of the property in the town, localized responsibility by dividing the

[68] See Chalmers, *The Social and Political Ideas of the Muckrakers*, 22.
[69] McClure, Speech at Race Betterment Conference, Jan. 10, 1914. McClure Papers.
[70] McClure (?) to D. A. Montgomery, Jan. 29, 1910, *ibid.*
[71] McClure, "The Science of Political and Industrial Self-Organization," 1933, manuscript in New York Public Library.
[72] *McClure's*, xxviii (Jan., 1907), 338; xxviii (April, 1907), 686.
[73] *Ibid.*, xxvii (Oct., 1906), 611.

departments among themselves, on the model of the British ministries.[74] As Turner explained, the most important actions of the commissioners were to lower governmental expenses, close the saloons, and chase the criminals out of town. Unimportant was the fact that the first commissioners were not popularly elected.[75] It was government by natural aristocracy.

In reality, McClure told his readers, the commission was "merely New England town government by selectmen— the most famous and successful single development of democracy in America."[76] He suggested editorially the commissioners who he thought could solve New York's municipal problems. The suggested commission consisted of Theodore Roosevelt as Mayor, J. P. Morgan as commissioner of finances, Leonard Wood as commissioner of police, William G. McAdoo as commissioner of public works, and Elihu Root as commissioner of law.[77] "Only," he thought, "by the most thorough and revolutionary reforms along this line is there hope for the future of American democracy."[78] But his democracy was not Jeffersonian; it was public acquiescence in the rule of the capable. When Memphis adopted the commission shortly thereafter, the youthful prohibitionist, Ed Crump, was catapulted into power.

McClure's advocated the commission as the solution to all subnational problems. State legislatures, predicted the magazine, would soon become obsolete, and "from three to five names will take the place of the present unworkable system."[79] This was heralded as the beginning of a truly national, unitary form of government whereby the states would be reduced to the status of European provinces. "Whatever this conscience of democracy is," asserted White, "it is binding us into a closer union than we have known before, making us one blood in our common aspiration."[80]

[74] *Ibid.,* 615.
[75] *Ibid.,* xxxv (May, 1910), 97.
[76] *Ibid.,* xxiv (Nov., 1909), 128.
[77] *Ibid.,* 128ff.
[78] *Ibid.*
[79] *Ibid.,* xxxvi (Nov., 1910), 119.
[80] White, *Old Order Changeth,* 168.

Within eight years after Turner's Galveston article, 350 cities with one-fifth of the nation's urban population had adopted the commission, and the number of reformed cities increased to 500 by 1917. Thereafter the city manager system became a more popular type of municipal government. The old mayoralty system with select and aldermanic boards passed generally into disuse.[81]

The extensive use of independent regulatory commissions, beginning with Roosevelt, who had sat on the Civil Service Commission, is evidence that the reformers placed great store in small appointed bodies of experts. That this resembled a business corporation could be questioned, but that it represented a major modification of traditional democracy cannot be denied.

It can be seen that the muckrakers—and on this question Miss Tarbell was not as outspoken as her colleagues—not only desired to imitate the most effective practices of their opponents in the shadow government; they wanted to see political power centralized and nationalized, much in the manner later advocated by Croly in *The Promise of American Life*. The locus of power was the executive branch, and it was there the popular Roosevelt "became a force for righteousness—the first leader the nation has developed since Lincoln."[82]

At no point does this predilection become more obvious than in the suspension of the muckraker animus against extra-constitutional prerogatives when the executive branch exercised them. Neither the antics of the Speaker of the House nor the courts fared well in muckraker reports, but Roosevelt's "extra-constitutional" intervention into the anthracite coal strike in Pennsylvania was considered enlightened.[83] It was only after the defeat of the Progressive Party in 1912 that the muckrakers became disillusioned with Roosevelt's methods, and even then the bard in Em-

[81] See Oswald Ryan, *Municipal Freedom: A Story of the Commission Government* (New York, 1915), 5; Henry Aubrey Toulmin, Jr., *The City Manager, A New Profession* (New York 1917), 268-79.

[82] White, *Old Order Changeth*, 144.   [83] *Ibid.*, 200.

poria continued to write him panegyrics. Except in the light of a Hamiltonian tradition, it is difficult to understand White's praise of Roosevelt's leadership: "Without his personality to dramatize the growing righteousness of the people, it is not difficult to imagine what calamity of misdirected radicalism might have been visited upon the nation. If that righteous wrath of the people at the selfish forces of society had not found expression through President Roosevelt, it would have been voiced through demagogues at an awful cost to the nation. His genius lies not in making sentiment, but in directing it into sane, conservative, workable laws."[84]

This view is expressed in *The Old Order Changeth*, a book which Hofstadter mislabels as "full of references to the intelligence, the self-restraint, the morality, the breadth of view of the average man, the emergent New Citizen."[85] In this volume, White, like his colleagues, placed more value on proper order than upon popular will. "There must always be a ruling class in America," he observed, and although he had an optimistic faith in the average man, he did not want "government by public clamor."[86] Government by the people was not "necessarily the best government," and unless properly led was no better than popular rule by the "red-headed or the one-eyed men or the short-haired women."[87] White feared lest the overzealous advocate of fundamental democracy "make a fetish of it."[88]

Hofstadter concludes that "although it was necessary for these Progressives to make some use of organization, they had a profound inherited distrust of it."[89] They seem not as concerned with the problem of organization as with efficiency and the structuring of power. Their aping of the shadow government, their dissatisfaction with the existing constitutional structure, and their appeal to the public

[84] *Ibid.*, 146. [85] Hofstadter, *Age of Reform*, 258.
[86] White, *Old Order Changeth*, 119, 131, 120.
[87] Emporia *Gazette*, Dec. 30, 1901.
[88] White, *Old Order Changeth*, 169.
[89] Hofstadter, *Age of Reform*, 260.

aimed at ousting the immigrant boss and the special financial interests bespeak their intents. Their distrust was directed towards an organization which they did not control. Once it was safely controlled by the proper leadership, they were willing to trust vast national powers to the executive branch. The moral, social, and economic problems of society were too urgent to maintain a Jeffersonian mistrust of government.

In conclusion, by 1910 the muckrakers, those at *McClure's* and those on the *American*, sought to defend the public interest against strong private political and economic groups which retarded the accommodation of government to progress. To effect this they relied upon the techniques of the shadow government. Reform meant bringing efficient, strong men into government, the creation of a political machine to support them, and the use, whenever possible, of appointed experts to supplement their labors. While institutional changes such as the direct primary, the initiative, and the referendum might help bring this transformation about, the muckrakers intended not to become "so absorbed in the *means* that we overlook the *end*."[90] Adaptation to the moral ends distilled from social Darwinism was more important than the democratic organization of government. Even during the Progressive campaign Baker could write that the rule of the people "is nothing," that it was untrue to say "majorities are always right."[91]

Supporting a structure of government that placed power in the hands of the executive department (with the Supreme Court hopefully being deprived of the right of judicial review), advocating a nationalism that equated state reform with state dissolution, and harboring a suspicion of popular irrationalism—admixed with a championing of racial justice, feminine rights, and temperance—identified the muckrakers with the pre-Civil War nationalism.[92] The

[90] Baker, Notebook "M," July 2, 1911, 5, Baker Papers.
[91] *Ibid.*, 11; Baker, Notebook "II," 1914, 91, *ibid.*
[92] See Baker, Notebook "K," 1908, 144, *ibid.*

state stood above the individual, and above the state the overarching laws of social and economic development, with which public law had to conform.[93]

What were the "great broad principles of economic or moral law" with which the state had to come to terms?[94] That is the subject of the remaining chapters.

[93] *McClure's*, XXII (Dec., 1903), 197.
[94] Baker, Notebook "C," 64, Baker Papers.

Chapter XIII. The Finale
of Laissez-Faire

THE COLLECTIVE mind of McClure's staff shows more diversity of view on economic questions than on political ones. McClure himself was less informed on these matters, and, beyond a few elementary guide posts, alllowed the staff to assert itself. It was also in this area that the collective mind underwent the greatest change—from an extreme friendliness towards trusts at the second inauguration of McKinley to a strong New Nationalist position during the Progressive period, when, in the final analysis, the first function of the redeemed state was envisioned as controlling the economic order. A study of these vicissitudes of thought throws more light upon the radical direction in which many of the Progressive muckrakers were going by 1912. Just as politics was the principal domain of Steffens and White, Baker and Miss Tarbell most assiduously pondered economic problems and were the special spokesmen on these questions.

In 1894 as a reporter watching the strikes and marches of Debs and Coxey, Ray Stannard Baker bought Benjamin Kidd's *Social Evolution*, the best book "at least for me at that time and in that mood."[1] Kidd, whose brand of social Darwinism resembled Lester Ward's, delineated in sharp focus the problems which for over a decade had been of little interest save to single taxers, socialists, Bellamy Nationalists, and certain academicians, such as the coterie around Ely and Commons who composed the American Economic Association and the American Political Science Association. Baker used Kidd's book as background reading while preparing *Our New Prosperity*. "No one," the Englishman wrote in a passage which Baker underlined, "who engages in a serious study of the period of transition

[1] Baker, *American Chronicle*, 58; Benjamin Kidd, *Social Evolution* (New York, 1894).

through which our Western civilization is passing at the present time can resist the conclusion that we are rapidly approaching a time when we shall be face to face with social and political problems, graver in character and more far-reaching in extent than any which have been hitherto encountered."[2] Kidd's description of individualists and collectivists, "into which society was slowly becoming organized," was the principal question which aroused Baker's interest.[3] That, in a word, was the largest problem confronting the country. The old laissez-faire competitive system, although imperfectly applied, created severe conflicts over control of the railroads, freight elevators, rebates, free passes, tariff, currency, business influence in government, and industrial violence. But during the muckraking period one question stood above all others—that of the trusts.

John Moody, who was to write with George K. Turner a *McClure's* series entitled "The Masters of Capital," published *The Truth about Trusts* in 1904. The book contained a diagram of the major combines. Commencing with the Spanish-American War, an estimated 300 trusts developed in a half-dozen years, led by Morgan's U.S. Steel, and by 1908 Burton J. Hendrick estimated their number at nearly 500.[4] Gabriel Kolko in *The Triumph of Conservatism* has recently challenged the contention that wealth was concentrating.[5] But his challenge is not completely persuasive. Relegated to a footnote is the significant fact that by 1909 almost one percent of all establishments in the United States accounted for 43.8 percent of the value of all products.[6] It still remains for someone to challenge Marx, Weber, Darwin, Acton, and Commons that monopolies of

[2] Kidd, *Social Evolution*, viii, copy in Baker Papers, Jones Memorial Library, Amherst, Massachusetts.

[3] *Ibid.*, 3.

[4] John Moody, *The Truth About Trusts* (Chicago, 1904), xi; *McClure's*, xxxi (Oct., 1908), 664.

[5] Gabriel Kolko, *The Triumph of Conservatism* (New York, 1963), 27-56.

[6] *Ibid.*, 309.

funds, characteristics, or power are unnatural processes. Against the new development of the trusts stood the almost impotent seven-hundred-word Sherman Act of 1890 and the earlier Interstate Commerce Act, enforced in 1904 by only four men in Roosevelt's Department of Justice. The philosophical problem which Kidd had foreseen a decade earlier—the one versus the many—confronted the country in a menacing manner.

Kidd concluded that the interest of the individual was not necessarily the interest of the many, as the Benthamites argued, that truly laissez-faire economics was nonexistent, and that as a result the socialization of wealth was destined to accelerate. It took Baker almost a decade to concur with these conclusions. A chapter in Baker's *Our New Prosperity*, published in 1900, dealt with the trust problem, but, as yet inarticulate in critical economic concepts, Baker had difficulty in explaining the novel phenomenon. He interpreted the outcry against "capital and monied combinations of every kind" as merely the "old, old writhing of the debtor under the crowding of the creditor."[7] Obviously Baker's ears were full of the din of the Populists and their cheap money crusade of 1896. In 1899 William Allen White had offered the same explanation: "Let a politician be out of an issue and he takes up the cause of the Great Plain People against the Tyrannical Trusts."[8] Several days at the Chicago Conference on Trusts only convinced White that "it would be as sensible to legislate against the church, or against matrimony, or against banks, or against government, as it would be to legislate against the Trusts as Trusts."[9]

These statements typify the *McClure's* group's passive attitude toward the concentration of wealth at the turn of the century. As the years went by, this posture changed,

---

[7] See Baker, *Our New Prosperity* (New York, 1900), 17-20; Chalmers, "The Social and Political Ideas of the Muckrakers," 195.

[8] *Emporia Gazette* (w), Sept. 14, 1899.

[9] *Ibid.*

undergoing at least three stages, each more critical and intense than the earlier.

With the inauguration of muckraking in 1903, *McClure's* first reaction to the monopolies was a haughty moral indictment of the commercial spirit, the profit motive, and the self-seeking nature of a business career. From beginning to end, as Miss Tarbell admitted in her autobiography, her *History of Standard Oil* was replete with references to the "ethical side" of business. She assumed that "there is no cure for business evils but in an increasing scorn of unfair play."[10] In this she was but following the early puritanical teachings of Richard T. Ely, who thought the religious ethic the proper means of limiting abuses of the economic order.[11] Having devoted over a dozen and a half articles to the history of Standard, following it from Pennsylvania to Ohio to Kansas, Miss Tarbell substantiated this belief with a focused portrait of John D. Rockefeller. The result convinced the tycoon that she was nothing more than a misguided woman. Her memorable "character" study of the tycoon began with quotations from chapter XVIII of Machiavelli's *The Prince* and attempted to demonstrate that it was Rockefeller's intent to be both loved and feared. The financier's public reputation was marked by kindness, piety, philanthropy and justice, but these were only the externals, she felt. Privately, he was amoral, ruthless, and "money mad."[12] George W. Alger, a progressive somewhat skeptical of muckraking, filed a minority view when he thought her work "exact in statement."[13] She concluded that the "basis of everything in business integrity is moral, not economical" and necessitates the recognition that "public interest is higher than your own."[14]

[10] Ida Tarbell, *History of Standard Oil* (2 vols., New York, 1904), II, 292.

[11] See "B. B.—Economic Order," 1933?, Tarbell Papers.

[12] *McClure's*, XXV (July, 1905), 227.

[13] *The Letters of Theodore Roosevelt*, V, 188; *McClure's*, XXIV (Dec., 1904), 223.

[14] *New York Herald Magazine*, April 1, 1928.

Miss Tarbell was the main purveyor of a "moral" history, a contempt for crass materialistic ethics, a position which she never seems to have changed, and her colleagues often shared this presupposition. "Greed is at the bottom of the evil," wrote White in the early days of the trusts, and Steffens echoed the sentiment: "the commercial spirit is the spirit of profit, not patriotism," of trade, not principle, of credit, not honor.[15] Property was a stewardship, wrote Baker, a moral "trust, held by the individual for the good of the whole people, & not to lavish" upon one's own selfish desires.[16] When he wrote "The Story of Life Insurance," Hendrick pressed the idea further and made a subtle criticism of Carnegie's *Gospel of Wealth*. He found Carnegie's benevolent law of compound interest threatening the law of human morality because the "people have forgotten the old ideals," and were inclined to commercialize life insurance, which, Hendrick held, was "not a business."[17] Instead, insurance was a trust, a sacred trust, which the people committed to the responsibility of a few capitalists.[18] If misused, the altruistic forces of the people, allied with democracy, were going to sweep away the financial plutocracy. This movement "in our national politics toward the more equitable distribution of our common wealth is from the Puritan's conscience," added the voice from Emporia.[19]

The exposure of a clandestine alliance between economic interests and political powers by *McClure's* slowly led the staff to a second and more sophisticated level of criticism. This stage was characterized by an attempt to discover the basic economic laws underlying the behavior of American industry. Miss Tarbell's work on Standard Oil, Moody's and Turner's "Masters of Capital" series, Hendrick's "His-

---

[15] *Emporia Gazette* (w), Sept. 14, 1899; Steffens, *Shame*, 7.
[16] Baker, Notebook "C," 1902-06, 125, Baker Papers; see White, *Old Order Changeth*, 243.
[17] *McClure's*, XXVII (May, 1906), 37.   [18] *Ibid.*, 38.
[19] White, *Old Order Changeth*, 167.

tory of Great American Fortunes," and numerous financial articles such as Baker's work on the railroads described the economic order with an increasing usage of radical, even Marxist, terminology.

But on the whole Miss Tarbell is a significant exception from this development, for on the trusts, as on the tariff, she followed the older teachings of Adam Smith's *Wealth of Nations*. Miss Tarbell never held any brief for monopolies under any guise, as was to be expected from her background. The announcement for her series on Standard was a credo of classical economics. The free market was a natural phenomenon, monopoly an attempt to pervert it.[20] Later in an article on "Commercial Machiavellianism" she elaborated: With monopoly the "captains of industry" besieged independent business in much the same way that Vicksburg had been cut off from its supply, and like mines under the breastwork, the monopolists, dedicated to things and success, not principles, controlled the lines of national credit.[21] Although Miss Tarbell seems never to have changed her mind, *McClure's* soon adopted the official position that concentration of wealth was more natural than the market posited by Adam Smith, and in the "Masters of Capital" the "inevitability of this movement has never been shown more clearly."[22] It was, of course, Karl Marx in *Das Kapital* who first argued that the concentration of wealth and of the monopolistic means of production into a few hands was inevitable.

No one accepted this stance more abruptly or completely than Ray Stannard Baker. Kidd's *Social Evolution* undoubtedly paved the way. Until 1905 Baker had identified himself with the conservative forces of stability. The governor of Colorado, "a banker himself, closely identified with conservative economic interests of the state, and therefore unlikely to make exaggerated statements" was the

[20] *McClure's*, XXII (Nov., 1903), 112.
[21] *Ibid.*, XXVI (March, 1906), 454. [22] *Ibid.*, XXXVI (Feb., 1911), 482.

lauded opponent of I. W. W. lawlessness.[23] With pleasure Roosevelt read this assessment, found it "absolutely fair & correct," and Baker accepted the President's private thanks in Washington, leaving under the impression that "there is no doubt that under the great weight of the problems which confront him, he is developing, getting a greater grasp on the deep principles—becoming, in short, more conservative."[24]

Prior to the bankers' panic of 1903 Baker disparaged the left which was "gropingly reaching toward socialism without knowing what socialism really is."[25] While socialism was the "extremest form of democracy," it was wholly impracticable until the ills of republicanism could be resolved. McClure was more intransigent, identifying both socialism and bossism with the "unreasoning, passionate gusts of popular opinion."[26] When a "distinguished and patriotic man, high in the public service" remarked that blighted economic conditions made socialism imminent, the magazine quickly noted that "he is mistaken. The coming 'ism' is not Socialism; the coming 'ism' is Patriotism."[27] Yet in a short while, principally under the influence of a Marxist analysis, Baker, like most of the *McClure's* group—with the exception of Miss Tarbell—felt the demise of capitalism at hand.

By the time of the schism and the founding of the *American,* Baker was already writing in his private notebook that the courts, by strict interpretation of "ancient law," were mere lackeys of the great trusts: "They stand for individualism, they deify competition & the doctrine of laissez-faire, they see nothing of the great new movements."[28] The newest movement was the restriction of capi-

---

23 *Ibid.,* XXII (May, 1904), 43.
24 Baker to Father, Jan. 29, 1905, Baker Papers.
25 *McClure's,* XXII (Dec., 1903), 197.
26 *Ibid.,* XXXVI (Nov., 1910), 119.   27 *Ibid.,* XXI (July, 1903), 336.
28 Baker, Notebook "J," 128ff, Baker Papers.

259

tal by the state, or, as White wrote John Phillips back at the editorial office, "the natural end of it all is the control of capital looking towards its abolition."[29] "Break the news gently to the shade of Karl Marks [*sic*]," he added, "but 'Babylon is fallen, is fallen, is fallen. . . .' "[30]

Babylon was being undermined by an unearned increment, concentrated in the hands of a do-nothing class. William Allen White coined the phrase "stolen value" to describe the spoils of the exploiter. It was not an exact correlation of surplus value, but rather resembled Aquinas' definition of usury as unfair profit. "I cannot, but believe," White wrote a skittish man taking exception to his use of the phrase, "that financial transactions, which place a burden upon the users of any commodity that is not found in the legitimate cost of that commodity, make 'Stolen Value.' "[31] Monopolistic profits were the case in point. While believing in an incentive, he could "not believe that the wrecker's profit, or that the pirate's profit is legitimate."[32] A half dozen years later, White was still confiding to Baker that only a preventive revolution would "stop America from considering seriously & with some enthusiasm the problem of the equation of him who earns what he does not get as he is related to him who gets what he does not earn."[33] In the meanwhile Baker was working his way to a more advanced position still.

Baker jeopardized his association with the *American* by insisting that the bourgeoisie was an exploiting leisure class. "Now the thing is *true*," he unsuccessfully protested when the offending passages were deleted from his article, "and to my mind essential as showing the comparative service to society of the workers and the stockholders (who get and do nothing, who receive much 'without turning a hand'). . . ."[34] His articles in the *American*, "represent-

[29] White to Phillips, Sept. 9, 1903, White Papers.
[30] *Ibid.*
[31] White to George F. Dominick, June 5, 1907, *ibid.*
[32] *Ibid.*   [33] White to Baker, Aug. 28, 1913, *ibid.*
[34] Baker to Boyden, April 9, 1912, Tarbell Papers.

ing the fundamental social conflict between the few and the many," unsettled even Roosevelt, who warmly advised amending this "twisted stress."[35] While seeing that "Socialism is, ultimately, the only way out" in 1908, Baker did not believe its millennial reign was imminent.[36] There were no responsible men to live in it. "When I attend Socialistic meetings and hear the intemperate clamor of half ignorant men (themselves not prepared to exercise the self-restraint so necessary to socialism, themselves not willing to become servants) I am afraid," he wrote.[37]

In a subtle way the Marxist analysis crept into *McClure's* great histories of corporate wealth. Burton J. Hendrick, who was to find little enticing in Croly's New Nationalism, observed concerning the makers of great American fortunes which he chronicled: "They have learned the lesson of the unearned increment too well."[38] Such talk did not yet rate well with McClure. He wrote from Europe that Hendrick could better spend his time by writing up "one of the great fundamental questions of the time," labor.[39] But hardly was the "History of Great American Fortunes" finished than John Moody and Turner retold the story of the masters of capital and the law of compound interest which caused the accumulation and concentration of great wealth.

The phrases "unearned increment" and "inevitable concentration of wealth" bespeak a familiarity with a radical economic terminology. Further, as in orthodox socialism, politics was exposed as the unequal partner of wealth. Steffens had blamed the businessman for municipal corruption, and belatedly the magazine followed his lead.

It was in *McClure's* that the concentration of the nation's railroads into six loci of power was first exposed, that Standard had its escutcheon permanently besmirched, and

---

[35] Roosevelt to Baker, June 3, 1908, Baker Papers.
[36] Baker, Notebook "J," 1907-1908, 127-28, *ibid.*
[37] *Ibid.*
[38] Quoted in Chalmers, "The Social and Political Ideas of the Muckrakers," 107-108.
[39] McClure to Cameron Mackenzie, May 21, 1908, McClure Papers.

that the old, old money of the Astors was deemed as malignant as that of such *nouveaux riches* as Thomas Fortune Ryan and his ilk among the street railway financiers. Having started their careers in almost complete ignorance of Marx, the journalists quickly graduated into a recognition that the "fetish of capitalism" was delivering national power to a plutocracy.[40] This was the principal burden, William Allen White asserted, of his *The Old Order Changeth*: "I am taking the movement to divorce business from politics, and control business by politics first in cities, second in states, third in the federal government, and it is remarkable how uniformly the people are working together all over America toward this common end."[41] White's remark came after the panic of 1907, which serves as an arbitrary dividing line between the muckrakers' analysis of the economic system and their adoption of anti-capitalist techniques. It coincided with a rather bitter panic and depression.

After diagnosing the nature of the plutocracy, the muckrakers proposed to capture the state and fortify it against the assaults from special economic interests. It was at this juncture that White tentatively suggested the creation of an economically neutral state as a disinterested arbiter between competing interests and classes.[42] Hofstadter has seen this olympian view of the state, untainted as it was by doctrinaire commitments, uninfluenced by vast alliances of interests called parties, as a part of the progressive intellectual ideology. Rather than a conclusion, White's neutral state was a temporary compromise worked out on the high road towards economic nationalism.

As long as the state lay entangled in the tentacles of Norris' *Octopus*, like a lady in distress, questions of how to obtain the public welfare remained paramount. The

---

[40] See Tarbell, *All in the Day's Work*, 135; White, *Autobiography*, 216.

[41] White to Phillips, Sept. 9, 1908, White Papers.

[42] White, *Old Order Changeth*, 136ff.

problems of whom the state should represent and what should be done with the trusts were neither mutually exclusive nor sequential, but they were so treated by the muckrakers. And so, almost imperceptibly, *McClure's* gravitated from political towards economic considerations after 1908. By the time of the insurgency against Taft over his tariff and conservation policies, the state was generally recognized as an instrument for the instigation of New Nationalism.

To return to the crucial trust question, it is in dealing with the large aggregations of wealth that the radical propensities of the muckrakers can be placed in perspective.

In May, 1906, Ellery Sedgwick had tersely described the three possible solutions to the trust problem as the positions of Eugene Debs, Herbert Spencer, and Theodore Roosevelt.[43] It was possible to socialize the trusts, to let them rule, or to attempt to preserve some vestige of the free market economy. These were basically the same alternatives offered by Judge Peter S. Grosscup in a *McClure's* article, "How to Save the Corporation."[44] Grosscup, holder of a Knox College degree, had gained fame by issuing an injunction against Debs and the newly organized American Railway Union in 1894 and later by reversing Kenesaw M. Landis' $29,000,000 fine on Standard Oil for accepting rebates. His decisions included an attempt to close the World's Columbian Exposition on Sunday and an enjoinment of the beef trust.[45]

Grosscup said that the development of the trusts must result in either paternalism, socialism, or some form of modified laissez-faire. Much in the manner of Louis Brandeis at a later date, he quickly dismissed corporate paternalism or state socialism which would destroy private opportunity. Feeling that the "antidote for monopoly is competition," Grosscup argued for the restoration of individual oppor-

---

[43] *American Magazine*, LXII (May, 1906), 112.
[44] *McClure's*, XXIV (Feb., 1905), 443ff.
[45] See *American Magazine*, LXI (Dec., 1905), 219.

tunity through a system of state controls, such as prohibition of stock-watering and other malpractices of Wall Street. As this pillar of conservatism saw it, this was the only way to broaden individual ownership in property and to save the private corporation.

Grosscup and Sedgwick were only following the alternatives already delineated by Jeremiah Jenks at Cornell, Richard T. Ely and John R. Commons at Hopkins and the University of Wisconsin, Henry C. Adams at the University of Michigan, and a score of other professional economists, including John Bates Clark and John Graham Brooks. While Commons and Ely would have nationalized all "natural monopolies"—principally public utilities—and destroyed others by cutting the tariff, more conservative economists voiced a disclaimer.[46] John Bates Clark wanted enforced competition, he wrote in 1905 in *The Control of Trusts*, yet his means of obtaining it precluded any tampering with the high tariff.[47] Jeremiah Jenks, who had published a volume at *McClure's* book company on the trusts, like Ely was much impressed by the Chicago Conference on Trusts. He saw a need for state-enforced and controlled competition. In 1900 he gave his assent to the general report of the United States Industrial Commission of which he was a member, advocating a systematic and universal accounting procedure for all interstate corporations—to be inspected by agents from the I.C.C. The Commission, with Jenks's support, went further and recommended government-regulated freight rates.[48] So even before the Northern Securities suit revealed Roosevelt's predilections in 1902, the trained economists had formed a battle line over the fate of laissez-faire, with Ely and Commons prepared to officiate at its demise.

[46] Richard T. Ely, *Monopolies and Trusts* (New York, 1900), 244, 256, 263-64.

[47] John Bates Clark, *The Control of Trusts* (New York, 1905), v, 42, 47, 60, 77.

[48] See Jeremiah Jenks, *The Trust Problem* (New York, 1900), 221ff, 235ff.

As progressivism became increasingly an economic movement, Grosscup's alternatives became more solidified positions. Eugene Debs, since 1898 the leader of American socialism, gained an increasing number of votes in his quixotic
bid for the presidency, but, of more consequence, Upton
Sinclair, David Graham Phillips, and Charles Edward Russell flocked to the red banner. In the tradition of Marx, the
socialists saw that their advantage lay in maintaining
an unreformed economic system because capitalism would
die more quickly without stitches or transfusions. "The
quicker the concentration of wealth is completed," Sinclair
taunted Baker as he prepared the "Railroads on Trial,"
the better it aids us & the over riding [*sic*] of all restraints
by the big bugs was part of the program we laid out two
generations ago."[49]

By necessity the muckrakers had to come to grips with
socialism, from which they had drawn so much of their own
analysis. Should they marry themselves to its conclusions as
well as to its analysis of capitalism? Sinclair tittered over
their fumbling attempts to find other paths. Miss Tarbell,
quite differently from her student days, wanted nothing
to do with socialism and hesitated to cite *Wealth Against
Commonwealth*, fearing that that bugbear was its purported
destination. Most of the *McClure's* group wrestled with the
problem—and none more sincerely than Ray Stannard
Baker.

To most of the muckrakers the concept of brotherhood
was more important than individualism, altruism more
worthy than self-interest, and public ownership of property, in many instances, more advantageous than private.
Their reasons varied somewhat. Their view of man's organistic unity, cohesiveness, was principally based on a belief
in a social evolution which will be discussed in more detail
later. Thus the classless longing of the socialists, which
would end the ceaseless dissensions of the industrial so-

[49] Upton Sinclair to Baker, Nov. 2, 1905?, Baker Papers.

ciety, was an alluring vision to the *McClure's* gang, among whom Walter Rauschenbusch's gospel enjoyed a high vogue. But while it was easy to view a race or a species as an organistic whole in terms of evolution, reform, as the ancient prophets claimed, lay in the individual heart. There were a few problems, perhaps even contradictions, in how the role of the individual was related to society.

Like Rousseau, the *McClure's* group could compromise man's particular will with general will. Although not so subtly as Rousseau, an editorial of February, 1906, delineated the twofold role of every citizen, subject and sovereign, whereby private and public interests were attuned.[50] In the former capacity man confronted the law and in the latter was responsible for the welfare of the state. While this fitted well with the magazine's defense of a Legislator, it proved a limitation towards the acceptance of any doctrine that not only submerged the individual interest but drowned it.

Still socialism had its appeal. Baker, like most of his colleagues, saw the benefits of municipal socialism which Ely and Commons had advocated in the pattern of European cities for several decades. More crucially, the muckrakers' sense of Christian responsibility squared with the ideals of the American counterparts of the Fabians—Jane Addams, Debs, and Victor Berger.

In fact the socialist cause eventually attracted a number of the muckrakers. Two were Lincoln Steffens, who suggested that the *American Magazine* be turned into a party organ, and his protégé, Walter Lippmann, whom Steffens helped to organize a socialist club at Harvard. But neither was ever willing to surrender his role as a free spirit for the sake of the party. "It looks yellow not to come in," Lippmann wrote Sinclair, "but you know that is not the reason. Each of us can do only a little, and he ought to try to do what he can do best."[51] Even Cleveland Moffett wrote the

[50] *McClure's*, XXVI (Feb., 1906), 448.
[51] Walter Lippmann to Sinclair, May 6, 1914, Sinclair Papers.

editor of the *Appeal to Reason,* "I agree with you in most things and realize that it is necessary to do a certain amount of exaggerating in order to make any impression on some of our hide-bound conservatives and privileged classes."[52] Yet he refused party membership. Brand Whitlock was willing to visit Sinclair at Edge Moor and use his oratorical talents for the socialist cause, but he also shied at joining the movement.[53]

The element which separated the orthodox socialists and the muckrakers, despite their allied sympathies, was a broad one and is worth further investigation.

First, the antics of Haywood's International Workers of the World, anarchistic and violently revolutionary, were as alien to the orderly world envisioned by these progressives as they were to the humane Debs and his partisan followers. The very progressive reforms which often employed Marxist concepts forestalled the Marxist laws of dialectical process. This was anathema to those, such as Sinclair, who wanted the capitalistic society to fall under its own weight in its final imperialistic stages. There was, too, a repugnance towards the internationalism which socialism espoused.

Perhaps purposely, the muckrakers were often confused with the socialists. Perhaps this pressure was one ingredient in forcing them to articulate their positions more definitely after Roosevelt's indictment of the movement. One zealous editor echoed the President's toxin: "Socialism—that's where these leaders of the magazines and newspapers are headed for. The Sentimentalist who looks to find there the Kingdom of Brotherly Love upon Earth, the honest man, hysterical with anger at the crimes of high finance, the brave fool spoiling for a fight, the good citizen who says to himself, 'that the evil is so great the whole must be swept away—' all alike are following the lead of the statesmen

[52] Moffett to Sinclair, June 17, 1918, *ibid.*
[53] Whitlock to Sinclair, Dec. 29, 1910, Dec. 6, 1911, *ibid.*

of the yellow press towards the ruinous experiment of straight-out socialism."[54]

Such criticism was not brushed aside quickly. Under this pressure Baker in particular attempted to analyze his own feelings on the question. There were two sorts of people interested in socialism, he wrote the year Taft was elected, those who wanted to achieve its goals and those who were "backing towards Socialism, repelled by the excesses of individualism."[55] The second group, of which he considered himself a member, saw in public ownership of property a handy weapon to threaten capital: "when the abuses from which they shrink are cured, they will part company straight-way with the extremist." Admiring the church-like fellowship of the socialists, Baker echoed a sentiment in 1907 already expressed in *McClure's*, "to me nothing could be more unreal or improbable than an ideal state before we possess ideal men upon which to found it. . . ."

Baker's humane sentiments, his longing for the ideal state, his friendship with New York's leading socialists—members of the radical "X Club"—and his inability to accept any of the palliatives for capitalism finally led him to the fringes of socialism. Mary W. Ovington, a radical herself, was soon writing that he was coming her way; "if you are not a Socialist you certainly are not 'anything' that is trying to do half-way work."[56] After seeing Taft's lack of success, Baker's inner struggle intensified. He became absolutely convinced that socialism was "ultimately, the only way out," but yet he was afraid that the "clamor of half ignorant men" might befog such a solution.[57] This inner dialogue continued for a half-dozen years. Wanting greater socialization of industry by seizing it from the "luxurious, idle, degenerating rich people," advocating the nationaliza-

[54] *American Magazine*, LXII (May, 1906), 111.
[55] Baker, Notebook "I," March 14, 1907, Baker Papers. The rest of this paragraph is from the same source.
[56] Mary W. Ovington to Baker, July 2, 1909, *ibid.*
[57] Baker, Notebook "J," 1907-1908, 127-28, *ibid.*

tion of railroads, on the other hand Baker could not surrender the position that character and "individual self-control is, after all, the final & firm basis of society."[58]

Long before the Progressive campaign Baker had moved beyond the question of whether environment could change man's character. He began to place his hope in the "enormous possibilities of achievement *when men work together.*"[59] "We Socialists," he wrote M. F. Woodlock, "believe that this principle has un-dreamed-of possibilities of further application to the good of human society."[60] In the final analysis society's cooperation in taming the blind forces of nature was going to prove more "useful" than competition, and "we believe in the ultimate almost unlimited application of this idea to human affairs. . . ."[61] This inevitable process was slow, he felt, prodded not by revolution but by education and experimentation.

This was the theme of "The Man Possessed," an incident in Baker's *The Friendly Road,* published in 1913. The new man, a better man, "who can regard himself as a function, not an end of creation, has arrived," he wrote.[62] Baker had also arrived at a highly personalized socialism.[63] This was the high-water mark of his commitment. He could not accept class warfare, materialism, or an attempt to build character through the control of environment. Rather, Baker took many of his socialist principles and liberally mixed them with instrumentalism. Having ghosted Robert La Follette's memoirs for the *American,* Baker, it would appear, ended up adopting most of the Senator's position on the practicality of economic experimentation, free from any rigid, ideological matrix.

Most of the *McClure's* group underwent a similar ideo-

58 Quotations from Chalmers, "The Social and Political Ideas of the Muckrakers," 207.
59 Baker to M. F. Woodlock, Sept. 8, 1913, Baker Papers.
60 *Ibid.*   61 *Ibid.*
62 David Grayson, *The Friendly Road* (New York, 1913), 255.
63 Semonche, "Progressive Journalist: Ray Stannard Baker, 1870-1914," 183.

logical crisis before moving onto the higher ground of New Nationalism. William Allen White explained his advanced social position on trusts by means of a dialogue between "Demos" and "Croesus." Demos was the people, hellbent upon socializing the products of progress, and Croesus was the exploiting master of capital. It was the capital of Croesus that bought the patents to inventions and monopolized their usage. Steam, particularly its employment in transportation, had given Croesus unusually large powers. Like Henry Adams, White saw the dynamo as a manifestation of progress, and, like Henry George, he saw it as an enslaver of Demos through its capture of the courts and political power. With Baker, White agreed that the solution to the dilemma of the individual versus the whole was to socialize the means of progress.

This included not only the forces of steam and transportation, but the very economic order that created them. As feudalism had been superseded by industrialism, he paraphrased the *Manifesto*, so capitalism, "with all its diabolical self-interest," would be socialized and used for the benefit of the totality of society.[64] Progressivism probably cultivated such sentiments: "It is possible that we are preparing the ground for a nationalization of industries that may pass from control to ownership—from industrial bonds to government bonds and then to the breaking up of great fortunes holding the government bonds by inheritance & income taxes."[65] As Demos learned to control capital, the problem of the distribution of wealth would be solved and public ownership of irrigation systems, railroads, and public utilities would presage the passing of the old order.[66]

Although McClure was unprepared to league with the socialists, he accepted much of White's analysis. As he told an Ottawa audience, laws were necessary to protect the peo-

[64] White, *Old Order Changeth*, 231, 234, 237ff, 241, 250.
[65] White to Baker, Aug. 28, 1913, Baker Papers.
[66] White to Phillips, Sept. 9, 1908, White Papers.

ple from the evil effects of progress. Only with the invention of paper and writing did forgery become a crime. At the core of modern wealth stood such industries as railroads, built on steam power, which developed during a period when the "slavery question kept new laws from being written."[67] The concentration of wealth alone did not frighten McClure as long as the state possessed positive powers to "maintain justice between the trusts and the people. . . ."[68] At one point McClure became so interested in socialism that he proposed with Richard T. Ely's assistance to make himself an expert in Marxist theory.[69] But the conversion never came. Nevertheless, with Baker and White he accepted municipal socialism, and looked forward, to the abhorrence of Roosevelt, to the nationalization of the railroads.[70]

Steffens' position on socialism was little different. "I would insist upon government ownership of grocery stores or churches," Steffens told an interviewer, "if they were responsible for the corruption of our public officials."[71] Although he favored the nationalization of all franchised businesses and worked and voted for Debs in 1908, Steffens was also attracted by socialism's heavenly city and not by its pronouncements on class warfare. All the same, the socialists considered him, like Baker, a comrade. Upton Sinclair remonstrated with him in the offices of *McClure's* that his articles were "enough to make a complete picture of the system," and the more pacific Debs wrote, "you have written from and been inspired by a social brain, a social heart, and a social conscience and if you are not a socialist I do not know one."[72] Debs was partially right, but mis-

[67] McClure, Speech to the Canadian Club, Nov. 26, 1910, McClure Papers.
[68] *Ibid.*
[69] Richard T. Ely to McClure, July 2, 1884, *ibid.*
[70] McClure to Robert McClure, Jan. 31, 1910, *ibid.*
[71] Quoted in Cheslaw, "An Intellectual Biography of Lincoln Steffens," 181-82.
[72] Steffens, *Autobiography*, 434; Steffens, *Letters*, I, 203.

taken in his anatomy. Steffens' heart and brain were always his own. In later years, after World War I, when he did render the party conspicuous service, he never bothered to join.

Practically the entire *McClure's* group, with the exception of Miss Tarbell, stood close to socialism during the years of the Taft administration. The country's conditions were ominous. Over half of the nation's workers earned less than the cost of the necessities of life. Most of the railroad stock in the country was watered. Even Samuel Hopkins Adams felt it was time to stop using socialism as a shibboleth, that "old game of trying to befool the people by a catchword," and to start using the governmental power to structure the economic order in some more reasonable way.[73]

A third stage of muckraker thought was precipitated by the Progressive movement. On the whole it represented a rejection of doctrinaire, monolithic socialism, and an attempt to find a more practical system, consistent with native institutions. But extensive nationalization and control of industry remained an ideological link between socialism and New Nationalism.

Before considering the journalists' conclusions during this period, it might be helpful to inspect their attitude towards two economic problems which, aside from Miss Tarbell's studies of the tariff and Standard Oil, best exhibit their regard for state action. It was this appeal for state control that finally led to New Nationalism. Let labor stand for Demos and railroads for Croesus.

Although McClure felt that organized labor was one of the few "terrible questions" of the time, the magazine's policy in 1904 solidified around the dialectical premise that the best industrial "condition is one in which there are strong organizations on both sides, each holding the other

[73] Quoted in Chalmers, *The Social and Political Ideas of the Muckrakers*, 57.

272

in check."[74] But the muckrakers viewed the growth of trade unions from 900,000 in 1900 to 2,000,000 in 1904 with mixed feelings. Often they identified, not with organized labor, but with the independent workman. Baker's famous article, "The Right to Work," which helped inaugurate muck-raking, was a lengthy study of non-union labor in the Pennsylvania coal fields.[75]

At issue was the union shop. Although Baker questioned its benefits, the union shop was defended in *McClure's* by John Mitchell himself.[76] Perhaps part of McClure's hesi-tancy in supporting a union shop, a part of his concern for the independent laborer, resulted from the serious labor problems which his magazine had suffered during its early years.

Another labor issue was the company union. In "Capital and Labor Hunt Together" in 1903, Baker attacked the cooperation between Chicago teamsters and employers be-cause the public was defrauded.[77] A more scathing attack against the company union was "The Trust's New Tool —The Labor Boss," also published in 1903. In this article Baker exposed Sam Parks, the Croker of the New York building trades, who sold out his colleagues to industry.[78] While a balm to independent unions, this article skirted the real issue of labor's role.

Unlike the liberal parties of Europe, few of the muck-rakers anticipated any amelioration of the economic plight through the efforts of the working class. Steffens, by 1914, was an exception. He was confident that the upper class,

[74] McClure to Cameron Mackenzie, May 21, 1908, McClure Papers; *McClure's*, XXIV (Dec., 1904), 139.

[75] *Ibid.*, XX (Jan., 1903), 323.

[76] Mitchell, president of the United Mine Workers, was a conserva-tive follower of Gompers. Mark Hanna's death, he remarked, was an "irreparable" loss to the cause of labor. (Marguerita Gree, *The Na-tional Civic Federation and the American Labor Movement, 1900-1925* [Washington, D.C., 1956], 61.)

[77] *McClure's*, XXI (Sept., 1903), 451.

[78] *Ibid.*, XXII (Nov., 1903), 30.

which he despised, would not "consider the people seriously until the workers have . . . their power to require the thing to be done."[79] For that reason, after Progressivism had failed, he occasionally took the podium at I. W. W. rallies in the west. By then they were the wave of the future.

While much less confident of the ability of the working class, William Allen White nevertheless hired only union laborers for the *Emporia Gazette* and specified in his contracts with publishers that his books be set by union laborers.[80] Yet he saw no antidote in the dominion of labor.

On the whole the muckrakers viewed the rule of labor as equally threatening as that of capital. Indeed, this is probably one reason why socialism did not have more appeal. The attempts of labor to exempt themselves from the trust statutes and to legalize the boycott brought a severe reprimand from Burton J. Hendrick in "The Battle Against the Sherman Law."[81] The magazine strongly supported additional legislation to bring labor under state control. The "Canadian Act," championed by Charles W. Eliot of Harvard, was vigorously advocated because it gave the government discretionary powers to delay strikes and lockouts in sectors of the economy vital to the general welfare.[82]

By 1910 the muckrakers were prepared to support state control of arbitration, wages, hours, and working conditions, usually in opposition to organized labor.[83] They wanted reform, but it had to emanate from a revitalized state—not from an interest group within it.

Leviathan was to save Demos. The same solution held for Croesus.

Like the fingers of a colossal hand, the railroads spread across the country with a nerve center located in the banking houses of Wall Street. The depression of 1893 and the

[79] Steffens to Laura Steffens, March 14, 1914, Steffens Papers.
[80] White to Alden S. Huling, Nov. 5, 1906, White Papers.
[81] *McClure's*, XXXI (Oct., 1908), 664.
[82] *Ibid.*, XXX (Dec., 1907), 149.
[83] See Irwin Yellowitz, *Labor and the Progressive Movement in New York State, 1897-1916*, 127, 130, 142.

panic of 1903, caused by the Northern Security fiasco, had done much to centralize control in the hands of a half-dozen men. The I. C. C., strengthened by the Elkins Act of 1903, did little to curb this monolithic power.[84]

When Roosevelt sought to augment the power of the I. C. C. further by means of the Hepburn rate-fixing bill, Baker became his frequent consultant. For over a year, while he wrote his "Railroads on Trial" series for *McClure's*, Baker called on the President. With the President's support he was even offered a desk in the Interstate Commerce Commission offices, use of a government stenographer, and full access to all unpublished documents and letters.[85] In return Baker's articles were usually submitted to the President for criticism prior to publication.

Roosevelt's appeal for railroad control finally came in his State of the Union address in December, 1905. "You have given me two or three thoughts for my own message," he wrote Baker earlier in the fall, "it seems to me that one of the lessons you teach is that these railroad men are not to be treated as exceptional villains, but merely as ordinary Americans, who under given conditions are by the mere force of events forced into doing much of what we complain."[86]

But the President, it appeared, was unprepared to accept *McClure's* conclusions on the railroad problem. Baker wanted an impartial governmental body (1) to establish exact or minimum rates and (2) to do justice between shippers in various communities on both long and short hauls. Roosevelt had no desire to open up the freight rate discrimination question upon which Baker had been writing, and he thought it probably unconstitutional to establish exact rates. The Hepburn Act finally established maximum rates and ignored short haul discrimination. "It is the easiest

[84] See Gabriel Kolko, *Railroads and Regulation, 1877-1916* (Princeton, 1965), 116.

[85] Baker to Father, Jan. 29, 1905, Baker Papers.

[86] Roosevelt to Baker, Sept. 13, 1905, Baker Papers, Princeton University.

thing in the world," the President explained, "to make a showing which will convince each of the two rival communities that there is discrimination against it, whatever is done."[87]

Nevertheless, Roosevelt used the *McClure's* series to help formulate his railroad policy. The magazine's dire picture of stock watering, surreptitious propaganda and advertising, and unjust rates and rebates became a part of the State of the Union message in 1905. In October the President mailed a copy to Baker for comment, but McClure intercepted it at the office and read it. "Boyden, *we* would not print it," he exclaimed, and forwarded it to Baker.[88]

By February, 1906, Roosevelt had almost maneuvered the passage of the Hepburn Bill. Baker visited Washington and questioned the President as to whether the measure was only a first step towards wider governmental action. "I believe that we cannot stop short of government ownership of the railroads," he told the chief executive.[89] Within months the Hepburn Bill was passed and Roosevelt had delivered his man-with-a-muck-rake speech.

Most of the editorial staff seems to have slowly yielded to Baker's conclusions. Originally both Phillips and McClure entertained some misgivings about the first railroad article.[90] But hardly was the "Railroads on Trial" series completed than McClure himself broached the question of public ownership—"the general theory of the reformation of society of which we are all thinking so much nowadays."[91] The magazine proposed that some elastic plan of control would have to be found to satisfy the new economic conditions of the country. State ownership was a possibility. *McClure's* was a proponent of scientific management, and state ownership would permit an opportunity to im-

[87] Roosevelt to Baker, Nov. 28, 1905, Baker Papers.
[88] Boyden to Baker, Oct. 17, 1905, *ibid.*
[89] Baker, Notebook "C," 70-77, *ibid.*
[90] Phillips to Baker, June 14, 1905, *ibid.*
[91] *McClure's*, XXVIII (Feb., 1907), 451.

plement Frederick Taylor's theories. On the other hand, the postal system did not appear to be as efficiently operated as most railroads. Although state control and private competition would probably prove the most effective plan, the door was left open to other solutions. Within three years McClure had finally reached the conclusion that government ownership of railroads in Europe, in which he was "interested tremendously," should prove a beneficial example for America.[92]

Leviathan was finally to rule Croesus.

A common idea can be seen to emerge from the muckrakers' highly critical investigations of the tariff, the trusts, labor, and the railroads: that relief could be found through vigorous state action.

Croly's *The Promise of American Life* became a text for New Nationalist advocates, those who were prepared to see the end of laissez-faire. Roosevelt kept a heavily annotated volume in his library at Oyster Bay. Baker, who examined the copy there, was soon reading one of his own, contending "it is the best thing of its kind I have seen."[93] It served as a sequel to Kidd's volume. Not all of the muckrakers concurred with Croly's conclusions that the trusts were inevitable and national control a necessity. But this became the position of Roosevelt, La Follette, and the Progressive Party, and those who voted for Roosevelt in 1912 generally agreed that the finale of laissez-faire was at issue. Phillips, McClure, White, Boyden, and Siddall all joined the Progressive revolt. Although Steffens and Baker favored La Follette, both being his intimate friends, Baker, by now suspicious of Roosevelt's motives, finally cast his vote for Wilson.[94] Regardless of their political persuasion, a dozen years of muckraking had brought the *McClure's* group to an advanced, if not radical, economic position. With Miss Tarbell alone in vigorous dissent, there seems to be agree-

[92] McClure to Robert McClure, Jan. 31, 1910, McClure Papers.
[93] Baker to Father, Dec. 12, 1910, Baker Papers.
[94] See Baker, Notebook "M," Aug. 31, 1912, 22, *ibid.*

ment with Sam "Golden Rule" Jones's statement to the Chicago Conference on Trusts: "We are not going back to the individualistic method of production."[95]

The conventional alternatives between New Nationalism and New Freedom presented themselves to the Progressives before the election of 1912. Partially in preparation for that campaign, in 1910 Baker ghosted the memoirs of Robert M. La Follette for the *American Magazine*. He had matured greatly since *The New Prosperity* was considered as a campaign document for McKinley in 1900. Writing for La Follette brought Baker into contact with the vigorous proponent of the "Wisconsin plan" and the avowed enemy of the plutocracy. La Follette meant to treat the Ballinger-Pinchot controversy and the Payne-Aldrich Tariff as peripheral issues and to make his main thrust at the industrial plight soon to be uncovered by the Pujo Committee. In the Fall of 1911 the Senator began drafting his second major bill on the trusts. He telegraphed John R. Commons and other experts to come to Wisconsin. For several days Commons, La Follette, Louis Brandeis, President Van Hise of the University of Wisconsin, Ray Stannard Baker, and George Record of New Jersey held discussions. The Senator greeted the group with the injunction that the "time had come when the Progressives should advance a constructive program. . . ."[96] La Follette then sat silently while the conversation raged: "raged is the word."

Like the Progressives and the country at large, the conference was soon divided on the trust question "along the fundamental lines of the individualistic & Socialistic tendencies of thought." Although "every man in the group was opposed to capitalism, of course, to the idea of property government, and everyone wanted to bring about more democratic conditions," a split developed between those

[95] Civic Federation of Chicago, *Chicago Conference on Trusts* (Chicago, 1900), 603.
[96] Baker, Notebook "L," Nov. 9, 1911, 61-62, Baker Papers. This paragraph and the following are from the same source.

advocating regulated competition and those advocating regulated monopolies. Commons, Van Hise, La Follette, and Baker were of the "Socialistic inclination" that an independent regulatory commission with broad powers to control industrial trade and price practices be established. Louis Brandeis, who was to become the principal instigator of the New Freedom, and Record, a single-taxer, dissented.

Only to a minor extent was this ambivalence reflected in the McClure group. Miss Tarbell, like the more traditional Burton J. Hendrick, supported the Brandeis position. With minimal state action Miss Tarbell confidently expected that "monopolistic features will be abolished" so that all men could possess "free and equal rights in the business world."[97] But allured as she was by "LaF. the fighter," Miss Tarbell's position never became dogmatic. A few months after the Wisconsin conference she wrote Baker as follows: "Do you realize that the shifting of the question to one of new governmental machinery is going to do for the trust & tariff question what the Panic of '93 & the Spanish American War did—Turn attention from them? While we are fighting over the kind of vote with which to dislodge the enemy, the enemy will do as he did in 93-4-5 & again 97-8—He built his entrenchment higher. You perhaps believe we can't do it without new tools, I don't yet, I know we can if we fight hard enough—but it is so much easier to get up steam over a new thing! *Do* come up & talk it over. Particularly I want to hear about La Follette. Don't let him think he's ended. He is not. . . . There's going to be a sweep to him. . . ."[98] Miss Tarbell was never very dogmatic about her greater concern for the tariff than for the trusts. She encouraged Baker's writing, even during the Red Scare, when there was some danger in doing so: "Don't be scared about your industrial articles. Just put down the way you feel, and don't think it is up to you to settle the whole busi-

[97] Quoted in Chalmers, "The Social and Political Ideas of the Muckrakers," 125.
[98] Tarbell to Baker, Feb. 29, 1912, Baker Papers.

ness. . . . All these things are in the paws of the gods, or whatever you want to call the forces that have their grip on us."[99]

Other staff members of the old *McClure's* group moved to New Nationalism with very little trauma. "Neither Fisher, Steffins [*sic*] or Boyden agree with Brandeis trust position," Baker wrote in 1914, still collecting allies.[100] Although suspicious of public management in a society of powerful interests, Lincoln Steffens continued to believe that industry was going "gradually to be taken over out of the hands of the profiteers. . . ."[101] The Russian Revolution and World War I sealed this conclusion.

Samuel Hopkins Adams, an important proponent of the Pure Food and Drug Administration, also strongly favored governmental control of the trusts through supervisory commissions which would declare, "You shall not charge one fraction of a mill above what will give you a fair return on a fairly estimated investment."[102] And William Allen White did not care "whether or not we shall sow for the socialists to reap. . . ."[103] "We are preparing the ground for a nationalization of industries," he wrote Baker a year after Roosevelt led the Progressive Party to defeat.[104] And to John Phillips he also confided, "the natural end of it all is the control of capital looking to its abolition."[105]

Sam McClure agreed that "a problem requiring the exercise of as great statesmanship as any government has ever put forth" was "how to maintain justice between the trusts and the people."[106] With it statistically safer to commit

[99] Tarbell to Baker, Dec. 15, 1919, *ibid.*

[100] Baker, Notebook "I," Jan. 12, 1914, 126, *ibid.*

[101] Steffens to Ella Winter, Dec. 20, 1919, Steffens Papers.

[102] Quoted in Chalmers, "The Social and Political Ideas of the Muckrakers," 159.

[103] White to Baker, Aug. 28, 1913, Baker Papers.

[104] *Ibid.*

[105] White to Phillips, Sept. 9, 1908, White Papers.

[106] McClure, Speech to the Canadian Club, Nov. 26, 1910, McClure Papers.

murder in Chicago than to work for the railroads, he seemed to regard as inevitable government ownership.[107]

John Phillips favored the "use of new tools of democracy" to keep open the doors of economic opportunity.[108] He used the *American* to support La Follette, whose position he adhered to. The public possessed a right to examine the rich and determine whether they received more than was justly due them. Like Grosscup, Phillips was concerned over diminished economic opportunity. "I have been interested in this idea," Phillips wrote to Emporia, "that all this political struggle and the movement that we are going through with has a very practical end. To a certain extent it is an exhibit of the instinct for self-preservation. We are trying by this means to keep open for the present and coming generations the road for opportunity . . . not simply to let them be doomed from the start to the definite service of a few men."[109] Phillips was thinking of his five children and "what chances they would have." Every generation seemed to have less opportunity than the last. "When I think of my father and my grandfather coming to their end with a very little saved up and being comfortable and happy on their small income, I see that that is not possible for our generation, and probably will be less possible for the next generation." His solution was New Nationalism.

In conclusion, most of the muckrakers saw the inevitable decline of laissez-faire at hand, and, indeed, insurgency was a blow aimed at the heart of the oligarchy, a blow that was to be delivered by the corporate "people," not by organized labor or any other faction of society. Although there was much divergency of thought, most were in favor of state-regulated monopolies by 1912. As Hofstadter has divided the Progressives, this means that most of the *McClure's* muckrakers were of the Hamiltonian persuasion.

107 *Ibid.*; McClure to Robert McClure, Jan. 31, 1910, *ibid.*
108 Phillips to White, Sept. 1, 1910, White Papers.
109 *Ibid.* The rest of this paragraph is from the same source. See also Phillips, *A Legacy to Youth*, 182ff.

A more detailed study of the economic theories of the muckrakers is David Chalmers' *The Social and Political Ideas of the Muckrakers*. Arranging the principal muckrakers from conservative to liberal, Chalmers finds no consistent economic theory. "Corporate power 'ought to be controlled,' they felt, but they rarely said how. With few exceptions they shied away from a more detailed study of and prescription for the evils of the financial mechanism itself."[110] "Most of these writers," he continues, "were not at home when dealing with economic problems."[111] Indeed, at *McClure's* the opposite appears to be the case. There was a preoccupation with economic problems after 1906, a flirtation with socialism on the part of many staff members, a widespread belief in nationalization of various sectors of the economy, and finally in 1912 a general coalescence in support of the Van Hise-Ely scheme of regulated monopolies. The majority were in favor of giving governmental commissions tremendous new powers, which, if applied, would have ended laissez-faire. Undoubtedly, a victory for the Progressive Party would have radically changed the nature of Pre-World War I reform.

While the purpose of the revitalized state was to rationalize, if not nationalize, economic power, there remained cer-

[110] See Chalmers, "The Social and Political Ideas of the Muckrakers," 140-41.

[111] *Ibid.* Gabriel Kolko in *The Triumph of Conservatism*, 160-61, supports this assertion: "It is significant that out of the entire muckraking literature, which was in effect a refutation of the existing theories on the character of the capitalist economy and state as well as a partial description of the operational nature of American institutions, no serious social or economic theory was formulated. In part this was due to the puerile character of many of the muckrakers, and their obscuring of many of the realities of the day by ascribing opposition to government control where there actually was none. . . . But all too many of the prominent muckrakers were journalists rather than thinkers, with commonplace talents and middle-class values, incapable of serious or radical critiques. A few at least were opportunists. Ray Stannard Baker. . . ."

tain ultimate altruistic aims to be achieved. Having seen a moral criticism of municipal government and business practices, a deep concern for criminality and lawlessness, and a quest for laws of human behavior, let us at long last deal with the question of ethics at *McClure's*.

Chapter XIV. "Society the Juggernaut; Man the Devotee?"

AFTER READING Kidd's chapter on "The Function of Religious Belief in the Evolution of Society" in *Social Evolution*, Baker questioned in his marginalia whether society was an avatar and man its devotee.[1] The nature of society, as well as the philosophical principles which governed it, was a metaphysical quest at *McClure's*. On the whole, answers were hewn from the heart of social Darwinism and Christianity. And indeed philosophical ethics, dealing with the behavior of society, became the basis of *McClure's* muckraking ideology.

In ethics these journalists showed a greater cohesiveness than in any other area. Alike, they all came from backgrounds of traditional Protestant Christianity, and, alike, they had their views modified by the new science, particularly social Darwinism. What happened in effect is that a social Christianity based on evolution replaced the old credal orthodoxy. Walter Rauschenbusch, that "true prophet," and William James were the principal men who allowed this adoption to be made so painlessly.[2] But during the muckraking years, many of the radical Christian tendencies continued to be expressed—sabbatarianism and temperance, for example. An understanding of the new ethics and how it replaced the old should allow some insight into the oft-repeated charges that the muckrakers were mere moralists. But before we view the emergence of an ethics based on social Darwinism and the Social Gospel at *McClure's*, it might be helpful to see how the muckrakers related their mission to religious purpose.

[1] Kidd, *Social Evolution*, copy in Baker Papers, Amherst.
[2] Baker, *American Chronicle*, 256; Phillips to Baker, Aug. 16, 1907, Baker Papers; Roseboro' to Tarbell, Nov. 14, 1938, Tarbell Papers.

284

The muckrakers, if it is possible to generalize, saw themselves as spiritual midwives of a new social order. The sentiments flooded Baker's diary as the popular press derided muckraking: "When there arise men who cry woe: your politics are rotten, your legislatures are corrupt, your business is immoral, you turn on them . . . & call them pessimists. . . . You may discover that some of them are prophets."[3] This was quickly acceded to by other social Christians. The Methodist founder of the ambitious International Reform Bureau agreed that *McClure's* was "one of the prophets that has attacked social evils more bravely and effectively than most of the preachers."[4] Such was McClure's intent. He saw the magazine "performing a certain mission" with God "in our plans."[5] There is no reason to believe that McClure ever changed his thinking, when as a young man he had written that "the *problem* of life, consists in the relation of man to God and the facts growing out of this relation."[6] "I want to study 'God in History,'" he said, "I want to study statecraft and government and law and institutions" as they reveal "this universal self-centered fact to life and its relations."[7] Many of the muckrakers could have agreed with Upton Sinclair, who wrote, "I want to give every second of my time and of my thought, every ounce of my energy, to the worship of my God and to the uttering of the unspeakable message that I know he has given me."[8]

These scattered references should give some indication of that religious fervor which played no small role in motivating muckraking. But the *Origin of Species* made it diffi-

[3] Baker, Notebook "I," 104, Baker Papers; see Baker, *The Spiritual Unrest* (New York, 1909), 281.

[4] Wilbur Fisk Crafts to McClure, Nov. 25, 1913, McClure Papers.

[5] McClure, Staff speech, fall, 1904, *ibid.*; McClure to Hattie McClure, April 23, 1896, *ibid.*

[6] McClure to Hattie McClure, April 30, 1882, *ibid.*

[7] *Ibid.*

[8] Upton Sinclair to Edwin Markham, 1901?, copy in Sinclair Papers, II, Lilly Library, University of Indiana.

cult to believe in the traditional creation story of the Old Testament. If this meant the erosion of a Bible-oriented ethics—then evolution itself became the source of a new ethics. How was an ethics to be forged from evolution?

Lincoln Steffens, having studied science under the Le Conte brothers at the University of California, after graduation became a pupil of Europe's foremost scholar of ethics, Wilhelm Wundt, at Leipzig. Hugo Munsterberg of Harvard, who wrote for *McClure's*, G. Stanley Hall, and probably John Phillips were also students of Wundt.

In the tradition of Kant and the German idealists, Wundt hoped to make moral philosophy the foundation of a metaphysics. Seeking an empirical foundation for ethics, he treated the history of custom and ethical ideas from a psychological point of view. The data of practical human existence could be arranged in two ways. First, each fact could be given equal value with every other and a helpless pluralism would result. This was the explicative method. Secondly, patterns could be discerned, and every fact evaluated in terms of its relationship to the cultural pattern. Ethics then became the science of normative values, the cornerstone of all practical sciences as logic was the basis of theoretical ones.

After the data were accumulated, Wundt thought subjective speculation discovered the postulates of the "normative idea" in the evidence. The normative idea obviously bore resemblance to Hegel's "idea" and his data of existence, the notion: the normative idea was particularized and dominant in individual acts as in universal law. One of the early German interpreters of Darwin, Wundt asserted that the normative idea was in a state of progressive revelation as society mastered its environment in epoch after epoch. Custom, and its offspring, habit and law, became subjects of investigation if one wished to discover the moral worth and purpose of ethics. With the disciplines of anthropology, sociology, and etymology, Wundt anticipated Freud and investigated dreams, myth, habits, and words, seeking the present revelatory stage of normative values.[9]

Although drawing upon Locke for epistemology and political theory, Wundt was generally hostile to British empiricism: "I am thoroughly opposed to its individualistic and utilitarian tendencies. . . ."[10] Committed to an evolving system of folk values, he could not brook a theory like utilitarianism which emphasized individual needs and aspirations. Society was the smallest organic unit of evolution, and its ethics, customs, laws, and habits were streamlining for natural survival. "Individualism as its name implies," he argued, "regards the individual as the sole legitimate end of morality; inferring, because the state and the law and order of the state exist *for* the individual, that therefore they are the voluntary creation of the individual."[11] But the state was a more highly developed union: the sum total of individuals. It was as natural as the family, and in terms of normative ideas it stood above both the individual and the family in significance.

The state was simply the organic projection of the folk society, much in the manner postulated by Hobbes. The chief ends of the state were legal protection and security, and by the law of social evolution these services were increasingly afforded. State development meant "the increased security of its members, and control of more abundant means of satisfaction of their needs and the unfolding of their powers."[12] The unconscious development towards "self-regulation" and altruism meant society could reasonably expect that "the moral basis of ownership should undergo change in the future."[13]

In most respects Wundt can be comfortably classified as a Hegelian idealist who had come to terms with Darwin.

9 Wilhelm Max Wundt, *Ethics: An Investigation of the Facts and Laws of the Moral Life*, trans. Edward Titchener et al. (3 vols., New York, 1908), I, vi-70; see also G. Stanley Hall, *Founders of Modern Psychology* (New York, 1912), 312ff.
10 *Ibid.*, I, vii.   11 *Ibid.*, I, 247.
12 *Ibid.*, I, 257.   13 *Ibid.*, I, 313, 259.

McClure's echoed Wundt's sentiments that law was a normative system of rules that should be kept attuned to evolving society, that "people" or "society" represented in total an organistic union of greater value than any association within the state, and that political reform consisted in the "conscious apprehension and systematic execution of determinate purposes" by statesmancraft in the fields of economics, law, society, and culture.[14] Steffens, of course, was the principal vehicle of this influence.

When Steffens returned to the United States in 1892, he had already finished the argumentative part of an essay on "Ethics and Evolution," leaving only the "deduction of some conclusions" to be made.[15] Confident that this work would give him an international reputation, he pondered going to Harvard "to get up the state of Am."[16] Although dissatisfied with metaphysics, Steffens reveals in this essay and in other writings the dominant influence of Wundt. Seeing himself a Feuerbachian materialist (although at times lapsing into the idealism of Hegel), Steffens contended: "My ethics is in what I have said. . . . The goods men believe to be goods (as proved by all their actions) though thinkers abhor, I would celebrate."[17] Ethics, in other words, was built upon the data of folk actions.

"Ethics and Evolution," after two laborious attempts, was left incomplete, but the intent to wring ethical principles from the evolutionary forces at work in society is clear. Steffens commenced: "The proposition, all that is, is the result of evolution, or, of growth out of what was, if not universally accepted, is at least so well established, that it may be assumed to be proved."[18] Evolutionary change, he felt in contradiction to Wundt, could also be towards "decline

---

[14] *Ibid.*, I, 275; III, 258, 261, 269, 272.
[15] Steffens to Joseph Steffens, Oct. 7, 1892, Steffens Papers.
[16] *Ibid.*
[17] Steffens to Fred Willis, April 1, 1893, *ibid.*
[18] Steffens, "Ethics and Evolution," manuscripts in the Steffens Papers. From these two manuscripts, intended as a small book, the following eight paragraphs are taken.

and decay"; otherwise it would be assumed that the present state was the "perfect end of universal striving."

Four basic areas of ethical studies interested the youthful Steffens: (1) the historical study of the laws of growth of moral ideas, (2) actual principles and motives of conduct, (3) "what ought to be," and, finally, (4) the practical means of achieving the theoretical ideal. His essay dealt principally with the Science of Morals, which "has for its data the facts of human conduct," and Theoretical Ethics, an analysis of the "ought."

He intended the Science of Morals to show "what is the actual state of present morals in a given society, what the forces which make for improvement & growth, and what the laws of that development." Steffens envisioned a field trip to a "social district" of the United States. There he would divide men according to occupations, seeking data about the motives of each group, "hoping ultimately to arrive at the actual fundamental motive of all conduct." He would pay attention to actual modes of behavior and distill "conscious & unconscious" purposes. All ideas not influencing conduct were to be disregarded. The facts would be complex; "it is a well-known fact that a businessman conducts his life on apparently different principles according as he engaged in his business, or in politics, according as he is among his family or in the society of his friends." This material, organized, would become the data for achieving a Theoretical Ethics. Indeed, Steffens' early muckraking pieces were intended for this purpose.

The aim of Steffens' Theoretical Ethics was to discover a basis for four principles of judgment: right, wrong, good, and bad. These values were not absolute or eternal, and yet they were not relative in the sense of being conditioned by human wants and social limitations. They were reflections of the law of natural selection. "There is," Steffens wrote, "such a thing as a judgment of nature upon conduct." His four ethical terms were defined by social Darwinism.

289

I. Right—conduct which makes for mere survival.
II. Good—conduct which furthers evolutionary process.
III. Wrong—conduct which hinders evolutionary process.
IV. Bad—conduct which hinders survival.

Survival was the first test of any mode of conduct. Nature was a severe judge of behavior, and at times its standards seem "to us cruel and revolting." If a herd of wild horses were attacked by wolves, some would take flight and some would stay and fight. "Nature takes no cognizance of the courage displayed in the fighters," for they would be destroyed. "She selects the cowardly and swift for the agent of the continuance of the horse species." The conduct of the fighters was bad, "that of the cowardly was right." Wundt himself would have agreed.

Beyond mere survival there was the development of life into higher organisms. "Thus the conduct of some individuals upon their organs and through a process of anatomical adjustment, brings about variations in structure." These acquired characteristics, which Lamarck, not Darwin, postulated, allowed individuals, families, and races to become mentally and biologically more adapted to evolution. This was Good—a greater value than mere survival. Degenerative forces at work in man, "like the Italians," resulted in a retrogression that was not as much a non-value as non-survival. Thus it was Wrong rather than Bad.

Human laws, customs, and religious beliefs were not deliberately founded upon the laws governing natural phenomena, but nature selected from man's creativity certain ideas and institutions for continuance which benefited its unknowable appetite. Some morals, customs, or habits survived which were neither of positive nor negative value to nature, but most were either Right or Good. Were these natural principles necessarily moral principles? "Having no standard, by which to show that the end proposed is a moral end, I have no course open but that hitherto pursued, viz: to show that all *ends*, human and moral, are subjected, in fact, to the test of conformity with natural ends." Moral rationalizations, like simple conduct, bend to the will of a progressive nature. Men who guided their conduct by principles incompatible with survival were bound to extinction or degeneration. But the scientist of morals should be wary of that "group of men, holding ideas of ends of conduct incompatible with survival, but following them not at all." Like the men who followed Good and Right principles, these men thrived.

Steffens, like Wundt, saw that evolutionary principles placed severe restrictions upon utilitarianism. Even if all men were hedonists bent upon individual pleasure, that characteristic itself resulted from nature producing men so organized. Natural selection retained "those whose pleasure was right," and rejected "those whose pleasure was wrong." Individualistic utilitarianism might help explain behavior, but it furnished no safe guide by which to direct conduct. In fact nature seemed to favor altruistic principles. The egoist might build his banks, railroads, and factories, but the end was bitter: "To the attainment of his millions the supposed egoist . . . has over-turned his intellectual & physical power. His children, whom he loves, are weaklings, mere entities, sometimes insane." This individualism quickly resulted in "the extinction of the race." The financier's supposed altruism in furnishing prosperity to thousands and in aiding the nation's economic development might be more real than the work of a hundred philanthropic societies, but nature's judgment was negative. The structural modification within an individual man was of greater importance than anything he might do. Although skeptical of individualism, Steffens was hesitant to follow Wundt's theory of social organism to an extreme.

All racial evolution went through the individual man, he said. Society, "sometimes spoken of as an organism but this is a mere figure of speech," was modified as it inherited individual advancements. Thus the individual anatomical modifications of moving from the country to the city, of making a discovery, or of writing a literary work contributed directly to the advancement of the species. Individual changes "must become the possession of the race" before progress occurred, he believed. The "race" and the "species" bespoke a higher evolutionary unit than man.

The state, as Steffens wrote in this early essay, was like custom, law, or belief. It was evolving towards "perfection." It was partly a cause and partly an *effect* of human evolution, but was an independent movement apart from the folk. Here again he disagreed with his teacher. Yet the influence of Wundt is obvious in most of what Steffens says about ethics and evolution, to wit: evolution selected customs and institutions for survival and progress, and ethics was the normative system of conduct which permitted a race or a species to survive and develop. Forty years later, when writing the re-education of Lincoln Steffens, his autobiography bears testimony that neither his notions of ethics nor his concern for natural law had left him.

At a later date Ray Stannard Baker was also influenced by the German theories of evolution. After Kidd's *Social Evolution* in 1894, Baker read Ernst Haeckel's *Natural History of Creation*.[19] Haeckel was the German equivalent of a Wallace or Huxley in his propagandizing of Darwin. His famous monistic law that ontogeny recapitulates phylogeny, that each organism in its development parallels the morphological changes of its ancestors, made him of interest to *McClure's*. Baker, whose father-in-law was, like Albert Hurd, a scientist and a former pupil of Louis Agassiz, sought Haeckel at Jena in 1900. Afterwards he wrote "The Search for the Missing Link."[20] Although Baker never accepted Haeckel's denial of the immortality of the soul, of the freedom of human will, or of the existence of a personal God, his conversion to social Darwinism at this time was com-

[19] See Baker, *American Chronicle*, 108-11.
[20] *McClure's*, XVII (Aug., 1901), 328.

plete in all other respects. Upon his return he wrote a modern version of the Parable of the Sower:

"I am this, a seed blown forth by the wind as likely to fall on stoney ground, to be the prey of bird or beast, or stronger than myself, taking my poor chance of finding the soil in which I may grow, may attain maturity, may blossom, fruit & reproduce. I am the . . . creeper, reaching out, ever experimenting, ever asking, ever hoping, ever seeking for a place where my tendrils may attach themselves. . . . The pine wears a million seeds & scatters them upon the world. Of all the million it is a chance not even one finds a growing space in the . . . earth & grows to treehood. We too are cast forth, swarms of human seed, thick spawn of men drifting about, driven by our winds, mostly dying, having made no growth, produced no flower, left no successors. And yet we are given higher power than the seed of the pine in that we can struggle. . . . Most men are cast into the world to be wasted, lost —& yet, wait, not lost either. Men, too, are produced like seeds in vast surplus. It is the scheme of nature which creates with careless hand, oversowing, overplanting so that by chance a few of her seed may grow, so that the species may be preserved, so that there may always be material for growth."[21]

Feeling that "perfection lies at the end of constant struggle & attainments of men," Baker accepted Steffens' assumptions regarding morality. "How can we play traitor to the struggle & drop—through sin—all the ground thus gained," he wrote, "for sin is treason to civilization."[22] In other words, he placed a moral value on struggle and survival, while failure was evil. Man's duty was to let his instinct go, to struggle upward. The source of natural evolution was clear: "Some of us say God: we know at least that it

21 Baker, Notebook "K & T," 1906?, Baker Papers.
22 Baker, Notebook "C," 1903-06, 144-45, *ibid.*

is Good."[23] Baker felt "there is comfort and satisfaction to know that good, after all, finally wins over evil."[24] With God in His world, men did progress slowly upward in the long run. But while natural law operated automatically, small discretionary powers were still reserved to man.

Men had to make progress themselves by struggling with their situations. With Lester Ward and the reform Darwinists he agreed, "we are not blind victims of the merciless law of natural selection, but, being endowed with consciousness, we have the power of turning upon ourselves and modifying natural law—within broad limits—to our own ends."[25] The extent to which this could be done, he never explained —but the idea had not yet suggested itself to Steffens.

Baker had asked Haeckel about the development of Germany. "Here in Germany," the Professor responded, "the tendency is all toward the centralization of power in the government, the removal of individual responsibility, and the working together of large masses of men as one man."[26] And Baker returned to America with a deep suspicion of "selfish individualism."[27] "The greatest individualists," he was soon writing, like Steffens, from a social Darwinist point of view, "have been the selfish, greedy kings of industry. . . ."[28] And soon he was advocating "a higher measure of responsibility of the citizen to the state" since after all "the freest man is the one who serves most."[29]

In writing on ethics Baker posed additional criticisms of individualism. Sin, went his complex definition, was "only a name for the divided life."[30] What Baker meant was that sin was contention in the social order. Sin was the political struggle between the few and the many, the economic struggle between labor and capital, and the social conflict between white and Negro. Sin was that which militated

---

[23] *Ibid.* [24] *Ibid.*, 23, 37. [25] *Ibid.*, 118-19.
[26] Baker, *American Chronicle*, 111.
[27] Baker, Notebook "C," 1903-06, 98-99, Baker Papers.
[28] *Ibid.* [29] *Ibid.*
[30] Baker, Notebook "L," 20, *ibid.*

against the growth of brotherhood and cohesiveness in society. This made individualism a creed fraught with dangerous possibilities. Man's greatest need was to develop a "social conscience" which transcended any class or individual action.[31] A social religion could give men this Hegelian "sense of unity" which was the "basic religious secret."[32] Religion became the "higher sense of good order and system" that would bring an end to sinful individual contention.[33]

Baker, like Steffens, saw the cohesive nature of the species, and became convinced that the failure to struggle upwards constituted a moral evil. He never clarified to what extent man should conform to the overarching laws of "good order and system," and to what extent, "within broad limits," they should be modified.

Like Baker and Steffens, the prophet in Emporia was deeply impressed by the social implications of Darwinism. Nowhere is this better expressed than in White's small volume, *A Theory of Spiritual Progress*.[34] The journey of "that mysterious thing called life, as it grows from chlorophyl into history" was upward bound "to an unknown port."[35] There was, he quoted Vernon L. Kellogg's *Darwinism Today*, a "determinate or purposive change" operated by an automatic modifying principle which impelled human evolution.[36]

Human evolution proved the primacy of "the instinct of race preservation."[37] The role of the individual in overall progress, said White, was small. In evolution "the individual was developed by his loyalty to the social unit."[38] Evolution had proved that the "partnership of society," in man as among the bees, was a greater instinct than self-preserva-

---

[31] Baker to Roosevelt, June 8, 1908, *ibid.*
[32] Baker, Notebook "L," 25, *ibid.*   [33] *Ibid.*, 112.
[34] William Allen White, *A Theory of Spiritual Progress* (Emporia, Kansas, 1910).
[35] *Ibid.*, 2, 4.   [36] *Ibid.*, 5.
[37] *American Magazine*, LXII (Oct., 1906), 577.   [38] *Ibid.*

tion. This meant that social behavior was endowed with an ethical quality much in the manner argued by Steffens.

Evolution meant that "changing habits of life have changed our morals" and that "customs grow stale and new ones replace them" as progress continues.[39] Sin was an action against evolutionary law and it led to the "consequent destruction" of its originator.[40] Steffens and Baker at various times could have agreed. "Sin and evil or whatever we may call life's somber forces that make for pain or unhappiness or sorrow," White wrote, "are infractions of the social code."[41] The social code then was "the sum of the customs of the people; it has the public sentiment behind it; it is more powerful than any human law."[42] As men conform to the customs of society, "the course of least resistance," the great evolutionary forces drive humanity forward.[43]

White felt that any modifications in the evolutionary process had to occur within "the vast social body of civilization."[44] His conception of society and its means of advancement compare with a notation made by Baker during his investigations of the industrial unrest. Labor unions, Baker wrote, had one advantage at least—they focused man's attention on a larger social group than the family. And they prepared the individual for still larger concepts of altruism such as the state.[45] William Allen White wrote in his essay that human sensibilities were slowly broadening. The cohesiveness of the social order was spreading from that of the "family to that of the tribe, from that to the clan, from that to the state, from that to the nation."[46] Although White had probably never heard of Wundt, he had paraphrased him.

The state, itself a reflection of custom, from "instinctive

---

[39] White, *A Theory of Spiritual Progress*, 8.

[40] *Emporia Gazette* (w), July 30, 1903.

[41] White, *A Theory of Spiritual Progress*, 11.

[42] *Ibid.*, 12.   [43] *Ibid.*, 14.   [44] *Ibid.*, 16.

[45] See Baker, Notebook "J," 116, Baker Papers; Baker, *American Chronicle*, 275.

[46] White, *A Theory of Spiritual Progress*, 19, 20.

folk charity" had an obligation "to make brothers of the weak so that they might grow strong and wise."[47] Thus White described the necessity of old age pension, workingmen's compensation, and various other Progressive schemes in terms of a folk consciousness. But later he wrote that the Progressive movement was an attempt to "change the environment of property so that whatever of poverty is due to environment may be removed."[48] Thus, like Baker, he showed that seeming inconsistent desire to come to terms with existent natural law in an active way. But, like Baker and Steffens, White derived a folk humanism, a suspicion of individualism, and a concept of ethics from evolution.

The other members of the *McClure's* group seem to have agreed with these general conclusions. Both John Phillips and McClure had studied Agassiz's Lamarckianism under Albert Hurd at Knox. Indeed, probably most of the muckrakers in principle accepted the inheritance of acquired characteristics. The role of environmental control was thus accentuated without contradicting the need for men to embrace custom at the societal level. Even the weak could join the folk. Miss Tarbell felt that the magazine should challenge some aspects of the old Darwinian theory, and then proposed the younger Agassiz to do it.[49]

Miss Tarbell, incidentally, wrote later that evolutionary theory came to her like "a revelation" describing the "divine method or process by which the beneficent spirit in the universe was to work out its intent."[50] From then forward, "evolution has never ceased to be a fundamental element in my religion."[51] How the divine intent was achieved in society she never explained.

Her editor was even less explicit. McClure's acquaintance with Herbert Spencer, "a great writer," helped motivate

47 *Ibid.*, 26, 30.
48 White to Phillips, Aug. 26, 1912, White Papers.
49 Joseph M. Rogers to Tarbell, April 11, 1900, Phillips Papers.
50 Tarbell, "My Religion," n.d., manuscript in Tarbell Papers.
51 *Ibid.*

him in his quest for a study of the nature of comparative governments. His interest in the evolution of ethical ideas, he said, inclined him to compare "results of government in the United States with the ideals that were in the minds of the founders of the country, and that are more or less dimly in the minds of everyone."[52] McClure was attracted to Hugo Munsterberg, Wundt's pupil, at Harvard. He commissioned him to do several studies in criminality. When Harry Orchard confessed at the Haywood trial in Boise, Idaho, in 1907, Munsterberg was present to apply German metaphysical ethics. Munsterberg's article preceded Orchard's confessions in *McClure's*.[53]

John Phillips, skeptical of Spencer's dogmas justifying individualism because the Englishman "has to twist himself about often to make the facts bear them," became an avowed follower of Thomas Huxley's agnosticism.[54] A skeptical positivism seemed to characterize Phillips throughout the muckraking years. Just prior to his studies at Leipzig, Phillips wrote, "I believe that a man can be unbiased —can stand in the midst of these . . . unsolved problems of life & the Universe & say 'I do not know' honestly & candidly—without getting up a specious semi-solution & being satisfied there with."[55] By the Progressive period Phillips had changed little. While believing that man was under "the control of forces that he does not quite direct—it sometimes seems to me as if I were an example of that," Phillips remained generally skeptical of speculative philosophy of any sort.[56] Having read Brooks Adams, he critically wrote Baker that "the report of facts, real things that lead to generalization, is more important, more difficult than the statement of the conclusion itself."[57] Speculation, he contended, had to be based on data, "not going

[52] *Philadelphia North American*, Aug. 15, 1905.
[53] *McClure's*, XXIX (Oct., 1907), 614; see McClure to unidentified, June ?, 1907, McClure Papers.
[54] Phillips to McClure, June 4, 1884, *ibid.*   [55] *Ibid.*
[56] Phillips to White, Sept. 24, 1912, White Papers.
[57] Phillips to Baker, May 27, 1908, Baker Papers.

too far beyond, not too much of a forecast, not too much of a solution," because "we can't really solve all the problems of civilization."[58] As a capable commonsense editor, he maintained a scientific detachment towards both facts and social theories. At this juncture, his own mind and the less probing one of Miss Tarbell met. She too was something of a literalist.

The muckrakers, then, as a whole accepted social Darwinism. While Phillips veered towards agnosticism, the other important muckrakers made their peace with evolution and took an ethics from its premise that all not conforming to natural law did not survive or advance. Evidently McClure, Steffens, Baker, White, and possibly Miss Tarbell felt social Darwinism highlighted the value of custom and the social entity while encouraging a fear of individualism.

It was evolution which tore the muckrakers from their traditional Christian moorings. With remarkable ease they synthesized their new values, supposedly based on science, with the altruism of the Golden Rule. The result, to use Henry May's term, was "radical social Christianity."[59] Almost the totality of Christian dogma dealing with divinity and inspiration was swept aside, and accentuated in its place were Christianity's social teachings, especially the Sermon on the Mount. The social aspects of Christianity were retained without accepting its highly developed rationalizations. This became a congenial position for many of the Progressives, and one to which many Single Taxers and Nationalists adhered.[60] As mentioned before, Charles M. Sheldon and Washington Gladden, along with Walter

---

[58] *Ibid.*

[59] See Henry F. May, *Protestant Churches and Industrial America* (New York, 1949), 235ff.

[60] George Mowry, *The California Progressives* (Berkeley and Los Angeles, 1951), 97-100; Edward Bellamy, *Equality* (New York, 1897), 340ff; Charles Howard Hopkins, *The Rise of the Social Gospel in American Protestantism, 1865-1915* (New Haven, 1940), 203f; for an interesting account of the conservative faith of George F. Baer et al. see Frederick Lewis Allen, *The Lords of Creation* (New York, 1935), 87-97.

Rauschenbusch and William James, prepared the way for this transition which presaged much of what Bergson was to say.

All of the muckrakers, perhaps even Phillips at times, seem to have shared the belief that God was immanent in the world, directing evolutionary progress. To Steffens, God was in Spencerian fashion "The Incomprehensible"; to White an "unseen power"; to Phillips, on occasion, the controller "of forces"; to Miss Tarbell "the greatest of realities" and a "beneficent spirit in the universe"; to Mc-Clure the divine giver of energy; and to Miss Roseboro' the "All Divine" who built the mysterious order.[61] These seemingly diverse views of God meant that the traditional conception of divinity had eroded to an almost deistic position.

Ray Stannard Baker retained more of his youthful religious enthusiasm than his colleagues. To Baker, God was not only immanent, but personal. His fervor becomes evident in his diaries: "If God give me power, *possess me,* shall I not follow? Shall I not do anything He asks?—oh, God, give me light, faith, fire, strength: let me fly, oh God! . . . Oh, God, take me out of this slough. Oh, let me see & feel Thy constant presence. . . ."[62] Baker's religious faith was quickened by a series of psychological experiences bordering on the mystical. This would have surprised Miss Roseboro', who thought all talk of communion with God nonsense. In the early days of muckraking, when the world seemed out of joint, Baker fled home to the quiet of his garden for solace. Here troubles flew away as the "earth

---

[61] Steffens to Dot Steffens, Feb. 4, 1892, Steffens Papers; Steffens to Riefer, Feb. 6, 1920, *ibid.*; Steffens, *The World of Lincoln Steffens,* eds. Ella Winter and Herbert Shapiro (New York, 1962), 92; *Emporia Gazette* (w), July 30, 1903; John Phillips to White, Sept. 4, 1912, White Papers; Tarbell, *All in the Day's Work,* 407; Tarbell, "My Religion," Ms in Tarbell Papers; McClure to Hattie McClure, Feb. 1, 1892, McClure Papers; McClure to Hattie McClure, April 30, 1882, *ibid.*; Roseboro' to Tarbell, Nov. 14, 1938, Tarbell Papers.

[62] Baker, Notebook "K," 131, Baker Papers.

became a place of peace & beauty," and he felt a new surge of "unspeakable love for human beings."[63] Alone in his garden, away from his friends, "I could feel God," and "repeated trials deepened this experience until it often seemed to me that I was literally passing into a new personality."[64] To his new personality, a religiously oriented alter ego, Baker gave a "quiet name," David Grayson.[65] The new personality fastened on Baker so strongly that frequently, "when I was suddenly addressed I found myself responding in a voice strange to me: to my embarrassment."[66] For the rest of Baker's life, this psychological cousin remained a part of his personality. Under the name Grayson, Baker published several volumes of pastoral fiction that would hardly have done credit to his journalistic name.

If, on the whole, with Baker as the major exception, God became more objective and non-personal, there was a similar retreat in other areas of dogma. By the muckraking period, questions of future rewards or punishments were considered mere speculations because "we do not know— we do not *know*," as Grayson put it.[67] Hell, even to Baker, was "puerile torments" conjured up by a "dreadful old doctrine."[68] To White the so-called hell was merely a present state of disobedience to that universal spiritual law which required the "gratitude of man to man."[69] If hell was lost, so was heaven.

Not even Tolstoy's *How I Came to Believe* could convince Baker that an Israelite heaven was any more feasible than the Buddhist. He chose to disbelieve in either.[70] Nor was McClure able to "form any higher conception of heaven" than life.[71] When a young Emporia woman immersed her old mother, who subsequently caught cold and died, Wil-

---

[63] Baker, Notebook "VII," *ibid.*   [64] *Ibid.*
[65] *Ibid.*   [66] *Ibid.*
[67] David Grayson, *Adventures in Contentment* (New York, 1906), 174.
[68] *Ibid.*, 124, 168ff.   [69] *Emporia Gazette* (w), July 30, 1903.
[70] Baker, Notebook "C," 1903-06, 118-19, Baker Papers.
[71] McClure to Hattie McClure, April 30, 1882, McClure Papers.

liam Allen White violently called down the wrath of heaven.[72] The blow was later softened when White admitted that heaven was only a "speculation."[73] White mocked the old-time religion which believed an electrocuted murderer "is supposed to be floating around on a pair of wings today" because a minister led him to believe "that in fifteen minutes by the prison clock, he would be choosing his harp."[74] The old-fashioned "hell sermon" and the hard sell for heaven were bankrupt, and the muckrakers were convinced that the "churches are finding this out."[75] This may not have been the universal opinion, but certainly it was the most articulated one.

If traditional theology had lost its footing, so had its defender, the church. Baker's *The Spiritual Unrest*, as he called his volume on that "settled institution," the church, became an important part of the ecclesiastical muckraking of *McClure's* and the *American*. Soon the Mormon Church and the revival of polygamy, the compromising past of Mrs. Mary Baker Eddy and the Christian Scientists, and the substandard tenements of Trinity Church were subjects of muckraker exposés.[76] Trinity Church in New York, on Wall Street, with its $50,000,000 endowment, was the "last resort of conservatism," Baker wrote.[77] All in all, it was "very little different from the other corporations" downtown, and "perhaps it was, if anything, worse because there was less accountability on the part of the board of directors (vestry)."[78] When Samuel Hopkins Adams labeled Trinity the "most active and successful enemy of tenement reform" in New York, the resulting imbroglio, which served as an impetus to the entire muckraking movement, precipitated a public debate which the affable editors saw printed and distributed to the credit of the magazine.[79]

[72] *Emporia Gazette* (w), July 9, 1903.
[73] *Ibid.*, July 30, 1903. [74] *Ibid.*, April 2, 1908.
[75] *Ibid.*, July 30, 1903.
[76] Baker, *The Spiritual Unrest*, 13.
[77] *Ibid.* [78] *Ibid.*
[79] Corporation of Trinity Church, *Correspondence Between the*

A parallel between authoritarian religious institutions and the trusts was quickly drawn in *McClure's* articles exposing the Mormons and the Christian Scientists. Through fourteen issues of *McClure's*, Georgine Milmine, a New York housewife whose articles were edited by Willa Cather and Mark Sullivan, documented the somewhat compromising methods by which Mrs. Eddy emerged as the absolute head of the Christian Scientist movement.[80] Mrs. Eddy was touted as the "priestess," the "old queen," and the "absolute ruler" of the church.[81] This sensational indictment was surpassed still later, in 1910, when Burton J. Hendrick beat the somewhat tired drum over the revival of church polygamy in Utah.[82] Almost a third of the Church's leadership was participating in this illegal practice, he asserted. To Baker these articles substantiated his thesis that "in some ways the church situation is more hopeful in China than it is in the United States."[83]

The church, by its selfish interests and great wealth, stood opposed to the altruistic forces inherent in social Darwinism. Not surprisingly, Baker's conclusions resembled those of Rauschenbusch in *The Church and the Social Crisis,* published in 1907: The churches were "all at sea; they can't keep religion inside their doors."[84] The churches, "as at present organized, hinder rather than help the spread of the true Spirit of Christianity" because they represented entrenched worldliness, he wrote in 1909, "and how much they represent it I never realized until I began the present studies in New York City."[85] To prevent religion from remaining a handmaiden of the capitalistic segment of the population, an ethical revival in human motives had to

---

Corporation of Trinity Church and McClure's Magazine (New York, 1905), 3, 15.
[80] Mark Sullivan, *The Education of an American* (New York, 1938), 202.
[81] *McClure's*, XXVII (Dec., 1906), 211.
[82] *Ibid.*, XXXVI (Dec., 1910), 242.   [83] Baker, *Spiritual Unrest*, 67.
[84] Baker to Phillips, April 25, 1908, Baker Papers.
[85] Baker to Father, May 2, 1909, *ibid.*

take place. In most respects Baker felt that the socialists had a "larger conception of what religion means than most of the churches."[86] After all, the socialists advocated the same "higher responsibility" of the citizen to the common good that Christ taught, and they found no room for "selfish individualism" so common in the organized churches.[87]

The other journalists greeted *The Spiritual Unrest* and muckraking of the churches with approval. Steffens wrote, "your church articles are very, very satisfying."[88] And Brand Whitlock told John Phillips he thought the articles excellent.[89] In Toledo, Whitlock had made Mayor Jones' vendetta against the churches his own, principally because the "church today as an institution is controlled by the rich."[90] And "Jesus despised them," came Steffens' reply.[91] The muckrakers enjoyed general agreement that the "politicians and the preachers" favored the rule of gold over the Golden Rule.[92] Viola Roseboro' probably summarized the staff's attitude when she said that the churches were "organized hypocrisy" permeated with "self-righteous piety."[93]

Because of social Darwinism, the muckrakers modified their faith and became social Christians in the full meaning of the term. They were prepared, in the name of brotherhood, to socialize the economic order. Muckraking they identified with *"the preaching of hell"* and Progressivism, a larger concept of brotherhood, with the "organiza-

---

[86] *Ibid.*

[87] Baker, Notebook "C," 98-99, *ibid.*; Baker, *Spiritual Unrest*, 254.

[88] Steffens to Baker, July 22, 1909, Baker Papers.

[89] Brand Whitlock to Phillips, June 11, 1909, Whitlock Papers.

[90] Brand Whitlock to Rev. Thomas Campbell, Jan. 17, 1905, *ibid.*; see Brand Whitlock, *The Letters of Brand Whitlock*, ed. Allan Nevins (New York, 1936), 81.

[91] Steffens to Whitlock, Feb. 16, 1910, Nevins Papers, Columbia University.

[92] Brand Whitlock, *Forty Years of It* (New York, 1925), 112ff.

[93] Jane Kirkland, *The Duchess of New Dorp*, I, 18.

tion of a church to lead the community to a better life."[94] And so they preached, occasionally in pulpits, always in print.

As Baker crossed the color line in the South, discovering unsuspected hostilities, he tried to convince President Roosevelt that the situation demanded the "teaching of the spirit of Jesus Christ—which works in the individual man."[95] The individual man had to replace his selfishness with a social consciousness. William Allen White also argued with the President that certain moral principles of brotherhood obligated social classes to each other, and he quoted Pope Leo XIII's *Rerum Novarum* in defense of a living wage for labor.[96]

Much of the fiction of these muckrakers bears the obvious stamp of social Christianity. The early David Grayson adventures posited as their thesis that the "greatest battle in the world today—the only real battle" was the battle for the "spiritual view of life."[97] White's novel, *A Certain Rich Man*, the "story of a malefactor of great wealth," was published in 1909, and elicited from Walter Rauschenbusch the compliment: "You preach the spirit against the flesh, righteousness against money, and love above all."[98] In New York a Wall Street banker walked into Dodd, Mead & Co., and asked for "One Millionaire," and was given White's book. He was "enormously impressed" by it, John Phillips wrote.[99] White was encouraged to follow this up nine years later with his final piece of fiction, *In The Heart of a Fool*.

Long after the muckraking period was past, Miss Tarbell articulated her social Christianity in an article for the

[94] Baker, Notebook "J," 116, Baker Papers; see Baker, *Spiritual Unrest*, 275.
[95] Baker to Roosevelt, June 8, 1908, Baker Papers.
[96] White to Roosevelt, Oct. 18, 1906, White Papers.
[97] Grayson, *Friendly Road* (New York, 1913), 101.
[98] Walter Rauschenbusch to White, July 9, 1910, White Papers.
[99] Phillips to White, Sept. 18, 1909, *ibid.*

McClure newspaper syndicate. Her credo would probably have sufficed for much of the staff.

It was impossible for Miss Tarbell to "remember the time when I did not have a conviction of divine goodness at work in the world."[100] Her faith underwent a severe shock when she discovered the world filled with "human suffering, inequalities, greed, ignorance, all so inconsistent with the notion of a merciful force active in the universe."[101] It soon became her desire to produce the "type of human being that can work out a brotherhood of man."[102] This was the travail of the Gospel in her view. She saw a divine striving, based on social Darwinism, towards brotherhood: "This conception of men in their relations to one another is not the fruit of doctrinal struggle, church organizations, of theologies however sound and essential, but rather of the travail of the spirit."[103] Any "permanent human betterment must rest on a . . . moral basis."[104] Selfish individualism, like that of Standard Oil, prevented this. "I accuse Mr. Rockefeller," she said in a Cleveland interview, "not of breaking the law or even the rules of business . . . , I judge him by the golden rule, and I claim that Mr. Rockefeller himself gives me the right" by claiming to be a Christian.[105] Miss Tarbell was joined by most of the other muckrakers in such moral stoning of the wicked.

Lincoln Steffens, like Jane Addams, Brand Whitlock, and Terence Powderly, used his autobiography to make a final argument for social Christianity and an indictment of orthodoxy. His position was perhaps the most extreme at *McClure's*. His famous vitriolic chapter entitled "The Churches Decide Against Christianity" deals with an experiment of faith. When the MacNamara brothers blew up the *San Francisco Times* in 1910, Steffens raced halfway around the world to defend them. He pleaded for a public

100 Tarbell, "My Religion," Tarbell Papers.
101 *Ibid.* 102 *Ibid.* 103 *Ibid.*
104 Tarbell, *All in the Day's Work*, 407.
105 Cleveland *Press*, n.d., clippings in Tarbell Papers.

acknowledgment of guilt by the men, the city, and the nation and an acknowledgment that environmental conditions fostered by capital made violence necessary. When the community failed to respond to the "suffering cries for help" and gave the bombers life sentences, Steffens smoldered for years and wrote in his *Autobiography*, "I recognized that it is no cynical joke, it is literally true, that the Christian churches would not recognize Christianity if they saw it."[106] To Steffens it was as if the traditional church were the Grand Inquisitor and an ethical humanism based on social Darwinism the inmate of the cell. Obviously a progressive Christianity was far different from that of the churches as a whole. In defeat Steffens gave up reading the New Testament and turned to the Old Testament for social principles. And perhaps it is not amiss to look at the result.

Becoming enamoured with Communism after the war, Steffens attempted to correlate the Old Testament with the Russian Revolution. The result was *Moses in Red*, published in 1926. While the Petrograd mobs "used to make me think of the mobs that followed Jesus about," it was the Exodus story that served as the prototype of the Bolshevik revolution.[107] His main thesis was that "we now have in current history another source of light upon ancient history."[108] Written in consultation with theologians in Paris and London, *Moses in Red* attempted to prove that "not Lenin, but Nature required the excesses of the Russian revolution; or, if you please, God."[109] The scientific comparison of the terror of Moses and Lenin was a serious essay on the natural laws of revolutionary progress. It was

[106] Steffens, *Autobiography*, 688.

[107] Steffens to Porterfield, editor of the San Diego *Sun*, May 11, 1918, Steffens Papers.

[108] Steffens to Brand Whitlock, Dec. 20, 1924, *ibid.*

[109] Steffens to Upton Sinclair, May 19, 1926; Sinclair Papers; see *The World of Lincoln Steffens*, ed. Ella Winter and Herbert Shapiro, for *Moses in Red*.

an updating of nature's system of ethics, of evolution's pound of flesh.

In conclusion, the muckrakers' social theories were built upon the principle of evolutionary societal progress, directed by a divine force. Man retained a certain free will to develop his social consciousness and conform to the folk system of values. And both the Golden Rule and the law of gravity were part of these normative values. But then so were laws, customs, and habits. Written law, which reflected the changing codes of habits, equally well expressed the sense of brotherhood of man and fatherhood of God implicit in the Sermon on the Mount. From this source came McClure's overriding concern with order and lawlessness.

The muckrakers may have joked about a "nig-nagging God" or about the myth of Adam, but on the whole their belief in man's brotherhood and the emergent Kingdom of God is evidenced by their great reform endeavor. Their preaching, their criticism of the profit motive in capitalism, their acceptance of the "supernatural spiritual impulse" of Christ, and their coming to terms with philosophical positivism mark them as radical Christian reformers.[110]

After the Bull Moose Party had bitten the dust in 1912, John Phillips asked William Allen White to compose the unwritten essay about the motives of Progressivism (a well-named movement). Write, said Phillips, on "The Law of Love." Baker, looking back at the years of muckraking, reflected a similar tone: "How I am driven back again & again upon Jesus Christ. The more I think of human ills & social remedies, the more I see that the teaching of Jesus Christ is the only solution. For, far beyond socialism . . . stands the unreached Christ in love and serenity."[111] In his mature years McClure still felt that "the one great rallying point is the Golden Rule; and the never failing guide

110 Hopkins, *The Rise of the Social Gospel,* 318-27; *Emporia Gazette* (w), July 30, 1903.
111 Baker, Notebook "J," 139, Baker Papers.

is the life and teachings of Jesus Christ."[112] And Steffens, discovering a new municipal reformer, could matter-of-factly report to Brand Whitlock, "I have found another Christian in politics."[113] Social Darwinism had moved the reform journalists to a social Christianity.

But such a progressive religion was shared by others. When one student at the State University of Kansas listed his religion as "Progressive" in 1911, William Allen White thought it the "creed of hundreds of thousands of men and women, who believe that religion is not a matter of going to church or 'professing' or 'getting the power,' but rather that religion is a matter of human service to bring about the coming kingdom of righteousness."[114] This religion of progress, he prophesied, "will change the world during this century as steam changed it in the past."[115] It all meant, said Steffens, only the "beginning of applied knowledge," and the race was young with "30 million years left ahead of us."[116]

Society was the juggernaut and man its devotee—and the muckrakers were the heralds of a new social order.

[112] McClure, "Liberty, Constitution and Free Enterprise," *Rural Progress Magazine*, n.d., in McClure Papers.
[113] Steffens to Whitlock, Nov. 16, 1905, Whitlock Papers.
[114] Emporia *Gazette* (w), Oct. 26, 1911.   [115] *Ibid.*
[116] Steffens to Cora Older, Jan. 3, 1919, Steffens Papers.

309

Chapter XV. "Two Revolts
Against Oligarchy"

THE MOST provocative and sensitive conclusion of what muckraking and Progressivism were all about was given by Theodore Roosevelt at Osawatomie, Kansas, in August, 1910.[1] There had been two great crises in the nation's history, the ex-President told his rain-drenched audience, the Revolution and the Civil War. The third epochal crisis was then at hand: "Exactly as the special interests of cotton and slavery threatened our political integrity before the Civil War, so now the great special business interests too often control and corrupt the men and methods of government. . . ."[2] Roosevelt's analogy went further: the Progressive "interest is primarily in the application to-day of the lessons taught by the contest of a half a century ago."[3]

Roosevelt was speaking to an audience who well understood what he meant. The brother of Gifford Pinchot, who sat on the stand with him, had just authored an article articulating this parallel with the Civil War. The *McClure's* article by Amos Pinchot was entitled "Two Revolts Against Oligarchy."[4]

The causes, Pinchot wrote, "of the political and industrial crises which we are passing through to-day are the same as the causes of the most momentous episode of our history, the Civil War."[5] A belief in the sacredness of property, that "ancient and feudal idea," made blood brothers of the slavocracy and the industrial plutocracy, for both clung tenaciously to that anachronistic and unjust precept.

"One has only to read the speeches and letters of North-

[1] See Amos Pinchot, *History of the Progressive Party, 1912-1916*, ed. Helen Hooker (New York, 1958), 166-67; and Forcey, *The Crossroads of Liberalism*, 121-52.

[2] Theodore Roosevelt, *The New Nationalism*, intro. William E. Leuchtenburg (New York, 1961), 27.

[3] *Ibid.*, 3.   [4] *McClure's*, xxxv (Sept., 1910), 581.

[5] *Ibid.*

ern leaders of thought before and during the war," it seemed to Pinchot, "to be struck by their peculiar resemblances to the utterances of the 'Insurgent' leaders of to-day."[6] As the cotton interests, planters and spinners, "intrenched and upheld by slavery," ruled formerly behind the three-fifths clause of the Constitution, in 1910 the special interests, "represented by the railroads and industrial trusts," dominated Congress.[7] Like the Kansas-Nebraska Act, which had stimulated the formation of the Republican Party, the Payne-Aldrich tariff was responsible for the Insurgency and proved that the "eternal and irrepressible conflict between the people and the great industrial interests for control of the government has again become acute."[8]

Representative government had been destroyed in Congress by the machinations of Aldrich and Cannon, and Taft, a prototype of Buchanan, a weak executive, was an accomplice in the crime. The regular Republicans had demonstrated their propertied allegiance by supporting the maladministration of Ballinger and by being party to plots to repeal the Sherman Act. So in the final analysis, asserted Pinchot, the radical Free Soilers had "stood in exactly the same relationship to the Whigs as the Insurgents of to-day stand in relation to the so-called 'regular' Republicans."[9]

There were many Progressives who saw such an obvious parallel. "It is always easy," wrote Jane Addams, who was born near Freeport, Illinois, and whose father was a Republican legislator in Illinois while Lincoln was President, "to overwork an analogy, and yet the economist who for years insisted that slave labor continually and arbitrarily limited the wages of free labor, and was, therefore a detriment to national wealth, was a forerunner of the economist of to-day who points out the economic basis of the social evil."[10] Hull House, in Miss Addams' opinion, was like a station on the underground railroad for the victims

6 *Ibid.*, 583.   7 *Ibid.*, 586.   8 *Ibid.*, 585.
9 *Ibid.*, 583.   10 *Ibid.*, XXXVII (Nov., 1911), 3.

of a social blight which exploited women. And just as the abolitionists had given the Negro the suffrage to doom slavery forever, she promised that the feminine vote would end white slavery. But first there needed to be a wide dissemination of propaganda, in the vein of *Uncle Tom's Cabin*, to convince those who would tolerate the social evil that only its complete abolition would satisfy moral law. In muckraker literature with its exposés Miss Addams saw the historical parallel becoming complete.

No less observant about the pattern of the political panorama unveiling itself before them were average citizens. A Chicago reformer wrote Steffens that his only hope for the solution to pressing contemporary ills lay in the success of the anti-slave agitation. "Read the letters of Phillips and Garrison; you will see that the sky looked to them as black as to us it seems now," he wrote in a letter which McClure printed:

> "When Garrison was a prisoner in Boston, when Phillips was a social outcast, when Charles Sumner was struck down in the Senate by Preston Brooks, what hope did any man see for abolitionism? And yet all these men lived to see the end of slavery among us. We shall be free, also, of this other thing, though it is harder. . . . It was never quite clear to the abolitionists how negro slavery was to be abolished. They only knew that it was hideous evil and they belted it day and night for twenty-six years. This is another evil of the same sort. . . . We'll get a cure when the national moral sense of the people is convalescent. . . . And *McClure's Magazine* is the magazine to make them think of it."[11]

Innumerable Civil War personages, many old reformers still alive and unconverted to plutocracy, used the pages of *McClure's* in a manner that gave personal continuity to the abolitionist ideals. Old Carl Schurz, who had campaigned for Lincoln in Illinois, wrote a pungent attack on

[11] *Ibid.*, XXIII (June, 1904), 222.

the new growth of peonage in the South and defended Roosevelt's friendship towards and use of Booker T. Washington. In writings published just before his death the old warrior was revealed as not only a supporter of Roosevelt, but also as an ally of W. E. B. Dubois.[12] In fact the founding of the N. A. A. C. P. soon afterwards, participated in by Miss Addams, Baker, Steffens, Dewey, Willard, Darrow, and Howells, inextricably linked the two reform movements.

Another figure who provided continuity between the old and the new was the New England novelist, Elizabeth Stuart Phelps. Miss Phelps, whose grandfather was an operator on the underground railroad, serialized her novels in *McClure's* and used the magazine to further, "the enfranchisement and elevation of my own sex," proclaiming that "while the abolition of American slavery was numerically first the abolition of the liquor traffic is not morally second."[13]

No one was more conscious of this parallel between abolitionists and progressives than the muckrakers themselves. A few months before Roosevelt drew his line in the sand at Osawatomie, William Allen White wrote his line on John Brown in the *Emporia Gazette,* in remembrance of that "crank" whose life "was the most precious single treasure ever offered to this union of states."[14]

White was concerned that the great national trusts, united in a community of interests against the people, were reviving anew the theory that property was more important than human rights. To the gallows John Brown had carried with him "the doctrine of vested rights in human beings, and it was executed with him," but, as White saw it, humanity faced similar battles in the exploitation of child labor,

[12] *Ibid.*, XXII (Jan., 1904), 259; Roosevelt to Baker, June 3, 1908, Baker Papers. For an opposing view see David W. Southern, *The Malignant Heritage: Yankee Progressives and the Negro Question, 1901-1914* (Chicago, 1968), 14ff, 60.

[13] *McClure's*, VIII (Nov., 1896), 77-78.

[14] *The Editor and His People*, ed. Helen Mahin, 280.

lack of workers' compensation, unsafe working conditions, and exorbitant monopoly prices to the public.[15] "The slaveholding oligarchy was never more solidly arrayed against the free people of the nation than is this bond-holding aristocracy to-day," White editorialized.[16] The spirit of John Brown was needed anew in the land, for "Brown's soul is not marching on if the sugar thieves steal from us, if the franchise grabbers put their clamps on future generations, if we let the steel trust and the wool trust and the lumber trust fatten on our tariffs, and stand by the congressmen who do these things."[17]

It was Ray Stannard Baker who most poignantly linked the third American Revolution with Beard's second one. To his father, an old G. A. R. veteran, he wrote, "this crusade against special privilege in high places is a real war, a real revolution. We may not have to go as far as you did, when you fought out the slavery question, with powder & blood. At the present, when any of us is wounded we bleed nothing but ink. But ink may serve the purpose. If it doesn't, I pity the country."[18]

The Knox-educated editors were in agreement. "What a curious thing it is that in entering upon this new era of intelligent and moral government," McClure wrote to Emporia, "the same parties that wanted to perpetuate slavery under the guise of state rights, are now trying to perpetuate corrupt government under the same guise."[19] Reminiscing over the Progressive movement fifty years later, White still agreed that the clamor against the trusts, the demand for railroad regulation, the desire for an income tax—in other words the use of the state to remedy human ills—stemmed originally from the creed of the "old Abolitionists, those

---

[15] *Ibid.* [16] *Ibid.*, 281. [17] *Ibid.*, 282.

[18] Baker to Father, Jan. 23, 1906, Baker Papers.

[19] McClure to White, Sept. 9, 1910, White Papers. Writing in 1926, John Phillips asserted, "Wealth and the passion for its increase corrupts the reason of the rich. . . . It affects them, as the institution of slavery affected many in the South for two generations." (John Phillips, "A Legacy to Youth," 187.)

who proclaimed the rights of men—Greeley, Garrison, Wendell Phillips," regardless of what party advocated them.[20] Such causes as feminism, racial justice, temperance, sabbath observance, and the development of public education—all so much a part of pre-Civil War reform—were integral elements of the Progressive program.

The Roosevelt who espoused these principles at Osawatomie was not the Roosevelt who left office in 1908. He still had the high-pitched voice, the glasses, the moustache, and the smile that looked like a grimace, but the program of New Nationalism which he proposed in this address and succeeding ones during the next month was based upon the conclusions which the muckrakers had made. Herbert Croly is often given credit for having changed Roosevelt's mind. It might be argued that *McClure's* had a greater effect on him than did *The Promise of American Life.* Though he named them in derision, Roosevelt imbibed their central doctrine.

American institutions, Roosevelt told his audience on the old battlefield, were threatened as at no time since the Civil War by the "lawless violence and corruption" of businessmen and politicians.[21] The state of lawlessness had developed "during the last forty years" because the growth of governmental authority had not kept pace with the power of industry and its interests.[22]

Roosevelt had carried a hair of Lincoln on inauguration day in 1905, and at Osawatomie he quoted the Great Emancipator freely on the primacy of labor. "I am for men, not property as you were in the Civil War. . . ."[23] Both labor and corporations were property and in the name of national interest both should be regulated. Trusts, "the

20 White, *Autobiography*, 216.

21 Roosevelt, *The New Nationalism*, 150. The *Chicago Economist* called Roosevelt's acceptance speech in August the "most impressive political document since the emancipation proclamation." Quoted in Wiebe, *Businessmen and Reform*, 124.

22 *Ibid.*, 42.

23 *Ibid.*, 36-38; Roosevelt, *Autobiography*, 385.

result of an imperative economic law," as well as the tariff, public domain, and public service corporations should be placed under the control of a governmental commission.[24]

Roosevelt wanted to avoid outright nationalization of the railroads, "if it can possibly be avoided. . . ."[25] Likewise, national controls on wages, hours of labor, and working conditions should be established. Laws were also needed to protect women and children, and to enact workmen's compensation.

The ex-President went further. Quoting Lincoln, he attacked judicial review, questioned states rights, and in the name of "national efficiency" challenged his audience to make the executive department the steward of public welfare.[26] To the Grand Army contingent present, Roosevelt explained, "you could not have won simply as a disorderly and disorganized mob. You needed generals. . . ."[27] Thus he promulgated the leadership principle as a plank of New Nationalism: "The leader leads the people; the boss drives the people."[28]

In his own way at Osawatomie, Roosevelt had given expression to the final aims of Progressivism. Its desire to rise above faction and section, its Bismarckian regard for the state and the executive, its assumption that laissez-faire was ended, and its moral cry for "law, order, and justice," were all there.[29]

In a sense the Progressive movement, coming exactly fifty years after the first national victory of the Republican Party, represents the successful culmination of muckraking. The phenomenal degree to which the Lincoln myth, freely invoked by Roosevelt, served as an impetus for muckraking and Progressivism is impressive. "Americans of Roosevelt's generation came close to transforming the Lincoln legend into a secular cult," writes William Leuchtenburg.[30] And

---

24 Roosevelt, *The New Nationalism*, 88, 98, 29.
25 *Ibid.*, 28.   26 *Ibid.*, 35; Roosevelt, *Autobiography*, 351.
27 Roosevelt, *The New Nationalism*, 38.   28 *Ibid.*, 172.
29 *Ibid.*, 157.   30 *Ibid.*, 9.

another historian, Ray Ginger, substantiates this almost undocumentable fact: "From the Civil War to 1900, Abraham Lincoln dominated the visions of the good society which were being projected to exonerate the successful and to inspire the young. To know what was good, men looked at Lincoln."[31] As David Donald has suggested in his *Lincoln Reconsidered*, virtually all men have made peace with their own individual Lincoln, used their image of him to effect their purpose. Doubtless the muckrakers created their own myths. But even more, they believed them and sought to implement the good works for which Lincoln had been martyred on Good Friday. So Progressivism was the resurgence of a decidedly Western moral imperative. Most historians have ignored the reform impetus of this source and looked elsewhere for the locus of Progressivism.

What brought these young Western Progressives to power was the revival of the Republican Party. Between 1876 and 1896 the Republicans had controlled the House of Representatives for only two terms. In the Senate the party had been more successful: six of the ten Congresses were Republican, but majorities had always been small. The campaign of 1896, between Bryan and McKinley, brought the urban Republicans, particularly from the Midwest, into power. Imbued with traditional Republican myths, these men were the founders and members of the fourscore civic reform organizations in the country at that time.

The traditional view that the silver issue drove larger numbers of urban voters, often foreign born, permanently into the Republican ranks is substantiated by recent scholarship. The Midwest, the cradle of Republicanism, became almost a one-party section and thus asserted itself in Republican councils. "Their swing to the Republicans in 1896," writes Stanley Jones, "was not an ephemeral phenomenon."[32] Illinois, for example, went Democratic only

[31] Ray Ginger, *Altgeld's America: The Lincoln Ideal Versus Changing Realities* (Chicago, 1965), 5.

[32] Stanley L. Jones, *The Presidential Election of 1896* (Madison, Wisc., 1964), 347.

317

once during the next thirty-six years, and that when Roosevelt split the party in 1912.

After the realignment of parties, the young Republicans —often with municipal reform experience—found themselves confronted with power in a newly industrial society. At first they re-articulated the old formulas about temperance and feminine rights. In a different context Hofstadter agrees that "Progressivism, at its heart, was an effort to realize familiar and traditional ideas under novel circumstances."[33]

While the old cluster of moral reforms were reapplied with great vigor, the traditional ethical impulse underwent significant modification. An original revulsion to lawlessness was transformed into a quest for order.[34] A radical social Christianity based upon the tacit assumptions of social Darwinism gave renewed urgency to the old imperatives. Valuing the social group over the individual permitted an indictment of individualism, an individualism that was splintering society apart into various sectional, racial, occupational, and political groups.

To reintegrate the fragments of society, the muckrakers and the Progressives wanted a strong unitary state which in turn would order and administer the economic system. To implement this program required power. While the Progressive Party was the revolutionary apparatus for seizing power, the muckrakers were the vanguard, the propagandizers.

Some historians have underestimated the ideology of this movement as well as the extent to which it was self-consciously revolutionary. John Chamberlain, in his *Farewell to Reform*, claims that the principal weakness of the muckrakers "lies in an insufficient thinking-out of the fundamental ideas on which their crusade is based. They

[33] Hofstadter, *Age of Reform*, 215.

[34] Robert Wiebe's provocative book, *The Search for Order, 1877-1920* (New York, 1967), 111-132, documents this. The organization of specialized laboring groups produced general social division and a search for stability.

do not see that most of the evils they attack are inevitable results of that national creed of individualism."[35] Indeed, this contradicts the expressed purpose of the *McClure's* group.

The origins of the movement have been seen better. Ray Ginger, in several volumes, including *Altgeld's America: The Lincoln Ideal Versus Changing Realities*, presents one of the better arguments for the continuity of history between the Civil War and the Progressive period. On the other hand, Richard Hofstadter, the principal historian of change, views the Progressive movement as a more or less discrete entity, with a chasm on either side. His masterful *Age of Reform* must be encountered by every historian of the period.

Hofstadter suggests numerous psychological and sociological motivations for the Progressive movement. His principal argument hangs on a status revolution which supposedly depressed the traditionally elite families into the middle class after the Civil War. Progressivism, he sees, is the reassertion of this group's authority. Samuel Hays, in *The Response to Industrialism*, argues the opposite: that Progressivism was an attempt on the part of a social elite to seize political power from the alien machine.

Class theories present grave difficulties, even to the voracious new computers. For example, did the second Charles Francis Adams quantitatively lose more status than the first, or did Oswald Garrison Villard fall below his esteemed father and grandfather? Was the assumption of a Pullman Company presidency by Robert Lincoln, the son of the President, a movement up or down, and was it improved or marred when his daughter eloped with a baseball player?

The men who made *McClure's* and the *American* came from the general Progressive backgrounds, now documented by Hofstadter, Louis Filler, and George Mowry.

[35] John Chamberlain, *Farewell to Reform* (New York, 1932), 142.

Their homes were the homes of small businessmen, doctors, and preachers, but the muckrakers were better educated, more highly remunerated, and probably, by any objective standard, in a better class than their parents. Their theories of society show them not to be particularly class conscious themselves.

While some writers have argued that the Progressives were simply anti-business, as Regier and Filler assume, Gabriel Kolko in *The Triumph of Conservatism, 1900-1916* claims that the movement was dominated by political capitalism intent upon protecting itself behind innocuous control commissions. The difficulty of Kolko's theory is that nationalization was seriously considered as an alternative to control, even by Roosevelt in his Osawatomie speech. Municipal socialization of water works, traction companies, electrical lighting facilities, and, in some instances, telephone companies, evidence the general direction of the Progressives. Regulatory commissions may appease the business sector they serve, but few are servile tools to financial interests.

To the extent to which financial interests clandestinely controlled political power, the muckrakers aimed their charges at the heart of the oligarchy. They wanted no special interests, not even the most powerful ones, to have a monopoly on government.

If numerous theories about the origins and nature of muckraking have been brandished about, others have circulated as to why it ended. As early as 1911, Baker was pestered with talk from Honolulu to New York that the muckraking organs were undergoing a "Morganization."[36] Three years later, Walter Lippmann wrote that he had confidentially been told twenty times of a nationwide scheme by financiers to suppress muckraking periodicals.[37]

Mounting costs, stabilized circulation, and increased competition generally drove the magazines to the wall.

[36] Baker to Belle La Follette, April 17, 1911, copy in Baker Papers.
[37] Walter Lippmann, *Drift and Mastery* (New York, 1914), 3, 4.

Baker correctly assayed the trend: "The magazine is drifting steadily toward greater control by the advertisers. It is edited not for the readers but for the advertisers."[38] Although only *Everybody's* and *Scribner's* carried more advertising, in December, 1911, McClure was finally forced to surrender his magazine to a group of financiers headed by his son-in-law, Cameron Mackenzie.[39] His long-standing debts had finally pulled him under. A few months earlier the Crowell Publishing Company, which already owned *The Woman's Home Companion* and *Farm and Fireside*, purchased the stock in the *American*.[40] Baker, White, and Miss Tarbell soon tired of the new management and left the magazine to the joint editorship of Boyden and Siddall, who transmogrified the journal into a pulp. The great muckraking voices had been stilled within months of Theodore Roosevelt's defeat at the polls. In 1912, as if in mourning, for the first year of his career Steffens did not publish a single word.[41]

Although most of the *McClure's* gang moved into free-lance work, for the next thirty years they corresponded, visited, reminisced, and in their mellow years learned to like sherry. On the *Red Cross Magazine* during the war or at Versailles afterwards, where Jaccaci entertained them all, they met. As the New Deal shifted gears to a war economy, they met for their little dinners. On some occasion, perhaps McClure's birthday, Miss Tarbell, Baker, Phillips, and perhaps others, would go to the Union Club. They talked quietly and listened as McClure told for the hundredth time about working seven years for Hattie and marrying her on twelve dollars a week. Everyone listened as if it were a fresh account. All rancor was forgotten. But the years did not erode the excitement of remembering a red hot issue being shipped from the Lexington Building.

38 Baker, Notebook "v," April 14, 1915, 58-59, Baker Papers.
39 See R. C. Wilson to White, Nov. 23, 1909, White Papers.
40 See Phillips to White, Jan. 14, 1911, *ibid.*
41 Cheslaw, "An Intellectual Biography of Lincoln Steffens," 188.

"I think often of the old days," Baker wrote Steffens in later years, "and never at any time of more interest than of those days at *McClure's* and the early years of the *American*, when we were saving the world—so blithely! We didn't know at the time quite how hard boiled it was."[42]

And Steffens, unchanged, intrigued with either communism or fascism, whichever way his fancy took him, wrote, "We Americans made a great mistake having that brief period of muckraking. It set back our death more years than we devoted to it."[43] "The breaking up of our brave little adventure," wrote Finley Dunne, soon to be among the coterie surrounding Harding, "is one of the saddest recollections of my life. . . ."[44]

McClure, having dictated one biography to Willa Cather, sat down years later to write another one. He listed in order the various chapters of his life that he knew so well. There was Knox College, the syndicate, the founding of *McClure's*, the Great War, Fascism. At this point his hand stopped; he marked out Fascism and wrote in Muckraking. It was only an incidental subject.

But on the whole the honored careers subsequently pursued by the individual members of the *McClure's* gang were often laden with a lament, once expressed by Baker: "I suppose they will return again, such times of awakening. The spirit of them is a little like the spirit of war and the purification that comes with it temporarily. It cannot remain because of our fallibility and the necessary, daily, practical struggle that must be, and perhaps properly, self-seeking. But others will return, I am confident, to the task which seemed once almost a mission and a call."[45]

[42] Baker to Steffens, April 28, 1930, Baker Papers.
[43] Steffens to Marie Howe, Dec. 28, 1919, Steffens Papers.
[44] Finley Peter Dunne to Tarbell, n.d., Tarbell Papers.
[45] Baker to Phillips, Dec. 20, 1920, Baker Papers.

Bibliographical Notes

THE BEST sources for the muckraking movement are periodicals. Until the availability of manuscript resources in recent years, scholars have concentrated their studies on these magazines. Serials, often edited before appearing in book form, must be read in the journals, in context, before their full impact can be realized. Unfortunately, most bound volumes, those of *McClure's* and the *American*, omit the exciting advertising pages. The *Index to McClure's Magazine; Volume I to XVIII* (New York, 1903) is helpful in tracing articles through the Spring of 1902, and the ably edited *Review of Reviews* is helpful in the same respect for the whole of muckraking literature. *McClure's Magazine* from 1893 to 1911 and *The American Magazine* from 1906 to 1915 are the best sources for following the public thought of the *McClure's* group.

Since McClure permitted his writers to publish often in other journals, these other articles must be inspected. Other useful journals have been the *St. Nicholas, Dial, Chautauquan, Munsey's, Collier's, Cosmopolitan, Century, Scribner's,* and *The American Magazine*. The *Knox Student* from McClure's student days throughout the Progressive period contains much valuable information, as do the *Knox Alumnus* and *The Wheelman*.

Newspapers, perhaps because of professional jealousies, are not always trustworthy. But the most valuable journals include the *Galesburg Evening Mail*, the *Galesburg Daily Mail, The Bureau County Republican*, the *Belleville Daily Advocate*, the *Chicago Record*, and the *New York Times*. Several additional papers are useful primarily for constructing a view of the public response to muckraking. These include the *New York Tribune*, the *Philadelphia North American*, the *New York Sun*, the *New York Herald*, and the *Emporia Gazette*. John Phillips' articles in the *Goshen Independent Republican* before World War II are an untapped source of information on the history of *Mc-Clure's* articles.

Recently available manuscript sources permit a new assessment of the muckraking movement. One of the most helpful collections is the Ray Stannard Baker Papers at the Library of Congress. Numerous journals and notebooks exhibit that sensitive journalist's wide experience with the leading Progressives, and, when carefully used, reveal a subjective reasoning that later was transformed into either muckraking articles or David Grayson fiction. The William Allen White Papers, also at the Library of Congress, are hardly as valuable for this period as the Baker Papers, since they deal principally with correspondence of the *Gazette*. Smaller collections of note at this same repository are those of Brand Whitlock, Finley Peter Dunne, Mark Sullivan, and Edwin Markham. The principal value of these collections is to show how the magazine's activities appeared to men not intimately connected with it. The Albert J. Beveridge Papers, the Theodore Roosevelt Papers, and the Booker T. Washington Papers were used to verify certain points.

The Lincoln Steffens Papers at Columbia University are stronger for the journalist's later career than for the muckraking period. Yet they are especially valuable as a check upon the authenticity of his autobiography. The published letters of Steffens do not always agree with the manuscripts. In fact, Steffens' almost illegible handwriting might well explain why some letters were abridged in those volumes. His unpublished manuscripts on "Ethics and Evolution" are in this collection. The Frederick Bancroft Papers, also at Columbia, shed light on McClure's continual concern with the Civil War. The Edmund Clarence Stedman Papers reveal much of the personality of Viola Roseboro'. The Thomas S. Jones, Jr. Papers, the Stephen Crane Papers, and the Allan Nevins Papers supply information for peripheral points.

324

The John H. Finley Papers, at the New York Public Library, relate to a later period; nonetheless they allow the young academician's considerable role in muckraking to be evaluated. In the same library a few items from the Tarbell Papers relate to McClure's bizarre behavior in 1904. The library also has possession of one of McClure's manuscripts, "The Science of Political and Industrial Self-Organization," written about 1933. This document is the musings of an old man, but in some instances it gives insights into certain phases of McClure's thought during the muckraking period.

Wagner College possesses the considerable and well-arranged Edwin Markham Papers. Not only do these documents give some indication of how *McClure's* treated its eminent writers, but they show that most sentiments felt by the *McClure's* group were shared by a wider public.

Princeton University has a collection of Ray Stannard Baker Papers more important to the era of Woodrow Wilson than to this study. The Margaret Oliphant Papers show McClure commencing his career. The Western Americana Papers contain a fascinating letter showing the economic plight of the Tarbell family after the formation of Standard Oil.

Perhaps the most crucial manuscripts for this study were the voluminous McClure Papers and John S. Phillips Papers at the Lilly Library, Indiana University. Although often dealing with daily problems, practically every letter written by McClure in the period is extant, permitting a penetrating insight into how the magazine functioned. The Phillips Papers, less full, have material vital to understanding how muckraking emerged and the staff finally split. Two collections of the Upton Sinclair Papers, at the same library, show the muckrakers' principal gadfly at work. The Century Papers are an unexplored source of material on publishing during the period.

The Eugene Field Papers at Washington University are disappointingly sparse. They reveal that Field knew some of the *McClure's* group, but there is little evidence that he influenced the founding of McClure's syndicate.

The Faculty Papers and the Bancroft Papers at Knox College are surprisingly full and reveal minutely the environment of the community during the post-Civil War years.

The principal collection of the Tarbell Papers is at Allegheny College, with others at the Oil Museum in Titusville. Miss Tarbell's manuscripts, library, and financial accounts are better preserved than those of her colleagues. Accurate figures on finances are usually quoted from these papers, which include a valuable diary of events for the spring of 1906.

The papers of Albert Brisbane, Stephen Crane, and Samuel Hopkins Adams at Syracuse University contain peripheral items germane to this study, while the Samuel Hopkins Adams Papers at Hamilton College are disappointingly incomplete.

A third collection of Baker Papers is located at the Jones Memorial Library, Amherst, Massachusetts. Its main value is that it contains much of Baker's library. Amherst College itself has a small collection of correspondence from Viola Roseboro' from a later period.

Harvard University possesses incidental papers of most of the important muckrakers—McClure, Phillips, Siddall, Jaccaci, and Tarbell, for instance—but its most valuable collection on this topic is the Bynner Papers, which show to some extent how the magazine procured good manuscripts.

The Cather Papers at Yale University, where miscellaneous manuscripts of such figures as Jaccaci are also located, give insight into what happened after the schism in 1906. The Cather Papers at the University of Virginia, in some respects a better collection, hold several letters of especial value.

The autobiographical resources for such a study as this are rich and varied. Lincoln Steffens' *Autobiography* (New York, 1931) is both the most comprehensive and the most subjective document of this kind. Miss Tarbell's *All in the Day's Work* (New York, 1938) avoids most controversial issues, as does McClure's earlier *My Autobiography* (New York, 1914). Both Baker's *American Chronicle* (New York, 1945) and William Allen White's *The Autobiography of William Allen White* (New York, 1946) are more informative. Both men apparently made good use of their vast manuscript materials, which gives their work a correspondingly high degree of accuracy. Curtis Brady's "The High Cost of Impatience," a manuscript memoir in the possession of Peter Lyon of New York City, deals ably with the advertising and financial problems at *McClure's* and John Phillips' "A Legacy to Youth," a manuscript in the possession of Dorothy P. Huntington of New York City, is an essay of paternal wisdom intended for his children.

Other important biographical accounts include Brand Whitlock's *Forty Years of It* (New York, 1914), John Moody's *The Long Road Home, An Autobiography* (New York, 1934), Will Irwin's *Propaganda and the News* (New York, 1936), Edward Bok's *The Americanization of Edward Bok* (New York, 1920), Mark Sullivan's *The Education of An American* (New York, 1938), Edwin Lefèvre, *Reminiscences of a Stock Operator* (New York, 1923), and Josiah Flynt, *My Life* (New York, 1908).

The muckrakers have also been written about with much zeal. Peter Lyon's *Success Story: The Life and Times of S. S. McClure* (New York, 1963) is a solid and readable apology for the muckraker's career written by his grandson. Robert C. Bannister, Jr., in his *Ray Stannard Baker: The Mind and Thought of a Progressive* (New Haven, 1966), presents ideas especially relevant to an understanding of Baker's relationship to David Grayson and his partisan support for Woodrow Wilson. R. M. Napier has prepared a useful *Bibliography of the Works of Ray Stannard Baker* (n.p., 1948). Elmer Ellis' *Mr. Dooley's America, A Life of Finley Peter Dunne* (New York, 1941) has more material on the *American* than on *McClure's*, but it is useful. A book not as well written but more informative is Jane Kirkland Graham's *Viola, the Duchess of New Dorp* (Danville, Ill., 1955), which is a highly subjective appraisal of Viola Roseboro'. A half dozen books have been written about William Allen White. Among the best are David Hinshaw's *A Man from Kansas, the Story of William Allen White* (New York, 1945) and Walter Johnson's *William Allen White's America* (New York, 1941).

Several printed collections of letters of great value are available. Walter Johnson's edition of the *Selected Letters of William White* (New York, 1947), Allan Nevins' edition of *The Letters and Journal of Brand Whitlock* (New York, 1936), and *The Letters of Lincoln Steffens* (New York, 1938), edited by Ella Winter and Granville Hicks, rank with E. E. Morison's edition of Theodore Roosevelt's *Letters* (Cambridge, 1951-1954) as essential materials on the nature of muckraking and its relationship to the larger political arena. *The Editor and His People: Editorials by William Allen White* (New York, 1924) edited by Helen Mahin, is another excellent primary source, showing particularly how White's views underwent great change early in his career.

Unpublished dissertations have often covered in excellent fashion smaller aspects of the muckraking movement. John E. Semonche's "Progressive Journalist: Ray Stannard Baker, 1870-1914," a doctoral dissertation (Northwestern, 1962), and Irving G. Cheslaw's "An Intellectual Biography of Lincoln Steffens," a doctoral dissertation (Columbia 1952) were the most useful. An area that could be developed much further is suggested by Gertrude Slichter's "The Influence of Foreign Reform Programs on the Progressive Movement," a doctoral dissertation (University of Illinois, 1962). Walter Gutman's "McClure's Magazine in the Era of the Muckrakers," a master's essay (Columbia, 1933), deals with the literary aspects of the magazine, and Ira Shimberg's "The Muckrakers," another master's essay (Columbia, 1927), deals with the same general subject. Jesse Sidney

Goldstein's "The Life of Edwin Markham," a doctoral dissertation (New York University, 1945), is the principal scholarly work dealing with the poet's life.

Perhaps the most important secondary work on publishing is Frank Luther Mott's *A History of American Magazines* (New York, 1938-1957), a work that has little sympathy for the muckrakers. More balance but less detail is afforded by James P. Wood's second edition of *Magazines in the United States* (New York, 1956). Dated but interesting is Algernon Tassin's *The Magazine in America* (New York, 1916), which gives some perspective to muckraking. Bernard A. Weisberger's *The American Newspaper* (Chicago, 1961) is an excellent source on the economic problems of publishing. George Britt's *Forty Years—Forty Millions: The Career of Frank A. Munsey* (New York, 1935) is a case study of how one publisher survived, and James Morgan's *Charles H. Taylor, Builder of the Boston Globe* (n.p., 1923) is another. Frank Luther Mott's *American Journalism* (New York, 1962) is a detailed survey of the field.

Numerous books have dealt with Progressive thought. Probably the most significant interpretation is Richard Hofstadter's *The Era of Reform: From Bryan to F. D. R.* (New York, 1955), which views Progressivism as a rather discrete manifestation of sociological and psychological forces. Other important intellectual studies of the period include Eric Goldman's *Rendezvous with Destiny* (New York, 1952), Daniel Aaron's *Men of Good Hope: A Story of American Progressives* (New York, 1951), and David W. Noble's *The Paradox of Progressive Thought* (Minneapolis, 1958) which describe the structure of thought of many important individuals but fail to deal with the muckrakers. Charles Forcey's impressive study, *The Crossroads of Liberalism: Croly, Weyl, Lippmann and the Progressive Era, 1900-1925* (New York, 1961) portrays the thinking of three journalists who had much in common with the *McClure's* group. David Chalmers' *The Social and Political Ideas of the Muckrakers* (New York, 1964) fills a gap left by the above studies but does not succeed in portraying the cohesive elements in the "mind" of the muckrakers. In some instances his dissertation by the same title (University of Rochester, 1955), is fuller than the published work.

Louis Filler's *Crusaders for American Liberalism* (New York, 1939) is the standard work on the muckrakers, one which puts the *McClure's* group into perspective. Supplementing this work are C. C. Regier's *The Era of the Muckrakers* (Chapel Hill, 1932) and Harold U. Faulkner's *The Quest for Social Justice* (New York, 1931).

Probably the most useful historical articles have been Samuel P. Hays, "The Politics of Reform in Municipal Government in the Progressive Era," in the *Pacific Northwest Quarterly*, LV (Oct., 1964), 157-69; Stanley K. Schultz, "The Morality of Politics: The Muckrakers' Vision of Democracy," in the *Journal of American History*, LII (Dec., 1965), 527-47; Will Irwin, "Strictly Personal; Viola Regina," in the *Saturday Review of Literature*, XVIII (March 3, 1945), 15-16; John Semonche, "Theodore Roosevelt's Muckrake Speech: A Reassessment," *Mid-American*, XLVI (April, 1964, 114-25; Robert S. Maxwell, "A Note on the Muckrakers," *Mid-American*, XLIII (Jan., 1961), 50-59; and Frank Luther Mott, "The Magazine Revolution and Popular Ideas in the Nineties," *Proceedings of the American Antiquarian Society at the Semi-annual Meeting Held in Boston*, April 21, 1954. Vol. 64, part 1 (April 21, 1954), 195-210. Peter Lyon, on July 31, 1963, and Dorothy P. Huntington, on December 23, 1967, in New York City, graciously granted interviews that were of help in formulating some of the generalizations found in this work.

Index

331

347

This book has been composed and printed by
Princeton University Press
Designed by Jan Lilly
Edited by R. Miriam Brokaw
Typography: Baskerville
Paper: Warren's Olde Style
Binding by Complete Books Company